PUBLISHER COMMENTARY

There is a reason the U.S. Air Force has one of the best cyberwarfare weapon system programs. This book pulls together 5 key Air Force publications on Cyberspace Security and Control System (CSCS).

AFI 17-2CSCS, VOL. 1	CYBERSPACE SECURITY AND CONTROL SYSTEM (CSCS) CYBERCREW TRAINING	11 May 2017
AFI 17-2CSCS, VOL. 2	CYBERSPACE SECURITY AND CONTROL SYSTEM (CSCS) STANDARDIZATION AND EVALUATIONS	11 Mar 2017
AFI 17-2CSCS, VOL. 3	CYBERSPACE SECURITY AND CONTROL SYSTEM (CSCS) OPERATIONS AND PROCEDURES	16 May 2017
AFM 17-1301	COMPUTER SECURITY (COMPUSEC)	10 Feb 2017
AFI 17-203	CYBER INCIDENT HANDLING	16 Mar 2017

These publications cover guidelines for planning and conducting cyberspace operations to support the warfighter and achieve national security objectives AFI 17-2CSCS outlines Initial Qualification Training (IQT) requirements for all crewmember personnel, Mission Qualification Training (MQT) and Upgrade and Specialized Training as well as Continuation Training. It provides procedures, evaluation and grading criteria used during performance evaluations on operational cyberspace weapon systems.

AFM 17-1301 establishes the Cybersecurity workforce security certification requirements relative to the function, category (technical or managerial), and level of the position. It covers Information Technology asset procurement stressing Unified Capabilities (UC) when modernizing IT and aligning with joint solutions, including the purchase of foreign-made commercial technology. It covers information systems access control, end point security, data spillage, data encryption, whitelisting, collaborative computing and teleworking.

AFI 17-203 provides broad guidance for implementing the Air Force (AF) and DoD Cyber Incident Handling Program. It provides a succinct description of the Categories of Events (0, 3, 5, 6, 8, and 9) and Incidents (1, 2, 4, and 7).

Why buy a book you can download for free? We print this so you don't have to.

When a new standard is released, an engineer prints it out, punches holes and puts it in a 3-ring binder. While this is not a big deal for a 5 or 10-page document, many cyber documents are over 100 pages and printing a large document is a time-consuming effort. So, an engineer that's paid $75 an hour is spending hours simply printing out the tools needed to do the job. That's time that could be better spent doing engineering. We publish these documents so engineers can focus on what they were hired to do – engineering.

A list of **Cybersecurity Standards** we publish is attached at the end of this document.

BY ORDER OF THE SECRETARY
OF THE AIR FORCE

AIR FORCE INSTRUCTION 17-2CSCS,
VOLUME 1

11 MAY 2017

Cyberspace

CYBERSPACE SECURITY AND
CONTROL SYSTEM (CSCS)
CYBERCREW TRAINING

COMPLIANCE WITH THIS PUBLICATION IS MANDATORY

ACCESSIBILITY: Publications and forms are available for downloading or ordering on the e- Publishing website at **www.e-Publishing.af.mil**

RELEASABILITY: There are no releasability restrictions on this publication

OPR: AF/A3CX/A6CX

Certified by: AF/A3C/A6C
(Brig Gen Kevin B. Kennedy)
Pages: 42

This instruction implements Air Force (AF) Policy Directive (AFPD) 17-2, *Cyberspace Operations* and references AF Instruction (AFI) 17-202, Volume 1, *Cybercrew Training*. It establishes the minimum AF standards for training and qualifying/certifying personnel for performing crewmember duties on the AF Cyberspace Security and Control System (CSCS) weapon system. This publication applies to all military and civilian AF personnel, members of the AF Reserve Command (AFRC), Air National Guard (ANG), third-party governmental employee and contractor support personnel in accordance with appropriate provisions contained in memoranda support agreements and AF contracts.

The authorities to waive wing/unit level requirements in this publication are identified with a Tier ("T-0, T-1, T-2, T-3") number following the compliance statement. See AFI 33-360, *Publications and Forms Management*, Table 1.1 for a description of the authorities associated with the Tier numbers. Submit requests for waivers through the chain of command to the appropriate Tier waiver approval authority, or alternately, to the Publication OPR for non-tiered compliance items. This instruction requires collecting and maintaining information protected by the Privacy Act of 1974 (5 U.S.C. 552a). System of Records Notices F036 AF PC C, Military Personnel Records System, and OPM/GOVT-1, General Personnel Records, apply. Units may supplement this instruction. All supplements will be coordinated through HQ AFSPC/A2/3/6T prior to publication. Process supplements as shown in AFI 33-360. Major Command (MAJCOM) supplements will be coordinated with USAF A3C/A6C. Guidance provided by the lead major command will contain specific training requirements unique to individual and crew positions.

Send recommended changes or comments to HQ USAF/A3C/A6C, 1480 Air Force Pentagon, Washington, DC 20330-1480, through appropriate channels, using AF Form 847, *Recommendation for Change of Publication*. When collecting and maintaining information protect it by the Privacy Act of 1974 authorized by 10 U.S.C. 8013. Ensure that all records created as a result of processes prescribed in this publication are maintained in accordance with AF Manual (AFMAN) 33-363, *Management of Records*, and disposed of in accordance with the AF Records Disposition Schedule (RDS) located in the AF Records Information Management System (AFRIMS). See Attachment 1 for a glossary of references and supporting information.

Chapter 1

GENERAL GUIDANCE

1.1. Training Objectives. This instruction prescribes basic policy and guidance for training United States Air Force Cyberspace Security and Control System (CSCS) crewmembers according to AFI 17-202 Volume 1, *Cybercrew Training*.

1.1.1. The overall objective of the CSCS training program is to develop and maintain a high state of readiness for the immediate and effective employment across a full range of military operations. Achieve mission readiness and effective employment through the development and mastery of core competencies for CSCS crewmembers.

1.1.2. The secondary objective is to standardize CSCS training requirements into a single source document.

1.2. Abbreviations, Acronyms and Terms. See Attachment 1.

1.2.1. For the purposes of this instruction, "certification" denotes a commander's action, whereas qualification denotes a formal Stan/Eval evaluation.

1.2.2. Key words explained.

1.2.2.1. "Will" or "shall" indicates a mandatory requirement.

1.2.2.2. "Should" indicates a preferred, but not mandatory, method of accomplishment.

1.2.2.3. "May" indicates an acceptable or suggested means of accomplishment.

1.2.2.4. "Note" indicates operating procedures, techniques, etc., which are considered essential to emphasize.

1.3. Responsibilities:

1.3.1. Lead Command. Air Force Space Command (AFSPC) is designated lead command for the CSCS weapon system. The lead command is responsible for establishing and standardizing crewmember training requirements in coordination with user commands. HQ AFSPC/A2/3/6 is authorized to manage all training course requirements and training tasks. HQ AFSPC/A2/3/6 will:

1.3.1.1. Chair a Realistic Training Review Board (RTRB) to review training requirements and programs for AF cyber units. RTRB participants will include applicable AFSPC active and reserve component representatives. All AF units with assigned CSCS crewmembers will be invited to send representatives and inputs.

1.3.1.2. Process all change requests.

1.3.2. All user MAJCOMs will:

1.3.2.1. Determine training requirements to fulfill primary (and secondary, if applicable) Designed Operational Capability (DOC) statement missions, as well as meet unit tasking.

1.3.2.2. Submit MAJCOM supplements to HQ USAF AF/A3CX/A6CX, through HQ AFSPC/A2/3/6T, for approval during topline coordination of the document. Copies of approved and published supplements will be provided by the issuing office to HQ USAF AF/A3C/A6C, HQ AFSPC/A2/3/6T, and applicable MAJCOM offices of primary responsibility (OPR).

1.3.2.3. Publish CSCS Ready Crewmember Program Training Memorandum (RTM).

1.3.2.4. Review subordinate unit supplemental instructions and training programs annually.

1.3.3. Wings and groups will:

1.3.3.1. Develop programs to ensure training objectives are met. The top training priority should be to train all designated crewmembers to Mission Ready (MR) status. Assist subordinate squadrons in management of training programs, ensure programs meet unit needs and provide necessary staff support. AFSPC wing/groups will assist AFRC unit training programs as required or requested IAW applicable unit support programs, memorandums of agreement, or memorandums of understanding. **(T-3)**

1.3.3.2. Attach Crewmember Position Indicator (CPI)-6/-8/-B/-D personnel to an operational squadron. See Attachment 3 for CPI explanation and definitions. **(T-3)**

1.3.3.3. Except when otherwise mandated, designate the training level to which each CPI–6/-8/-B/-D will train. Upon request, provide AFSPC/A2/3/6T (through MAJCOM/A3T or equivalent) with a list of MR and Basic Mission Capable (BMC) manning positions. Review programs and manning position designations annually. **(T-3)**

1.3.3.4. Develop additional training requirements and/or programs as necessary to meet unit mission requirements. Units may include these requirements in local training procedures. **(T-3)**

1.3.4. Squadrons. The SQ/CC's top training priority should be to train all designated crewmembers to MR or BMC. Squadrons will:

1.3.4.1. Squadron Training (DOT) is responsible for maintaining training forms and unit certification documents for all squadron personnel and personnel attached to the squadron for cyberspace operations **(T-3)**.

1.3.4.2. Unit Stan/Eval will maintain the letter of certification (i.e., letter of Xs) summarizing crewmember certifications; this letter will be signed by the OG/CC, SQ/CC or SQ/DO and may be maintained via electronic storage. **(T-3)**

1.3.4.3. Ensure adequate continuity and supervision of individual training needs, experience and proficiencies of assigned and attached crewmembers. **(T-3)**

1.3.4.4. Ensure review of training and evaluation records of newly assigned crewmembers and those completing formal training to determine the training required for them to achieve BMC or MR status and to ensure provisions of this volume are met. **(T-3)**

1.3.4.5. Ensure Ready Cybercrew Program (RCP) missions are oriented towards maintaining mission ready proficiency and tactical employment. Provide guidance to ensure only effective RCP missions are logged. **(T-3)**

1.3.4.6. Determine missions and events in which individual MR crewmembers will maintain mission ready certification/qualification. **(T-3)**

1.3.4.7. Determine missions and events in which individual BMC crewmembers will maintain basic certification/qualification. **(T-3)**

1.3.4.8. Determine utilization of BMC crewmembers. **(T-3)**

1.3.4.9. Determine how many and which crewmembers will carry special certifications (mission commander, etc.) and qualifications (instructor, etc.). **(T-3)**

1.3.4.10. Assist the wing or group in the development of unit training programs. **(T-3)**

1.3.4.11. Monitor individual assigned and attached crewmembers currencies, proficiencies, and requirements. **(T-3)**

1.3.4.12. Ensure crewmembers participate only in sorties, missions, events, and tasks for which they are qualified/certified and adequately prepared, trained, and current. **(T-3)**

1.3.4.13. Ensure flight commanders or designated representatives monitor quality of training, identify training deficiencies, and advise SQ/CC of additional training needs. **(T-3)**

1.3.4.14. Execute unit-level crewmember certifications described in this instruction. **(T-3)**

1.3.5. Individual crewmembers will:

1.3.5.1. Be responsible for monitoring and completing all training requirements. **(T-3)**

1.3.5.2. Ensure they participate only in operational activities for which they are qualified/certified, current, and prepared. **(T-3)**

1.4. Processing Changes. Process changes using the AF Form 847, *Recommendation for Change of Publication*, IAW AFI 33-360, through local and MAJCOM training channels to USAF/A3CS for approval. **(T-3)**

1.5. Training. Cybercrew training is designed to progress an individual from Initial Qualification Training (IQT), through Mission Qualification Training (MQT), to annual Continuation Training (CT). Additional training requirements to the CSCS weapon system include Requalification Training (RT), Upgrade Training, and Instructor Training.

1.5.1. Ready Cybercrew Program (RCP). RCP is the CT program designed to focus training on capabilities needed to accomplish a unit's core tasked missions and fulfill the DOC statement mission requirements. Upon completion of IQT and MQT, crewmembers will have received training in all the basic mission-sets of the unit. After MQT completion, crewmembers will then be assigned to a MR or BMC manning position within the unit and maintain the appropriate level of proficiency and currency per the RCP tasking memorandum.

1.5.2. Initial Qualification Training (IQT). Training needed to qualify for basic crewmember duties in an assigned crew position for a specific weapon system, without regard for the unit's operational mission. See **Chapter 2**.

1.5.3. Mission Qualification Training (MQT). The purpose of MQT is to qualify crewmembers in assigned crew positions to perform the command or unit mission IAW the unit's DOC statement. See Chapter 3.

1.5.4. Continuation Training (CT). The CT program provides crewmembers with the volume, frequency, and mix of training necessary to maintain proficiency in the assigned certification/qualification level.

1.5.5. Requalification Training (RT). RT is designed to provide the training necessary to requalify a crewmember with an expired qualification evaluation or loss of currency exceeding 6 months (for currency items specified in Chapter 4).

1.5.6. Mission Ready (MR). A crewmember who satisfactorily completed IQT and MQT, and maintains qualification and proficiency in the unit mission.

1.5.6.1. All CPI-1/-2/-A/-Z designated positions will maintain certification/qualification status. The OG/CC may require other CPI-6/B positions not assigned to the squadron to be certified/qualified. See Attachment 4 for CPI explanation and definitions. (T-3)

1.5.6.2. MR crewmembers will maintain currencies that affect MR status, accomplish all core designated training (missions and events), and all mission related training. Failure to complete required MR training or maintain currencies will result in regression to BMC. Failure of an MR crewmember to maintain BMC currencies will result in regression to non-MR (NMR) status. MR crewmembers, regressed to BMC, may perform missions and events in which they are certified at the discretion of the SQ/CC. (T-3)

1.5.7. Basic Mission Capable (BMC). A crewmember that satisfactorily completed IQT and MQT, is qualified in some aspect of the unit mission, but does not maintain MR status. The crewmember must be able to attain full MR status as specified in MAJCOM-provided guidance.

1.5.7.1. Assign BMC-coded positions to crewmembers with the primary job of performing wing supervision or staff functions that directly support cyber operations (e.g., numbered air force staff, wing staff, OSS personnel, etc.). (T-3)

1.5.7.2. Regular Air Force BMC crewmembers and activated ARC BMC crewmembers must be able to attain MR status and, if required, certification/qualification in 30 days (respectively) (T-2).

1.5.7.3. BMC crewmembers accomplish all mission related training designated by the RTM   (T-3).

1.5.7.4. Current, proficient, and certified/qualified BMC crewmembers may participate in missions as determined by the SQ/CC.

1.5.7.5. Failure to complete required BMC training results in regression to non-BMC (N-BMC) status. While N-BMC, SQ/CC will determine missions the crewmembers may perform and the supervision required. (T-3)

1.6. Training Concepts and Policies:

1.6.1. Units will design training programs to achieve the highest degree of readiness consistent with safety and resource availability. Training must balance the need for realism against the expected threat, crew capabilities, and safety. This volume provides training guidelines and polices for use with operational procedures specified in applicable operational publications. **(T-3)**

1.6.2. Design training to achieve mission capability in squadron-tasked roles, maintain proficiency, and enhance mission accomplishment and safety. RCP training missions should emphasize either basic combat skills, or scenarios that reflect procedures and operations based on employment plans, location, current intelligence, and opposition capabilities. Use of procedures and actions applicable to mission scenarios are desired. **(T-3)**

1.6.3. Unless specifically directed, the SQ/CC determines the level of supervision necessary to accomplish the required training. An instructor is required if mission objectives include introduction to new or modified tasks and/or instruction to correct previous discrepancies. **(T-3)**

1.7. Experienced Crewmember Requirements. CSCS crewmembers are declared experienced on the weapon system when they meet the requirements in Table 1.1. **(T-3)**

Table 1.1. Experienced Crewmember Requirements (T-2).

Position	Declared Experienced (Hours)	Notes
Boundary Protection Operator (CSCS-BPO)	450	1
Client End Point Protection Operator (CSCS-CPO)	450	1
Directory Services Operator (CSCS-DSO)	450	1
Infrastructure Operator (CSCS-IFO)	450	1
Monitoring Management Operator (CSCS-MMO)	450	1
Storage and Virtualization Operator (CSCS-SVO)	450	1
Vulnerability Assessment Operator (CSCS-VAO)	450	1
Vulnerability Remediation Operator (CSCS-VRO)	450	1
Crew Commander (CSCS-CC)	850	1, 2, 3, 4
Operations Controller (CSCS-OC)	450	1, 5
1. Crewmembers begin acquiring experience hours upon the successful completion of MQT.		
2. Requires the successful completion of 67 CW Mission Commander Course.		
3. CSCS-CC responsibilities can be assumed by crewmembers, not additional personnel.		
4. Msn/CC / Pkg/CC are responsibilities assumed by CSCS-CC when executing large force employment missions.		
5. The Operations Controller position can be assumed by crewmembers, not additional personnel.		

1.7.1. Specialized Training. Specialized training is any special skill necessary to perform the unit's assigned mission not required by every crewmember. Specialized training consists of upgrade training, such as instructor upgrade, etc.

1.7.2. Specialized training is accomplished after the crewmember is assigned MR or BMC status. Unless otherwise specified, crewmembers in MR or BMC positions may hold special mission qualifications or certifications as long as any basic training requirements are accomplished. Table 1.2 identifies Specialized Mission Training Requirements. **(T-3)**

Table 1.2. Minimum Upgrade and Specialized Mission Training Requirements.

Upgrading From	Upgrading To	Prerequisites	Tasks & Events to Complete Upgrade	Notes
Any Position	Instructor	Experienced (any position); Instructor Training Course	Instructor Qual & SQ/CC certification	
* Commanders must ensure each candidate has the ability, judgement, technical expertise, skill, and experience when selecting a crewmember for upgrade or specialized mission training.				

1.8. RCP Guidance and Management:

1.8.1. The RCP training cycle is aligned with the fiscal year and executed IAW the RCP Tasking Memo (RTM). Each RCP status (i.e., MR or BMC) is defined by a total number of RCP missions, events, and associated currencies as determined by Higher Headquarters (HHQ) guidance and unit commanders. **(T-3)**

1.8.2. The total number of missions and events for MR or BMC is the primary factor for maintaining an individual's RCP status. Failure to accomplish all training requirements may lead to an individual's regression by the SQ/CC, IAW HHQ guidance. **(T-3)**

1.8.3. An effective RCP mission requires accomplishing a tactical mission or training mission, and completion of the RCP mission/events.

1.8.4. Log non-effective sorties when a training sortie is planned and started, but a majority of valid training for that type of mission is not accomplished due to system malfunction, power failures, etc. Non-effective sorties will be logged and reported appropriately. **(T-3)**

1.8.5. Progression from BMC to MR requires:

1.8.5.1. A 1-month lookback (4 months for ARC) at the MR mission rate. **(T-3)**

1.8.5.2. Certification/qualification in all core missions and events required at MR. **(T-3)**

1.8.5.3. Confirmation the progressed crewmember can complete the prorated number of mission and event requirements remaining at MR by the end of the training cycle. Refer to Proration of Training, paragraph 4.10. **(T-3)**

1.8.5.4. Completion of mission-related training, to include a current certification as applicable to the assigned unit's DOC statement. **(T-3)**

1.8.6. MR and BMC crewmember will complete the required monthly mission/events requirements. If unable, refer to Regression, paragraph 4.9 **(T-3)**.

1.8.7. End of cycle training requirements are based on the crewmember's experience level, as outlined in paragraph 1.7, on the last day of the current training cycle. **(T-3)**

1.9. Training Mission Program Development:

1.9.1. RTM MR or BMC mission and event requirements apply to all MR and BMC crewmembers, as well as those carrying special mission certifications/qualifications (see Attachment 2). The standard mission requirements listed in the RTM establish the minimum number of missions per training cycle for MR and BMC levels of training. The RTM takes precedence over this volume and may contain updated requirements, missions, events, or tasks not yet incorporated into Attachment 2. The RTM applies to all CSCS Cybercrew personnel. **(T-3)**

1.10. Training Records and Reports:

1.10.1. Units will maintain crewmember records for individual training and evaluations IAW:

1.10.1.1. AFI 17-202V1, *Cybercrew Training* **(T-3)**

1.10.1.2. AFI 17-202V2, *Cybercrew Standardization and Evaluation Program* **(T-3)**

1.10.1.3. Any additional HHQ supplement to the above-mentioned volumes **(T-3)**

1.10.2. Track the following information for all crewmembers (as applicable):

1.10.2.1. Mission-related training (e.g., tactics training, crew resource management training, etc.). **(T-3)**

1.10.2.2. Requirements and accomplishment of individual sorties, mission types, and events cumulatively for the training cycle. **(T-3)**

1.10.2.3. RCP mission requirements and accomplishment using 1-month and 3-month running totals for lookback commensurate with CT status (MR or BMC). **(T-3)**

1.10.2.3.1. One-Month Sortie Lookback: Total individual RCP sorties tracked for a 30-day time period. This lookback is used to assess individual progress in achieving the Total Sorties (minimum) required for the 12-month training cycle.

1.10.2.3.2. Three-Month Sortie Lookback: Total individual RCP sorties tracked for a 90-day time period. This lookback is used to assess individual progress in achieving the Total Sorties (minimum) required for the 12-month training cycle.

1.10.2.3.3. ARC will use 4 and 6 month lookbacks. Utilize loopback to assess individual progress to achieve the Total Sorties (minimum) required for the training cycle. **(T-3)**

1.11. Crewmember Utilization Guidance:

1.11.1. Commanders will ensure wing/group crewmembers (CPI-1/-2/-A) fill authorized positions IAW Unit Manning Documents (UMD) and crewmember status is properly designated (see Attachment 3 for CPI explanation and definitions). The overall objective is for crewmembers to perform mission-related duties. Supervisors may assign crewmembers to valid, short-term tasks (escort officer, operational review board (ORB), etc.,) but must continually weigh the factors involved, such as level of crewmember tasking, proficiency, currency, and experience. For inexperienced crewmembers in the first year of their initial operational assignment, supervisors should limit non-crew duties to those related to unit mission activities. **(T-3)**

1.11.2. Use evaluators as instructors for any phase of training to capitalize on their expertise and experience. If an evaluator is an individual's primary or recommending instructor, the same evaluator shall not administer the associated evaluation. **(T-3)**

1.12. Sortie Allocation and Unit Manpower Guidance:

1.12.1. In general, inexperienced CPI-1/-2/-A/-Z crewmembers should receive priority over experienced crewmembers. **(T-3)**

1.12.2. There is no maximum sortie requirement for MR crewmembers. The RTM defines the minimum sortie requirements for crewmembers per training cycle. **(T-3)**

1.13. Training on Operational Missions. Unless specifically prohibited or restricted by weapons system operating procedures, specific theater operations order (OPORD), or specific HHQ guidance, the OG/CC exercising operational control may approve upgrade, certification/qualification or special certification/qualification training on operational missions. In order to maximize efficient utilization of training resources, units will take maximum advantage of opportunities to conduct appropriate CT items that may be conveniently suited to concurrent operational mission segments. **(T-3)**

1.14. In-Unit Training Time Limitations:

1.14.1. Comply with the time limitations in Table 1.3. Crewmembers entered in an in-unit training program leading to qualification, requalification, or certification will be dedicated to that training program on a full-time basis (the OG/CC is the waiver authority). **(T-3)**

1.14.2. Training time start date is the date when the first significant training event (a training event directly contributing to qualification, certification, or upgrade) has begun, or 45-days (90 days ARC) after being attached or assigned to the unit after completion of the Formal Training Unit (FTU); whichever occurs first. Training time ends with the syllabus completion. **(T-3)**

1.14.3. If member is projected to exceed the training cycle, units will notify the OG/CC (or equivalent) in writing before the crewmember exceeds upgrade training time limits in Table 1.3. SQ/CCs may extend listed training times up to 60 days (120 days ARC) provided appropriate justification is documented in the crewmember's training folder. **(T-3)**

1.14.3.1. Include training difficulty, unit corrective action to resolve and prevent recurrence, and estimated completion date.

Table 1.3. In-Unit Training Time Limitations Active Duty (Calendar Days). (T-3).

Training	Crew Personnel	Notes
Mission Qualification Training	60	1,4
Requalification	45	2,4
Mission Certification	30	2,4
Instructor Upgrade	45	2,4
BMC to MR	30	2, 3, 4
Notes:		
1. Training time begins upon reporting to the unit, after completion of IQT with the first training event.		
2. Training time begins with the first training event.		
3. BMC crewmember must be able to attain MR status and, if required, certification / qualification in 30 days or less for those missions/events in which they maintain familiarization only.		
4. 180 days for ARC.		

1.15. Periodic and End-of-Cycle Training Reports.

1.15.1. Periodic Reporting. Squadrons will submit a quarterly training report to MAJCOM/A3T (or equivalent) by the 15th of every 4th month of the training cycle (if the 15th falls on a weekend/holiday, then by the next business day). Reports will consist of a SQ/CC memo summarizing previous report results/issues, current training plan summary and significant shortfalls/limiting factors (LIMFACS) affecting training. **(T-3)**

1.15.2. End-of-Cycle Reporting. Squadrons will submit an End-of-Cycle Training Report NLT 15 October. Report all deviations from the training requirements in this volume or the RTM, after proration at the end of the training cycle. **(T-3)**

1.16. Waiver Authority:

1.16.1. Waivers. Unless another approval authority is cited ("T-0, T-1, T-2, T-3"), waiver authority for this volume is the MAJCOM/A3 (or equivalent). Submit requests for waivers using AF Form 679 through the chain of command to the appropriate Tier waiver approval authority. If approved, waivers remain in effect for the life of the published guidance, unless the waiver authority specifies a shorter period of time, cancels in writing, or issues a change that alters the basis for the waiver.

1.16.2. With MAJCOM/A3 (or equivalent) approval, waiver authority for all requirements of the RTM is the OG/CC. Additional guidance may be provided in the memo. Unless specifically noted otherwise in the appropriate section, and also with MAJCOM/A3 (or equivalent) approval, the OG/CC may adjust individual requirements in Chapter 4 and Chapter 5, on a case-by-case basis, to accommodate variations in crewmember experience and performance. **(T-2)**

1.16.3. Formal School Training and Prerequisites. Any planned exception to a formal course syllabus (or prerequisite) requires a syllabus waiver. Submit waiver request through MAJCOM/A3T (or equivalent) to the waiver authority listed in the course syllabus. If required for units' designated mission, events waived or not accomplished at the formal school will be accomplished in-unit before assigning MR status. **(T-2)**

1.16.4. In-Unit Training Waiver. MAJCOM/A3T (or equivalent) is approval/waiver authority for in-unit training to include syllabus and prerequisite waivers. Before approval, review the appropriate syllabus and consider availability of formal instruction and requirements. All in-unit training will utilize formal courseware in accordance with AFI 17-202V1. MAJCOMs will coordinate with the FTU to arrange courseware delivery to the unit for in-unit training. **(T-2)**

1.16.5. Waiver authority for supplemental guidance will be as specified in the supplement and approved through higher level coordination authority. **(T-2)**

1.16.6. Units subordinate to a NAF will forward requests through the NAF/A3T (or equivalent) to the MAJCOM/A3T (or equivalent). Waivers from other than the MAJCOM/A3 (or equivalent) will include the appropriate MAJCOM/A3 (or equivalent) as an information addressee. (T-2)

Chapter 2

INITIAL QUALIFICATION TRAINING

2.1. General. This chapter outlines CSCS IQT requirements for all crewmember personnel.

2.2. Formal Training. CSCS IQT includes training normally conducted during FTU formal syllabus courses.

2.3. Local Training. In circumstances when FTU training is not available within a reasonable time period, local IQT may be performed at the unit IAW the provisions of this chapter. Local IQT will be conducted using appropriate FTU course syllabi and requirements. When local IQT is authorized, the gaining unit assumes responsibility for providing this training. **(T-3)**

2.3.1. Requests to conduct local IQT will include the following:

2.3.1.1. Justification for the local training in lieu of FTU training. **(T-3)**

2.3.1.2. Summary of individual's mission related experience, to include dates. **(T-3)**

2.3.1.3. Date training will begin and expected completion date. **(T-3)**

2.3.1.4. Requested exceptions to FTU syllabus, with rationale. **(T-3)**

2.4. Mission-Related Training. Current and available reference materials, such as AFTTP 3-1.CSCS, other applicable AFTTP 3-1s and 3-3s, unit guides, and other available training material and programs, will be used as supporting materials to the maximum extent possible. **(T-3)**

2.5. Mission Training:

2.5.1. Mission sequence and prerequisites will be IAW the appropriate FTU syllabus (unless waived). **(T-3)**

2.5.2. Training will be completed within the time specified by the syllabus. Failure to complete within the specified time limit requires notification through channels to MAJCOM/A3 (or equivalent) with crewmember's name, rank, reason for delay, planned actions, and estimated completion date. **(T-3)**

2.5.3. Crewmember in IQT will train under the appropriate supervision directed by the FTU syllabus until completing the QUAL evaluation. **(T-2)**

2.5.4. FTU syllabus mission objectives and tasks are minimum requirements for IQT. However, additional training events, based on student proficiency and background, may be incorporated into the IQT program with SQ/CC authorization. Additional training due to student non-progression is available within the constraints of the FTU syllabus and may be added at SQ/CC discretion.

2.6. IQT for Senior Officers:

2.6.1. All senior officer training (Colonel selects and above) will be conducted at the FTUs unless waived IAW AFI 17-202v1. **(T-2)**

2.6.2. Senior officers must meet course entry prerequisites and will complete all syllabus requirements unless waived IAW AFI 17-202v1. **(T-2)**

2.6.3. If senior officers are trained at their assigned base, they will be considered in a formal training status for the course duration. Their duties will be delegated to the appropriate CDs or CVs until training is completed. Waiver authority for this paragraph is MAJCOM/CC (submitted through MAJCOM/A3 or equivalent). **(T-2)**

Chapter 3

MISSION QUALIFICATION TRAINING

3.1. General .   MQT is a unit-developed training program that upgrades IQT-complete crewmembers to BMC or MR status to accomplish the unit DOC statement missions. Guidance in this chapter, which represents the minimum, is provided to assist SQ/CCs in developing their MQT program, which must have OG/CC approval prior to use. Squadrons may further tailor their program for individual crewmembers, based on current qualifications (e.g., United States Air Force Weapons School (USAFWS) graduate, Instructor), certifications (e.g., MC, Stan/Eval), experience, currency, documented performance, and formal training. Squadrons may use applicable portions of MQT to create a recertification program for crewmembers that regressed from MR to BMC status. **(T-3)**

3.1.1. MQT will be completed within 90 calendar days (180 days for ARC) starting from the day after IQT completion or the crewmember's first duty day in the gaining unit if IQT was completed prior to arrival. If the crewmember elects to take leave prior to entering MQT, the timing will begin after leave termination. Training is complete upon SQ/CC certification of MR or BMC status (subsequent to the successful completion of the MQT MSN qualification evaluation). Notify MAJCOM/A3T (through MAJCOM/A3TT or equivalent) either if training exceeds the 90-day time period or there is a delay beginning MQT (e.g., due to security clearance) that exceeds 30 days (180 days for ARC). **(T-3)**

3.2. Mission-Related Training:

3.2.1. Units will develop instructions addressing areas pertinent to the mission as determined by the SQ/CC. Training accomplished during IQT may be credited towards this requirement. **(T-3)**

3.2.2. Mission-related training may be tailored to the individual's background and experience or particular local conditions. Current and available reference materials, such as AFTTP 3-1.CSCS, other applicable AFTTP 3-1s and 3-3s, unit guides, and other available training material and programs, will be used as supporting materials to the maximum extent possible. **(T-3)**

Table 3.1. Mission-Related Training Requirements.

Code	Event	Crew Position	Notes
GTR001	Unit Indoctrination Training	All	1
GTR002	Weapons and Tactics	All	1
GTR003	Risk Management	All	1, 2
1. Accomplish upon arrival after each permanent change of station. See Attachment 2 for event description.			
2. Previously qualified crewmembers transferring between units need to re-accomplish this event if they have lost currency or as determined by the SQ/CC.			

3.2.3. Mission-related training will support the mission and concept of operations of the individual squadron; incorporate appropriate portions of AFTTP 3-1.CSCS and other mission-related documents. **(T-3)**

3.3. Initial Certification

3.3.1. Initial Certification of MR crewmembers will be completed within 30 days after completing MQT (recommended, but not required for BMC crewmember). Failure to comply will result in regression to NMR until complete. Suggested briefing guides are at Attachment 3. Each crewmember will demonstrate to a formal board a satisfactory knowledge of the squadron's primary DOC statement missions. Board composition will be established by the SQ/CC. Desired composition is SQ/CC or SQ/DO (chairman), weapons and tactics, training, intelligence, and other mission-area expert representatives. **(T-3)**

3.4. Mission Training:

3.4.1. At SQ/CC discretion, applicable missions from those listed below will be used to build the unit MQT program. MQT programs should use profiles typical of squadron missions.

3.4.2. Supervision. A squadron instructor is required for all training missions unless specified otherwise. **(T-3)**

3.4.3. Minimum Sortie Requirements. The minimum sorties required in a local MQT program will be IAW the MQT course syllabus (not required if portions of the MQT program are used to recertify crewmembers that regressed from MR to BMC). Reference the paragraphs below for further details and recommended sortie flows the SQ/CC may use to develop the unit's MQT program. **(T-2)**

3.4.4. Mission sequence and prerequisites will be IAW the appropriate unit MQT course syllabus (unless waived) **(T-2)**.

3.4.5. Mission Objectives: Be familiar with local area requirements and procedures. Specific Mission Tasks: local area familiarization, emergency procedures and other tasks determined by the unit. **(T-3)**

3.4.6. Individual events may be accomplished anytime during MQT, however all events will be accomplished prior to SQ/CC certification of MR or BMC status **(T-3)**.

3.4.7. Mission Types. Current Special Instructions (SPINS) define CSCS mission types.

    3.4.7.1. Reference standing SPINS for mission type definitions.

3.4.8. Training will be completed within the time specified by the syllabus. Failure to complete within the specified time limit requires notification through channels to the MAJCOM/A3T or equivalent with crewmember's name, rank, reason for delay, planned actions, and estimated completion date. **(T-3)**

3.4.9. Crewmembers in MQT will train under the appropriate supervision as annotated in the FTU syllabus until completing the qualification evaluation. **(T-2)**

3.4.10. FTU syllabus mission objectives and tasks are minimum requirements for MQT. However, additional training events, based on student proficiency and background, may be incorporated into the MQT program with SQ/CC authorization. Additional training due to student non-progression is available within the constraints of the FTU syllabus and may be added at SQ/CC discretion.

3.5. MQT for Senior Officers:

3.5.1. All senior officer training (Colonel selects and above) will be conducted at the unit. **(T-2)**

3.5.2. Senior officers must meet course entry prerequisites and will complete all syllabus requirements unless waived by the MAJCOM/A3. **(T-2)**

3.5.3. Senior officers will be considered in a formal training status for the duration of the course. Their duties will be delegated to appropriate CDs or CVs until training is completed. Waiver authority for this paragraph is the MAJCOM/CC (submitted through the MAJCOM/A3). **(T-2)**

Chapter 4

CONTINUATION TRAINING

4.1. General. This chapter establishes the minimum crewmember training requirements to maintain MR or BMC status for an assigned training status. The SQ/CC will ensure each crewmember receives sufficient training to maintain individual currency and proficiency **(T-3)**.

4.2. Crewmember Status. SQ/CCs will assign crewmembers a status using the following criteria:

4.2.1. Mission Ready (MR). A crewmember member who satisfactorily completed IQT and MQT, and maintains qualification, certification, currency and proficiency in the command or unit operational mission.

4.2.1.1. The crewmember shall be able to attain full unit mission certification to meet operational tasking within 30 days **(T-2)**.

4.2.2. Non-Mission Ready (NMR). A crewmember that is unqualified, non-current or incomplete in required continuation training, or not certified to perform the unit mission.

4.2.3. MR and BMC crewmembers will accomplish and/or maintain RCP requirements, for their respective status, and the appropriate events in the RCP tables in this Instruction and the RTM. **(T-3)**

4.2.4. Crewmembers will maintain all required certifications to operate on the network or will be subject to decertification if those requirements are not met. **(T-3)**

4.3. Training Events/Tables. Standardized training event identifiers and descriptions are located in Attachment 2. Units will include unit-specific events to include a description in their local training documentation. **(T-3)**

4.3.1. Crediting Event Accomplishment. Credit events accomplished on training, operational missions and satisfactory evaluations or certifications toward RCP requirements and establish a due date. Use the date of successful evaluation as the date of accomplishment for all mission-related training events accomplished during a formal course. A successful evaluation establishes a new current and qualified reference date for all accomplished events. For training during IQT or requalification training, numbers of events accomplished prior to the evaluation are not credited to any crew position. In all cases, numbers of events successfully accomplished during the evaluation or certification are credited toward the crew position. **(T-3)**

4.3.2. For an unsatisfactory evaluation, do not log CT requirements for those events graded U/Q3 (according to AFI 17-202V2) until re-qualified. **(T-3)**

4.3.3. Instructors and evaluators may credit up to 50 percent of their total CT requirements while instructing or evaluating.

4.4. Continuation Training Requirements. Completion and tracking of continuation training is ultimately the responsibility of the individual crewmember. Crewmembers should actively work with their supervisors, unit schedulers and training offices to ensure accomplishment of their continuation training requirements. Attached crewmembers are responsible for reporting accomplished training events to their attached unit. **(T-3)**

4.4.1. Mission-Related Training Events. Crewmembers will comply with requirements of Table 4.1. Failure to accomplish events in Table 4.1 leads to NMR status **(T-2)**.

4.4.1.1. Weapons and Tactics Academic Training. Units will establish a weapons and tactics academic training program to satisfy MQT and CT requirements. Training is required semi-annually during each training cycle. SQ/CCs will provide guidance to unit weapons shops to ensure all crewmembers are informed/reminded of all CSCS weapons, systems and mission-specific TTP **(T-2)**.

4.4.1.1.1. Academic instructors should be Weapons Instructor Course (WIC) graduates.

4.4.1.1.2. Instruction should include (as applicable), but is not limited to **(T-3)**:

4.4.1.1.2.1. Applicable AF Tactics, Techniques, and Procedures (AFTTP) 3-1 and 3-3 series publications, AFI 17-2CSCS Volume 3, *Cyberspace Security and Control System (CSCS) Operations Procedures*, and other documents pertaining to the execution of the unit mission.

4.4.1.1.2.2. Specialized training to support specific weapons, tactics, mission capabilities, rules of engagement (ROE), and other mission related activities.

4.4.1.2. Risk Management (RM). Crewmembers will participate in RM training once every training cycle. Briefings will include the concepts outlined in AFPAM 90-803, *Risk Management (RM) Guidelines and Tools*. RM training will be tracked. Failure to complete RM training will result in NMR status.

Table 4.1. CSCS Cybercrew Mission-Related CT Requirements.

Code	Event	Position	Frequency	Notes
GTR002	Weapons & Tactics	All	179d	1, 2
GTR003	Risk Management	All	365d	1, 2
Notes: 1. "d" is the maximum number of days between events. 2. Failure to complete this event within the time prescribed leads to NMR status. Crewmembers will not be able to accomplish unsupervised crew duties until the delinquent event is accomplished or waived. **(T-3)**				

4.4.2. Mission Training Events. Crewmembers will comply with requirements of the RCP Tasking Memorandum (RTM) for their respective position. Total sorties and events are minimums which ensure training to continually meet all DOC tasked requirements and may not be reduced except in proration/waiver. Unless specifically noted the OG/CC is the waiver authority for all RCP requirements and for all provisions in Chapter 4 and Chapter 5 of this volume. Failure to accomplish events in these tables may lead to NMR status. **(T-3)**

4.5. Specialized Mission Training. Specialized training is normally accomplished after a crewmember is assigned MR or BMC status. Unless otherwise specified, crewmembers in MR or BMC positions may hold special mission certifications as long as additional training requirements are accomplished. (See **Chapter 5**) **(T-3)**

4.5.1. The SQ/CC will determine which crewmembers will train for and maintain special mission qualifications and certifications. **(T-3)**

4.6. Currencies, Recurrencies and Requalification.

4.6.1. Currency. The RTM defines currency requirements for MR and BMC crewmembers. Crewmembers may not instruct, evaluate or perform any event in which they are not qualified and current unless under instructor supervision. **(T-3)** Currency may be established or updated by:

4.6.1.1. Accomplishing the event as a qualified crewmember provided member's currency has not expired. **(T-3)**

4.6.1.2. Accomplishing the event as a qualified crewmember under supervision of a current instructor. **(T-3)**

4.6.1.3. Events satisfactorily performed on any evaluation may be used to establish or update currency in that event. **(T-3)**

4.6.2. If a crewmember is non-current, thereby requiring recurrency, that mission or event may not be performed except for the purpose of regaining currency. Non-current events must be satisfied before the crewmember is considered certified/qualified (as applicable) to perform those events unsupervised. Loss of currencies affecting MR status will require regression to BMC (see paragraph 4.9); loss of currencies not affecting MR status does not require regression **(T-3)**.

4.7. Loss of Instructor Status and Requalification/Recurrency. Instructors may lose instructor status for the following:

4.7.1. Loss of currency for greater than 180 days. **(T-3)**

4.7.2. They become noncurrent in a mission or event which causes removal from MR or BMC status and the SQ/CC deems that loss of currency is of sufficient importance to require complete decertification (but not a complete loss of qualification). **(T-3)**

4.7.2.1. If the affected crewmember retains instructor qualification IAW AFI 17-202V2, recertification will be at the SQ/CC's discretion. **(T-3)**

4.7.2.2. If the SQ/CC does not elect to decertify the individual or if the individual becomes non-current in missions or events, which do not require removal from MR status, instructor status may be retained, but the instructor will not instruct that mission or event until the required currency is regained. **(T-3)**

4.7.3. Instructor Lack of Ability. Instructors serve solely at the discretion of the SQ/CC. Instructors should exemplify a higher level of performance and present themselves as reliable and authoritative experts in their respective duty positions. Instructors exhibiting substandard performance should be reviewed for suitability of continued instructor duty. **(T-3)** Instructors will be decertified if:

4.7.3.1. Awarded a less than fully qualified grade in any area of the evaluation regardless of overall crew position qualification. **(T-3)**

4.7.3.2. Failure of a qualification. **(T-3)**

4.7.3.3. SQ/CC deems instructor is substandard, ineffective, or providing incorrect procedures, techniques, or policy guidance. **(T-3)**

4.7.3.4. Decertified instructors may regain instructor status by correcting the applicable deficiency and completing the training and/or evaluation as specified by the SQ/CC. **(T-3)**

4.8. Regression.

4.8.1. MR or BMC Regression for Failure to Meet Lookback. Only RCP training missions and cyberspace operations sorties may be used for lookback. If the crewmember does not meet lookback requirements throughout the training cycle, SQ/CC can regress the crewmember from MR to BMC or NMR. **(T-3)**

4.8.1.1. Failure to meet one-month lookback requires a review of the crewmember's three-month sortie history. If the three-month lookback is met, the crewmember may, at SQ/CC discretion, remain in MR or BMC status. Failure to meet the three-month lookback will result in regression to BMC or NMR/N-BMC, as applicable, or the crewmember may be placed in supervised status at the SQ/CC's discretion. If probation is chosen, the only way to remove a crewmember from probation and preserve the current status is to reestablish a 1-month lookback at the end of the probation period. ARC utilizes 4-month lookback and 6-month lookback instead of 1-month and 3-month. **(T-3)**

4.8.1.2. Lookback computations begin following completion of MQT. The crewmember must maintain 1-month lookback until a 3-month lookback is possible. SQ/CCs may apply supervisory rules as described in paragraph 4.8.1.1 if a new MR or BMC crewmember fails to meet currency and proficiency requirements during the 1-month lookback while establishing 3-month lookback. In addition, 1-month lookback will start the first full month of MR or BMC status. **(T-3)**

4.8.1.3. ARC replaces 1-month lookback with 4-month lookback and 3-month lookback with 6-month lookback. **(T-3)**

4.8.2. Regression for Failed Evaluations. Crewmembers who fail a periodic evaluation are unqualified and will regress to NMR as applicable. Crewmembers will remain NMR until successfully completing required corrective action(s), re-evaluation and SQ/CC re-certification **(T-3)**.

4.8.3. Failure to Maintain Standards. If a qualified crewmember demonstrates lack of proficiency or knowledge, the SQ/CC may elect to regress the individual to NMR as applicable. These crewmembers will remain NMR until successful completion of corrective action as determined by the SQ/CC, an evaluation if required, and re-certification by the SQ/CC. **(T-3)**

4.9. End-of-Cycle Requirements. Crewmembers who fail to complete mission or event requirements by the end of training cycle may require additional training depending on the type and magnitude of the deficiency. Refer to paragraph 4.11 for proration guidance. In all cases, units will report training shortfalls to the OG/CC. **(T-3)**

4.9.1. Crewmembers failing to meet annual RCP events or minimum total sortie requirements may continue CT at MR or BMC as determined by lookback. The SQ/CC will determine if additional training is required.

4.9.2. Failure to meet specific MR or BMC mission type requirements will result in one of the following:

4.9.2.1. Regression to NMR if the SQ/CC determines the mission type deficiency is significant. To regain MR or BMC status, the crewmember will complete all deficient mission types. These missions may also count toward the total requirements for the new training cycle. **(T-3)**

4.9.2.2. Continuation at MR or BMC status if total RCP missions and lookback are maintained and the mission type deficiencies are deemed insignificant by the SQ/CC. The SQ/CC will determine if any additional training is required to address shortfall. **(T-3)**

4.9.3. Failure to accomplish missions/events required for Special Mission capabilities or certifications/qualifications will result in loss of that certification/qualification. The SQ/CC will determine recertification requirements. Requalification requirements are IAW AFI 17-202V2 applicable HHQ guidance, and AFI 17-2CSCS Volume 2, *Cyberspace Security and Control System (CSCS) Standardization and Evaluations*. **(T-3)**

4.10. Proration of Training.

4.10.1. Proration of End-of-Cycle Requirements. At the end of the training cycle the SQ/CC may prorate any training requirements precluded by the following events: initial arrival date in squadron, emergency leave, non-mission TDYs, exercises, or deployments. Ordinary annual leave will not be considered as non-availability. Other extenuating circumstances, as determined by the SQ/CC, that prevent the crewmember from mission duties for more than 15 consecutive days may be considered as non-availability for proration purposes. **(T-3)** The following guidelines apply:

4.10.1.1. Proration will not be used to mask training or planning deficiencies. **(T-3)**

4.10.1.2. Proration is based on cumulative days of non-availability for mission duties in the training cycle. Use Table 4.2 to determine the number of months to be prorated based on each period of cumulative non-mission duty calendar days. **(T-3)**

4.10.1.3. If MQT is re-accomplished, a crewmember's training cycle will start over at a prorated share following completion of MQT. **(T-3)**

4.10.1.4. No requirement may be prorated below one. Prorated numbers resulting in fractions of less than 0.5 will be rounded to the next lower whole number (one or greater). **(T-3)**

4.10.1.5. Newly assigned crewmembers achieving MR or BMC status after the 15th of the month are considered to be in CT on the first day of the following month for proration purposes. A prorated share of RCP missions must be completed in CT. **(T-3)**

4.10.1.6. A crewmember's last month on station prior to PCSing may be prorated provided 1 month's proration is not exceeded. Individuals PCSing may be considered MR for reporting purposes during a period of 60 days from date of last mission/sortie, or until loss of MR currency, port call date, or sign in at new duty station, whichever occurs first.

4.10.1.7. Activated Reserve Augmentation Unit (RAU) members will maintain active duty proficiencies and currency requirements prorated for the duration they are on orders. **(T-3)**

4.11. Operational Missions. The following procedures are intended to provide flexibility in accomplishing the unit's CT program. Sorties conducted during operational missions will be logged. These sorties count toward annual RCP requirements and will be used for lookback purposes. Operational missions and events may be used to update proficiency/currency requirements if they meet the criteria in Attachment 2. **(T-3)**

4.11.1. Example: Capt Jones was granted 17 days of emergency leave in January and attended SOS in residence from March through April for 56 consecutive calendar days. The SQ/CC authorized a total of two months proration from his training cycle (two months for the 73 cumulative days of non-availability).

Table 4.2. Proration Allowance.

CUMULATIVE DAYS OF NON-MISSION ACTIVITY	PRORATION ALLOWED (Months)
0 – 15	0
16 – 45	1
46 – 75	2
76 – 105	3
106 – 135	4
136 – 165	5
166 – 195	6
196 – 225	7
226 – 255	8
256 – 285	9
286 – 315	10
316 – 345	11
Over 345	12

4.12. Regaining MR or BMC Status.

4.12.1. If MR or BMC status is lost due to failure to meet the end of cycle event requirements, re-certification/re-qualification is IAW paragraph 4.10. **(T-3)**

4.12.2. If MR or BMC status is lost due to failure to meet lookback IAW paragraph 4.10, the following applies (timing starts from the date the crewmember came off MR or BMC status):

4.12.2.1. Up to 90 Days.   Complete a SQ/CC approved recertification program (documented in the individual's training folder) to return the crewmember to MR or BMC standards.   Upon completion of the recertification program, the MR or BMC crewmember must also meet the subsequent 1-month lookback requirement prior to reclaiming MR or BMC status.   The missions and events accomplished during the recertification program may be credited towards their total/type mission and event requirements for the training cycle as well as for their monthly mission requirement. In addition, all RCP event currencies must be regained. The SQ/CC will approve any other additional training prior to MR recertification. **(T-3)**

4.12.2.2. 91-180 Days.   Same as above, plus open/closed book qualification examinations (IAW AFI 17-202V2. Open/closed book exams will be documented IAW AFI 17-202V2. **(T-3)**

4.12.2.3. 181 Days and Beyond. Reaccomplish a SQ/CC-directed MQT program to include a formal MSN evaluation IAW AFI 17-202V2, applicable HHQ guidance, and AFI 17-2CSCS V2. **(T-3)**

Chapter 5

UPGRADE AND SPECIALIZED TRAINING

5.1. General. This chapter outlines duties and responsibilities for units to upgrade, certify, and maintain currency/proficiency for special capabilities, and certifications/qualifications. SQ/CCs may tailor programs for individuals based on previous experience, qualifications, and documented performance. These capabilities and certifications/qualifications are in addition to unit core missions and do not apply to every crewmember assigned or attached to the unit.

5.2. Requirements. Requirements for upgrade and special mission training are listed in Table 1.2. Additionally, commander endorsement is required to ensure each candidate has the ability, judgment, technical expertise, skill and experience when selecting a crewmember for upgrade or specialized mission training. Prerequisites are waiverable by SQ/CC. **(T-3)**

5.3. Instructor Upgrade. This section establishes the minimum guidelines for instructor upgrade.

5.3.1. Instructor Responsibilities. An AF instructor shall be a competent subject matter expert adept in the methodology of instruction. The instructor shall be proficient in evaluating, diagnosing, and critiquing student performance, identifying learning objectives and difficulties, and prescribing and conducting remedial instruction. The instructor must be able to conduct instruction in all training venues (e.g., classroom, training devices, ops floor, mission execution, etc.). **(T-3)**

5.3.1.1. Instructor Prerequisites. SQ/CCs will consider ability, judgment, technical expertise, skill, and experience when selecting a crewmember for instructor upgrade. **(T-3)**

5.3.1.2. For instructor minimum requirements, see Table 5.2. All instructor candidates will be MR in their unit's mission. USAF Weapons School (USAFWS) graduates are instructor qualified **(T-2)**.

5.3.1.3. Training. Instructor training will include methodology of instruction, Air Force tasking process, mission planning, and unit mission employment at the minimum (e.g., tasked mission types). The instructor candidate must be able to conduct instruction in all training venues (e.g., classroom, training devices, ops floor, mission execution, etc.). **(T-3)**

5.3.1.4. Testing. Units will develop tests based on the training requirements in AFI 17-202V1, HHQ Supplements, this publication, and other relevant guidance. Tests will be closed book and consist of a minimum of 25 questions. To receive credit for this training each instructor candidate must pass the test with a minimum score of 80 percent. Units will develop and maintain an instructor test master question file. **(T-3)**

5.3.1.5. Qualification and Certification. All instructor candidates will demonstrate to an evaluator their ability to instruct and perform selected tasks and items according to applicable directives.   Following successful completion of instructor training and evaluation, the SQ/CC or designated representative will personally interview the candidate and review instructor responsibilities, scope of duties, authority, and philosophy. The SQ/CC will certify a new instructor by placing a letter of certification in the training folder and indicate qualifications on a letter of Xs **(T-2)**.

WILLIAM J. BENDER, Lt Gen, USAF
Chief, Information Dominance and Chief
Information Office

Attachment 1

GLOSSARY OF REFERENCES AND SUPPORTING INFORMATION

References

AFPD 17-2, *Cyberspace Operations*, 12 April 2016

AFI 17-202 Volume 1, *Cybercrew Training*, 2 April 2014

AFI 17-202 Volume 2, *Cybercrew Standardization and Evaluation Program*, 15 October 2014

AFI 17-2CSCS Volume 2, *Cyberspace Security and Control System (CSCS) Standardization and Evaluations*

AFI 17-2CSCS Volume 3, *Cyberspace Security and Control System (CSCS) Operations Procedures*

AFI 33-360, *Publications and Forms Management*, 1 December 2015

AFMAN 33-363, *Management of Records*, 1 March 2008

AFPAM 90-803, *Risk Management (RM) Guidelines and Tools*, 11 February 2013

Prescribed Forms

None

Adopted Forms

AF Form 847, *Recommendation for Change of Publication*

Abbreviations and Acronyms

AF— Air Force

AFI— Air Force Instruction

AFMAN— Air Force Manual

AFPD— Air Force Policy Document

AFRC— Air Force Reserve Command

AFRIMS— Air Force Records Information Management System

AFSPC— Air Force Space Command

AFTTP— Air Force Tactics, Techniques and Procedures

ANG— Air National Guard

ARC— Air Reserve Components

BCQ— Basic Cyber Qualified

BMC— Basic Mission Capable

C2— Command & Control

CC— Commander

CD— Deputy Commander

CPI— Cybercrew Position Indicator

CSCS— Cyberspace Security and Control System

CSCS-BPO - CSCS Boundary Protection Operator

CSCS-CC - CSCS Crew Commander

CSCS-CPO - CSCS Client End Point Protection Operator

CSCS-DSO - CSCS Directory Services Operator

CSCS-IFO - CSCS Infrastructure Operator

CSCS-MMO - CSCS Monitoring Management Operator

CSCS-OC - CSCS Operations Controller

CSCS-SVO - CSCS Storage and Virtualization Operator

CSCS-VAO - CSCS Vulnerability Assessment Operator

CSCS-VRO - CSCS Vulnerability Remediation Operator

CT— Continuation Training

CV— Vice Commander

CW— Cyberspace Wing

DO— Director of Operations

DOC— Designed Operational Capability

EXP— Experienced

FLT— Flight

FTU— Formal Training Unit

HHQ— Higher Headquarters

HQ— Headquarters

IAW— In Accordance With

IP— Internet Protocol

IQT— Initial Qualification Training

LIMFAC— Limiting Factor

MAJCOM— Major Command

MC— Mission Commander

MQT— Mission Qualification Training

MR— Mission Ready

N-BMC – Non-Basic Mission Capable

NGB— National Guard Bureau

NMR – Non-Mission Ready

OG— Operations Group

OPORD— Operations Order

OPR— Office of Primary Responsibility

OSS— Operations Support Squadron

PCS— Permanent Change of Station

RAU— Reserve Augmentation Unit

RDS— Records Disposition Schedule

RCP— Ready Cybercrew Program

ROE— Rules of Engagement

RTM— RCP Tasking Memorandum

SPINS— Special Instructions

SQ— Squadron

TDY— Temporary Duty

USAF— United States Air Force

USAFWS— United States Air Force Weapons School

WIC— Weapons Instructor Course

Terms

Additional Training—Any training recommended to remedy deficiencies identified during an evaluation that must be completed by a specific due date. This training may include self-study, Crew Training Device or simulator. Additional training must include demonstration of satisfactory knowledge or proficiency to examiner, supervisor or instructor (as stipulated in the Additional Training description) to qualify as completed.

Attached Personnel—This includes anyone not assigned to the unit but maintaining qualification through that unit. AFRC, ANG, and HAF augmented personnel are an example of attached personnel.

Basic Cyber Qualified (BCQ)—A crewmember member who satisfactorily completed IQT. The crewmember will carry BCQ only until completion of MQT. BCQ crewmembers will not perform RCP-tasked events or sorties without instructor crewmembers.

Basic Mission Capable (BMC)—A crewmember member who satisfactorily completed IQT and MQT, but is not in fully certified MR status. The crewmember accomplishes training required to remain familiarized in all and may be qualified and proficient in some of the primary missions of their weapon system BMC requirements. These crewmembers may also maintain special mission qualification.

Boundary Protection Operator (CSCS—BPO) – Allows/denies/redirects/logs network traffic in, though, and from base firewalls and proxies. Additionally, evaluates, detects, prevents, and implements counter-measures to protect network hosts, data, voice, and key mission systems from unauthorized network activity.

Certification—Designation of an individual by the certifying official (normally the SQ/CC) as having completed required training and being capable of performing a specific duty.

Client End Point Protection Operator (CSCS—CPO) – Remediates vulnerabilities and weaknesses identified in cyberspace terrain and associated software suites utilized by Air Force Information Systems and net-centric capabilities.

Continuation Training (CT)— Training which provides crewmembers with the volume, frequency, and mix of training necessary to maintain currency and proficiency in the assigned qualification level.

Currency—A measure of how frequently and/or recently a task is completed. Currency requirements should ensure the average crewmember maintains a minimum level of proficiency in a specific event.

Cybercrew Position Indicator (CPI)—Codes used to manage crewmember positions to ensure a high state of readiness is maintained with available resources.

Cyberspace Operations (CO)—The employment of cyberspace capabilities where the primary purpose is to achieve objectives in or through cyberspace.

Directory Services Operator (CSCS-DSO)—Provides authentication and accessibility to clients in the Air Force Network domain.

Experienced Crewmember (EXP)—A crewmember who has met the minimums listed in the RTM, has completed MQT and maintains CMR/BMC requirements of this instruction, and who, in the commander's judgment, exhibits a high degree of experience, professionalism, and proficiency to support unit missions.

Infrastructure Operator (CSCS-IFO)—Employs both configuration and security policies on network components to enforce policies and techniques that effectively and securely route network traffic.

Initial Qualification Training (IQT)—Weapon system-specific training designed to address system specific and/or positional specific training leading to declaration of BCQ as a prerequisite to Mission Qualification Training (MQT).

Instructor—An experienced individual qualified to instruct other individuals in mission area academics and positional duties. Instructors will be qualified appropriately to the level of the training they provide.

Instructor Training—Training designed to declare a member as instructor qualify.

Instructor Event—An event logged by an instructor when performing instructor duties during the sortie, or a portion thereof. Instructor qualification required and used for the mission or a mission element. Examples include upgrade sorties, re-establishing currencies, etc. Instructors will log this event on evaluation sorties.

Mission—A set of tasks that lead to an objective, to include associated planning, brief, execution, and debrief.

Mission Qualification Training (MQT)—Following IQT, MQT is a formal training program used to qualify crewmember members in assigned crew positions to perform the unit mission. This training is required to achieve a basic level of competence in the unit's primary tasked missions and is a prerequisite for MR or BMC declaration.

Mission Ready (MR)—The status of a crewmember member who satisfactorily completed IQT, MQT, and maintains certification, currency and proficiency in the command or unit operational mission.

Monitoring Management Operator (CSCS-MMO)—Provides situational awareness of cyberspace terrain and weapons system component health monitoring solutions for the CSCS.

Proficiency—A measure of how well a task is completed. A crewmember is considered proficient when they can perform tasks at the minimum acceptable levels of speed, accuracy and safety.

Qualification (QUAL)—Designation of an individual by the unit commander as having completed required training and evaluation and being capable of performing a specific duty.

Ready Cybercrew Program (RCP)—Annual sortie/event training requirements for crewmembers to maintain mission ready/combat mission ready (MR) status.

Sortie—The actions an individual cyberspace weapon system takes to accomplish a mission and/or mission objective(s) within a defined start and stop period.

Specialized Mission Training—Training in any special skills (e.g., tactics, weapon system capabilities, responsibilities, etc.) necessary to perform the unit's assigned missions that are not required by every crewmember. Specialized training is normally accomplished after the crew member is assigned MR or BMC status, and is normally in addition to MR or BMC requirements. This training may require an additional certification and/or qualification event as determined by the SQ/CC.

Squadron Supervisor—May include all or some of the following depending on specific guidance and SQ/CC concurrence: SQ/CC, SQ/DO, ADOs, and FLT/CCs.

Storage and Virtualization Operator (CSCS-SVO)—Performs backup, recovery, and archiving via storage area networks (SAN).

Supervised Status—The status of a crew member who must perform the mission under the supervision of an instructor.

Supervisory Crewmember or Staff Member—Personnel in supervisory or staff positions (CPI-6/8/B/D) who actively conduct cyber operations.

Training Level—Assigned to individuals based on the continuation training status (basic cyber qualification, basic mission capable, or mission ready/combat mission ready) they are required to maintain.

Training Period—Any training period determined by the wing in which training requirements are performed.

Upgrade Training—Training needed to qualify to a crew position of additional responsibility for a specific weapon system (e.g., special mission qualifications). See special mission event training.

Vulnerability Assessment Operator (CSCS—VAO) – Identifies vulnerabilities within cyberspace terrain and associated software suites utilized by Air Force Information systems and net-centric capabilities. In addition, identifies and assesses the weaknesses in cyberspace terrain through which adversaries may gain/maintain access to the AFNet.

Vulnerability Remediation Operator (CSCS—VRO) – Remediates vulnerabilities within cyberspace terrain and associated software suites utilized by Air Force Information systems and net-centric capabilities.

Attachment 2

GLOSSARY OF MISSION, SORTIE AND EVENT DEFINITIONS

A2.1. Mission and Sortie Definitions:

A2.1.1. See 624th Operations Center portal for latest information.

A2.2. Mission, Sortie and Event Identifiers and Descriptions:

A2.2.1. Mission-Related Training. Mission-related training is training required of all crewmembers as part of their CT program. Where conflict exists between this guidance and the RTM, the RTM takes precedence. Training accomplished during IQT/MQT may be credited toward CT requirements for the training cycle in which it was accomplished.

A2.2.1.1. GTR001 Unit Indoctrination Training (CSCS Fundamentals).

A2.2.1.1.1. Purpose: Each newly assigned crewmember will complete CSCS Fundamentals, a unit indoctrination program, prior to performing unsupervised primary crew duties. This is one-time training after a permanent change of station/assignment.

A2.2.1.1.2. Description: This training is required for all newly assigned and attached crewmembers. The unit will publish specific requirements. This training will prepare crewmembers for the unit's operational mission. The training will familiarize them with local procedures, facility/support agencies; introduce any unit/mission unique procedures, and other information as determined by the SQ/CC. Familiarization will be to standards established in the unit conducting the training.

A2.2.1.1.3. OPR: Unit/DOT

A2.2.1.1.4. Course Developer: Unit/DOT

A2.2.1.1.5. Training Media: Lecture

A2.2.1.1.6. Additional Information: Document Unit Indoctrination Training in the individual's Training IQF for assigned and attached personnel.

A2.2.1.2. GTR002 Weapons and Tactics Training.

A2.2.1.2.1. Purpose: To provide the crewmember with the information necessary for effective and successful execution of the unit's assigned mission.

A2.2.1.2.2. Description: GTR002 will be administered using courseware developed by the unit. The course will be based on information found in at a minimum AFTTP 3-1.CSCS, AFTTP 3-1.General Planning, and AFTTP 3-1.Threat Guide, AFI 17-2CSCS V3 as well as other documents relevant to the execution of the unit's mission (e.g. AFTTP 3-1.ACD / AFINC / CVA/Hunter, AFTTP 3-1/3-3.AOC, etc.)

A2.2.1.2.3. OPR: Unit/DOK

A2.2.1.2.4. Course Developer: Unit/DOK

A2.2.1.2.5. Training Media: Lecture

A2.2.1.2.6. Instructor Requirements: Academic instructors should be WIC graduates or have attended the applicable academic portion(s) of school, if possible.

A2.2.1.2.7. Additional Information: Instructors teaching GTR002 may receive credit for their GTR002 requirement.

A2.2.1.3. GTR003 Crew Risk Management (CRM) Training.

A2.2.1.3.1. Purpose: Provide crewmembers with unit CRM training according to AF Pamphlet 90-803, Risk Management (RM) Guidelines and Tools, other RM resources, and MAJCOM Supplements.

A2.2.1.3.2. Description: GTR003 will be administered using unit developed courseware. CRM training introduces the common core CRM subjects to provide crewmembers with the information necessary to enhance mission effectiveness. Training should create a cultural mindset in which every crewmember is trained and motivated to manage risk and integrates CRM into the mission and activity planning process ensuring decisions are based upon risk assessment of the operation/activity. CRM training will be tailored to meet the unique mission needs and operational requirements of each organization and to the personnel within the organization.

A2.2.1.3.3. OPR: Unit

A2.2.1.3.4. Course Developer: Unit

A2.2.1.3.5. Training Media: Lecture

A2.2.1.3.6. Additional Information: CRM instructors teaching GTR003 may receive credit for their GTR003 requirement.

A2.3. CSCS Events Training. The following is a list of tactical events to be used for fulfilling continuation training requirements. It is recommended that Unit/DOT integrate tactics training into each of these scenarios.

A2.3.1. EV001 Malicious Email

A2.3.1.1. Purpose: Detect and defeat a malicious email

A2.3.1.2. Description: A coordinated effort to employ the weapon system to counter nefarious email which may contain malicious logic and/or malicious URLs.

A2.3.1.3. OPR: Unit/DOT

A2.3.1.4. Course Developer: Unit/DOT

A2.3.1.5. Training Media: Weapon system, table top exercise, or simulator

A2.3.1.6. Instructor Requirements: Certified CSCS Instructor

A2.3.1.7. Additional Information: Student assessment via instructor observation

A2.3.2. EV002 Data Exfiltration Attempt

A2.3.2.1. Purpose: Detect and defeat a Data Exfiltration Attempt

A2.3.2.2. Description: A coordinated effort to employ the weapon system to counter the adversary conducting data exfiltration from the AFIN.

A2.3.2.3. OPR: Unit/DOT

A2.3.2.4. Course Developer: Unit/DOT

A2.3.2.5. Training Media: Weapon system or simulator

A2.3.2.6. Instructor Requirements: Certified CSCS Instructor

A2.3.2.7. Additional Information: Student assessment via instructor observation

A2.3.3. EV003 Rogue Network Devices

A2.3.3.1. Purpose: Detect and remove a rogue network device

A2.3.3.2. Description: A coordinated effort to employ the weapon system to counter and remove a rogue network device from the CSCS.

A2.3.3.3. OPR: Unit/DOT

A2.3.3.4. Course Developer: Unit/DOT

A2.3.3.5. Training Media: Weapon system, table top exercise, or simulator

A2.3.3.6. Instructor Requirements: Certified CSCS Instructor

A2.3.3.7. Additional Information: Student assessment via instructor observation

A2.3.4. EV004 AFIN Malware Propagation

A2.3.4.1. Purpose: Detect and isolate propagating malware

A2.3.4.2. Description: A coordinated effort to employ the weapon system to counter and/or isolate malicious logic propagating on the AFIN.

A2.3.4.3. OPR: Unit/DOT

A2.3.4.4. Course Developer: Unit/DOT

A2.3.4.5. Training Media: Weapon system, table top exercise, or simulator

A2.3.4.6. Instructor Requirements: Certified CSCS Instructor

A2.3.4.7. Additional Information: Student assessment via instructor observation

A2.3.5. EV005 Host to Host Exploitation

A2.3.5.1. Purpose: Detect and defeat AFIN host compromise

A2.3.5.2. Description: A coordinated effort to employ the weapon system to counter inter host exploitation on the AFIN.

A2.3.5.3. OPR: Unit/DOT

A2.3.5.4. Course Developer: Unit/DOT

A2.3.5.5. Training Media: Weapon system, table top exercise, or simulator

A2.3.5.6. Instructor Requirements: Certified CSCS Instructor

A2.3.5.7. Additional Information: Student assessment via instructor observation

A2.3.6. EV006 C2 Channel ID

A2.3.6.1. Purpose: Detect and defeat an adversary C2 channel on the AFIN

A2.3.6.2. Description: A coordinated effort to employ the weapon system to counter an adversary C2 channel on the AFIN.

A2.3.6.3. OPR: Unit/DOT

A2.3.6.4. Course Developer: Unit/DOT

A2.3.6.5. Training Media: Weapon system, table top exercise, or simulator

A2.3.6.6. Instructor Requirements: Certified CSCS Instructor

A2.3.6.7. Additional Information: Student assessment via instructor observation

A2.3.7. EV007 Weapon System Component Compromise

A2.3.7.1. Purpose: Detect and respond to Weapon System compromise

A2.3.7.2. Description: Identify and counter threats to components of the CSCS Weapon System.

A2.3.7.3. OPR: Unit/DOT

A2.3.7.4. Course Developer: Unit/DOT

A2.3.7.5. Training Media: Weapon system, table top exercise, or simulator

A2.3.7.6. Instructor Requirements: Certified CSCS Instructor

A2.3.7.7. Additional Information: Student assessment via instructor observation

A2.3.8. EV08 Identify True Source IP

A2.3.8.1. Purpose: Correlate true source IP of potentially malicious traffic

A2.3.8.2. Description: A coordinated effort to employ the weapon system to track down and identify true source IP address.

A2.3.8.3. OPR: Unit/DOT

A2.3.8.4. Course Developer: Unit/DOT

A2.3.8.5. Training Media: Weapon system, table top exercise, or simulator

A2.3.8.6. Instructor Requirements: Certified CSCS Instructor

A2.3.8.7. Additional Information: Student assessment via instructor observation

A2.3.9. EV09 System Reconstitution

A2.3.9.1. Purpose: Detect and respond to degraded/disruption in system service

A2.3.9.2. Description: A coordinated effort to employ the weapon system to stage and deploy server backups or machine images to reconstitute network loss.

A2.3.9.3. OPR: Unit/DOT

A2.3.9.4. Course Developer: Unit/DOT

A2.3.9.5. Training Media: Weapon system, table top exercise, or simulator

A2.3.9.6. Instructor Requirements: Certified CSCS Instructor

A2.3.9.7. Additional Information: Student assessment via instructor observation

A2.3.10. EV010 Data (Domain) Spill

A2.3.10.1. Purpose: Detect and respond to data spill event

A2.3.10.2. Description: A coordinated effort to employ the weapon system to detect and mitigate a data spill event.

A2.3.10.3. OPR: Unit/DOT

A2.3.10.4. Course Developer: Unit/DOT

A2.3.10.5. Training Media: Weapon system, table top exercise, or simulator

A2.3.10.6. Instructor Requirements: Certified CSCS Instructor

A2.3.10.7. Additional Information: Student assessment via instructor observation

A2.3.11. EV011 Cross-Domain Violation

A2.3.11.1. Purpose: Detect and respond to cross-domain violation

A2.3.11.2. Description: A coordinated effort to employ the weapon system to detect and isolate incidents of cross-domain violations.

A2.3.11.3. OPR: Unit/DOT

A2.3.11.4. Course Developer: Unit/DOT

A2.3.11.5. Training Media: Weapon system, table top exercise, or simulator

A2.3.11.6. Instructor Requirements: Certified CSCS Instructor

A2.3.11.7. Additional Information: Student assessment via instructor observation

A2.3.12. EV012 Support to Forensics Access

A2.3.12.1. Purpose: Support to forensics investigations

A2.3.12.2. Description A coordinated effort to employ the weapon system to enable access for and support system forensics.

A2.3.12.3. OPR: Unit/DOT

A2.3.12.4. Course Developer: Unit/DOT

A2.3.12.5. Training Media: Weapon system, table top exercise, or simulator

A2.3.12.6. Instructor Requirements: Certified CSCS Instructor

A2.3.12.7. Additional Information: Student assessment via instructor observation

A2.3.13. EV013 Enumerate Blue Terrain

A2.3.13.1. Purpose: Teach principals of enumerating friendly forces cyberspace terrain

A2.3.13.2. Description: A coordinated effort to employ the weapon system to detect and identify systems located within blue or friendly space.

A2.3.13.3. OPR: Unit/DOT

A2.3.13.4. Course Developer: Unit/DOT

A2.3.13.5. Training Media: Weapon system, table top exercise, or simulator

A2.3.13.6. Instructor Requirements: Certified CSCS Instructor

A2.3.13.7. Additional Information: Student assessment via instructor observation

A2.3.14. EV014 Quarantine Malicious Host/Service

A2.3.14.1. Purpose: Execute the quarantine of network host(s)/service(s)

A2.3.14.2. Description: A coordinated effort to employ the weapon system to detect and respond to malicious hosts/services.

A2.3.14.3. OPR: Unit/DOT

A2.3.14.4. Course Developer: Unit/DOT

A2.3.14.5. Training Media: Weapon system, table top exercise, or simulator

A2.3.14.6. Instructor Requirements: Certified CSCS Instructor

A2.3.14.7. Additional Information: Student assessment via instructor observation

Attachment 3

CREWMEMBER RESOURCE MANAGEMENT

A3.1. Crewmember inventory requires close management at all levels to ensure a high state of readiness is maintained with available resources. To manage crewmember inventory, Cybercrew Position Indicator (CPI) codes are assigned to identify these positions.

Table A3.1. Cybercrew Position Indicator (CPI) Codes.

CPI Codes	Explanation	Remarks
1	Crewmember position used primarily for weapon system operations (Officer).	See Note 1
2	Crewmember position used primarily for weapon system operations (Government Civilians).	See Note 1
3	Staff or supervisory positions at wing level and below that have responsibilities and duties that require cyberspace operations expertise but which do not require the incumbents to operate the weapon system.	See Note 2
4	Staff or supervisory positions above the wing level that have responsibilities and duties that require cyberspace operations expertise but which do not require the incumbents to operate the weapon system.	See Note 2
6	Staff or supervisory positions at wing level and below that have responsibilities and duties that require the incumbents to actively perform cyberspace operational duties on the weapon system.	See Note 2
8	Staff or supervisory positions above the wing level that have responsibilities and duties that require the incumbent to actively conduct cyberspace operations on the weapon system.	See Note 2
A	Crewmember positions used primarily for weapon system operations (Enlisted).	See Note 1
B	Staff or supervisory positions at wing level and below that have responsibilities and duties that require the incumbents to actively perform cyberspace operational duties on the weapon system.	See Note 2
C	Staff or supervisory positions at wing level and below that have responsibilities and duties that require cyberspace operations expertise but which do not require the incumbents to actively operate the weapon system.	See Note 2
D	Staff or supervisory positions above the wing level that have responsibilities and duties that require the incumbent to actively conduct cyberspace operations on a weapon system.	See Note 2
E	Staff or supervisory positions above the wing level that have responsibilities and duties that require cyberspace operations expertise but which do not require the incumbents to actively operate the weapon system.	See Note 2
Z	Crewmember positions used primarily for weapon system operations (Contractor).	See Note 1

Notes:
1. CPI-1, 2, A and Z are for officers, enlisted, government civilian, and contractor personnel assigned to operational squadrons or formal training programs. The primary duty of these personnel is to operate the weapon system to conduct cyberspace operations.
2. CPI-3, 4, 6, 8, B, C, D, and E identify crewmember members assigned to supervisory or staff positions. These positions require cyberspace operations experience with some requiring weapon system operation (CPI-6, 8, B, and D).

BY ORDER OF THE SECRETARY
OF THE AIR FORCE

AIR FORCE INSTRUCTION 17-2CSCS,
VOLUME 2

11 MAY 2017

Cyberspace

CYBERSPACE SECURITY AND
CONTROL SYSTEM (CSCS)
STANDARDIZATION AND
EVALUATIONS

COMPLIANCE WITH THIS PUBLICATION IS MANDATORY

ACCESSIBILITY: Publications and forms are available for downloading or ordering on the e- Publishing website at **www.e-Publishing.af.mil**

RELEASABILITY: There are no releasability restrictions on this publication

OPR: HQ USAF/A3CX/A6CX

Certified by: HQ USAF/A3C/A6C
(Brig Gen Kevin B. Kennedy)
Pages: 31

This Instruction implements Air Force (AF) Policy Directive (AFPD) 17-2, *Cyberspace Operations*, and references Air Force Instruction (AFI) 17-202 Volume 2, *Cybercrew Standardization and Evaluation Program*. It establishes the Crew Standardization and Evaluation (Stan/Eval) procedures and evaluation criteria for qualifying crew members in the Cyberspace Security and Control System (CSCS) weapon system. This publication applies to all military and civilian AF personnel, members of AF Reserve Command (AFRC) units and the Air National Guard (ANG). Refer to paragraph 1.3 for information on the authority to waive provisions of this AFI. This publication may be supplemented at the unit level, but all direct supplements must be routed through channels to HQ USAF/A3C/A6C for coordination prior to certification and approval.

The authorities to waive wing/unit level requirements in this publication are identified with a Tier ("T-0, T-1, T-2, T-3") number following the compliance statement. See AFI 33-360, *Publications and Forms Management*, Table 1.1 for a description of the authorities associated with the Tier numbers. Submit requests for waivers through the chain of command to the appropriate Tier waiver approval authority, or alternately, to the Publication OPR for non-tiered compliance items. Send recommended changes or comments to the Office of Primary Responsibility (OPR) (HQ USAF/A3C/A6C, 1480 Air Force Pentagon, Washington, DC 20330-1480), using AF Form 847, *Recommendation for Change of Publication*; route AF Forms 847 from the field through the chain of command. This Instruction requires collecting and maintaining information protected by the Privacy Act of 1974 (5 U.S.C. 552a). System of records notices F036 AF PC C, Military Personnel Records System, and OPM/GOVT-1, General Personnel Records, apply. When collecting and maintaining information protect it by the Privacy Act of 1974 authorized by 10 U.S.C. 8013. Ensure all records created as a result of processes prescribed in this publication are maintained in accordance with (IAW) AF Manual (AFMAN) 33-363, *Management of Records*, and disposed of in accordance with the AF Records Disposition Schedule (RDS) located in the AF Records Management Information System (AFRIMS). See Attachment 1 for a glossary of references and supporting information.

Chapter 1

GENERAL INFORMATION

1.1. General. This instruction provides cyberspace operations examiners and cybercrew members with procedures and evaluation criteria used during performance evaluations on operational cyberspace weapon systems. For evaluation purposes, refer to this AFI for evaluation standards. Adherence to these procedures and criteria will ensure an accurate assessment of the proficiency and capabilities of cybercrew members. In addition to general criteria information and grading criteria, this AFI provides specific information and grading criteria for each crew position, instructor upgrade qualification and Stan/Eval examiner objectivity evaluations.

1.2. Recommendation for Change of Publication. Recommendations for improvements to this volume will be submitted on AF Form 847, *Recommendation for Change of Publication*, through the appropriate functional chain of command to HQ USAF/A3CX/A6CX. Approved recommendations will be collated into interim or formal change notices, and forwarded to HQ 24 AF/A3T for HQ 24 AF/A3 approval.

1.3. Waivers. Unless another approval authority is cited ("T-0, T-1, T-2, T-3"), waiver authority for this volume is the MAJCOM/A3 (or equivalent). Submit requests for waivers using AF Form 679 through the chain of command to the appropriate Tier waiver approval authority. If approved, waivers remain in effect for the life of the published guidance, unless the waiver authority specifies a shorter period of time, cancels in writing, or issues a change that alters the basis for the waiver.

1.4. Procedures:

1.4.1. Standardization and Evaluation Examiners (SEEs) will use the grading policies contained in AFI 17-202V2 and the evaluation criteria in this instruction volume for conducting all AFSPC and AFSPC-oversight units' weapon system performance, Cybercrew Training Device (CTD) and Emergency Procedures Evaluations (EPE). All evaluations assume a stable platform and normal operating conditions. Compound emergency procedures (multiple, simultaneous emergencies) will not be used.

1.4.2. Each squadron will design and maintain evaluation profiles for each mission/weapon system that includes information on each crew position. These profiles, approved by OG/OGV, should outline the minimum number and type of events to be performed/observed to satisfy a complete evaluation. Evaluation profiles will incorporate requirements established in the applicable grading criteria and reflect the primary unit tasking **(T-3)**.

1.4.3. All evaluations fall under the Qualification (QUAL), Mission (MSN) or Spot (SPOT) categories listed in AFI 17-202V2. For dual/multiple qualification or difference evaluations that do not update an eligibility period, list as "SPOT" on the front of the AF Form 4418, *Certificate of Cybercrew Qualification*, and explain that it was a difference evaluation under "Mission Description." **(T-3)**

1.4.3.1. Schedule all evaluation activity on one mission/sortie to the greatest extent possible. All performance phase requirements should be accomplished during a training (or operational if training not available) mission/sortie. If a required event is not accomplished during a mission/sortie, OG/CC is the waiver authority for the event to be completed in the CTD. This may be delegated no lower than SQ/CC unless otherwise authorized in position specific chapters of this instruction volume. **(T-2)**

1.4.3.2. During all evaluations, any grading areas observed by the evaluator may be evaluated. If additional training is identified for areas outside of the scheduled evaluation, document the training required under the appropriate area on the AF Form 4418. **(T-2)**

1.4.3.3. This AFI contains a table of requirements for the written requisites and a table for the grading criteria for various evaluations. Each table may include a "Note" which refers to a general note found in the individual grading criteria, and/or a number, which refers to a note shown below the table. To complete an evaluation, all areas annotated with an "R" must be successfully completed. **(T-2)**

1.4.3.4. Unit examiners may administer evaluations outside of their organization to include administering evaluations between AFSPC, AFRC and ANG provided written agreements/understandings between the affected organizations are in-place. Written agreements/understandings shall be reviewed and updated annually **(T-3)**.

1.4.4. Momentary deviations from tolerances will not be considered in the grading, provided the examinee applies prompt corrective action and such deviations do not jeopardize safety. Cumulative deviations will be considered when determining the overall grade. The SEE will state the examinee's overall rating, review with the examinee the area grades assigned, thoroughly critique specific deviations, and recommend/assign any required additional training **(T-2)**.

1.4.5. SEEs will not evaluate students with whom they have instructed 50% of the qualification/upgrade training or those they recommend for qualification/upgrade evaluation without SQ/CC approval. **(T-3)**

1.4.6. All crewmembers for the mission/sortie (to include students, instructors, examinees, and evaluators) will participate in and adhere to all required mission planning, mission briefing, mission execution, and mission debriefing requirements. All crewmembers must be current on CIF and meet all Go/No-Go requirements IAW AFI 17-202 series instructions, this instruction and all applicable supplemental guidance prior to operating, instructing or evaluating on the weapon system **(T-2)**.

1.5. General Evaluation Requirements:

1.5.1. Publications Check. In units where crewmembers are individually issued operating manuals, checklists, crew aids, etc., for use in conducting operations, a publications check will be accomplished for all evaluations. The publications check will be annotated in the Comments block of the AF Form 4418 only if unsatisfactory. List of Effective Pages (LEP) and annual "A" page checks in individually issued operating manuals must be accomplished, documented and current. Unit OGV will list the required operating publications in the local CIF Library and/or local supplement to AFI 17-202V2. NOTE: In units where such resources are not individually issued but made available/accessible for common use, the squadron Stan/Eval office will list those items (version and date) and ensure the accuracy and currency of the information contained in those resources for common use. **(T-2)**

1.5.2. Written Examinations:

1.5.2.1. The requisites in Table 1.1 are common to all CSCS crew positions and will be accomplished IAW AFI 17-202V2, all applicable supplemental guidance and unit directives. These will be accomplished prior to the mission/sortie performance phase unless in conjunction with an N/N QUAL. NOTE: An N/N evaluation conducted in the examinee's eligibility period and meeting all required QUAL profile requirements affords the examinee to opt for the N/N evaluation to satisfy a periodic QUAL, in which the examinee may complete written and EPE requisites after the performance phase. However, the written examination(s) and EPE must be completed prior to the examinee's expiration date **(T-2)**.

1.5.3. Emergency Procedures Evaluations (EPE). Every Qualification evaluation, which updates an expiration date, will include an EPE. Qualification EPEs will evaluate the crewmember's knowledge and/or performance of emergency procedures, to include use of emergency equipment. Use the Emergency Procedures/Equipment grading criteria for all emergency situations. Use Systems Knowledge/Operations grading criteria to evaluate general systems operation. An EPE will be accomplished orally and may be accomplished prior to the mission with any unit SEE conducting a scenario-based evaluation using question/answer (Q&A) techniques, preferably during the SEE pre-brief with the examinee. Units will determine scenarios for EPEs. The SEE will assign an overall EPE grade. The evaluation criteria for EPEs is defined in Area 8, para 2.4.8. Document the accomplishment and result of the EPE in the Written Phase block of Section II Qualification on the AF Form 4418 **(T-2)**.

Table 1.1. Crew Position Specific Requirements - Written Examinations (T-2).

Examination Type	CC QUAL	OC QUAL	BPO QUAL	CPO QUAL	DSO QUAL	IFO QUAL	MMO QUAL	SVO QUAL	VAO QUAL	VRO QUAL
CLOSED BOOK (Note 1)	R	R	R	R	R	R	R	R	R	R
OPEN BOOK (Note 1)	R	R	R	R	R	R	R	R	R	R
EPE (Note 2)	R	R	R	R	R	R	R	R	R	R
R – required NOTES: 1. The CLOSED BOOK and OPEN BOOK exams consists of 25-50 questions derived from applicable operations manuals and governing directives. OG/OGV will determine the necessary number of questions to be included for each weapon system and crew position. 2. The Emergency Procedure Examination (EPE) is required for all INIT QUAL and subsequent periodic QUAL evaluations covering duties in the member's primary crew position. See paragraph 1.5.3. for procedures/requirements for conducting EPEs.										

1.5.4. Qualification (QUAL) Evaluations. These evaluations measure a crewmember's ability to meet grading areas listed on Table 1.2. at the end of this chapter and defined in **Chapter 2** of this instruction. IAW AFI 17-202V2 and lead MAJCOM guidance, QUAL evaluations may be combined with MSN evaluations. When practical, QUAL evaluations should be combined with Instructor evaluations, as applicable for the crew position. **(T-2)**

1.5.5. Mission (MSN) Evaluations. IAW AFI 17-202V2 and lead MAJCOM guidance, the requirement for a separate MSN evaluation may be combined with the QUAL evaluation. The various procedures and techniques used throughout the different weapon system variants are managed through a training program, which results in a mission certification. Mission certifications will be IAW AFI 17-202 Volume 1, *Cybercrew Training*, AFI 17-2CSCS Volume 1, *Cyberspace Security and Control System (CSCS) Cybercrew Training*, and all applicable supplements and will be documented in the appropriate training folder. MSN evaluation grading areas are also listed on Table 1.2. at the end of this chapter and defined in **Chapter 2** of this instruction. **(T-2)**

1.5.5.1. For cybercrew members who maintain multiple mission certifications, recurring evaluations need only evaluate the primary mission events as long as currency is maintained in all other required training events. **(T-2)**

1.5.6. Instructor Evaluations. Grading areas for these evaluations are listed on Table 1.2. at the end of this chapter. See **Chapter 3** of this instruction for amplified information and grading area definitions.

1.5.7. Stan/Eval Examiner (SEE) Objectivity Evaluations. Grading areas for these evaluations are listed on Table 1.2. at the end of this chapter. See **Chapter 4** of this instruction for amplified information and grading area definitions. **(T-2)**

1.5.8. No-Notice Evaluations. OG/CC will determine no-notice evaluation procedures/goals **(T-3)**.

1.6. Grading Instructions. Standards and performance parameters are contained in AFI 17-202V2 and this instruction. A three-level grading system is used for most areas; however, a "Q-" grade will not be indicated under critical areas.

1.6.1. Critical Area/Subarea. Critical areas are events that require adequate accomplishment by the examinee to successfully and safely achieve the mission/sortie objectives and complete the evaluation. These events, if not adequately accomplished could result in mission failure, endanger human life, or cause serious injury or death. Additionally, critical areas/subareas apply to time-sensitive tasks or tasks that must be accomplished as expeditiously as possible without any intervening lower priority actions that would, in the normal sequence of events, adversely affect task performance/outcome. If an examinee receives a "U" grade in any critical area, the overall grade for the evaluation will be "Q-3." Critical areas are identified by "(C)" following the applicable area title. **(T-2)**

1.6.2. Non-Critical Area/Subarea. Non-critical areas are events or tasks deemed integral to the performance of other tasks and required to sustain acceptable weapon system operations and mission execution. If an examinee receives a "U" grade in a non-critical area then the overall grade awarded will be no higher than "Q-2." An examinee receiving a "Q-" grade in a non-critical area or areas may still receive a "Q-1" overall grade at evaluator discretion. An overall "Q-3" can be awarded if, in the judgment of the flight examiner, there is justification based on performance in one or several areas/sub areas. Non-critical areas are identified by "(N)" following the applicable area title. **(T-2)**

1.6.3. If an examinee receives a "U" grade in a non-critical area then the overall grade awarded will be no higher than "Q-2." An examinee receiving a "Q-" grade in a non-critical area or areas may still receive a "Q-1" overall grade at evaluator discretion. An overall "Q-3" can be awarded if, in the judgment of the SEE, there is justification based on performance in one or several areas/sub areas. **(T-2)**

1.6.4. The SEE must exercise judgment when the wording of areas is subjective and when specific situations are not covered. **(T-2)**

1.6.5. Evaluator judgment will be the final determining factor in deciding the overall qualification level. **(T-2)**

Table 1.2. Crew Position Specific Requirements - Performance Phase Evaluations (T-3).

AREA/TITLE	Category C, N	Crew Position										Upgrade	
		CC	OC	BPO	CPO	DSO	IFO	MMO	SVO	VAO	VRO	INSTR	SEE
1. Mission Planning	N	R	R	R	R	R	R	R	R	R	R		
2. Systems / Equipment Knowledge	N	R	R	R	R	R	R	R	R	R	R		
3. Briefing	N	R	R	R	R	R	R	R	R	R	R		
4. Positional Changeover Brief	N, Note 1	R	R	R	R	R	R	R	R	R	R		
5. Operations Check Procedures	N	R	R	R	R	R	R	R	R	R	R		
6. Situational Awareness	C	R	R	R	R	R	R	R	R	R	R		
7. Safety	C	R	R	R	R	R	R	R	R	R	R		
8. Emergency Equipment / Procedures	N	R	R	R	R	R	R	R	R	R	R		
9. Crew Discipline	C	R	R	R	R	R	R	R	R	R	R		
10. Crew Coordination	N	R	R	R	R	R	R	R	R	R	R		
11. Communication	N	R	R	R	R	R	R	R	R	R	R		
12. Task Management	N	R	R	R	R	R	R	R	R	R	R		
13. Reports, Logs and Forms	N	R	R	R	R	R	R	R	R	R	R		
14. Post Mission Activity	N	R	R	R	R	R	R	R	R	R	R		
15. Crew Debrief	N	R	R	R	R	R	R	R	R	R	R		
16. Composite Force/Mutual Support	N	R	R										
17. Mission Management	N	R	R										

18. Patrol Procedures	N		R	R	R	R	R	R	R	R		
19. Cyberspace Collection	N		R	R	R	R	R	R	R	R		
20. Cyberspace Strike	N		R	R	R	R	R	R	R	R		
21. Cyberspace Control	N		R	R	R	R	R	R	R	R		
22. Secure Procedures	N		R	R	R	R	R	R	R	R		
Instructor Grading Criteria												
23. Instructional Ability	N										R	
24. Instructional Briefings/Critique	N										R	
25. Demonstration and Performance	N										R	
Stan/Eval Examiner Objectivity Evaluation Criteria												
26. Compliance with Directives	N											R
27. SEE Briefing	N											R
28. Performance Assessment /Grading	N											R
29. Additional Training Assignment	N											R
30. Examinee Debrief	N											R
31. Supervisor Debrief	N											R
32. SEE Performance/Documentation	N											R

C – critical; N – non-critical; R – required

NOTES:

1. Applicable for shift/crew changeovers.

Chapter 2

CREW POSITION EVALUATIONS AND GRADING CRITERIA

2.1. General. The grading criteria contained in this chapter are applicable to evaluations for CSCS Crew Commanders (CC), Operations Controllers (OC) Boundary Protection Operators (BPO), Client End Point Protection Operators (CPO), Directory Services Operators (DSO), Infrastructure Operators (IFO), Monitoring Management Operators (MMO), Storage and Virtualization Operators (SVO), Vulnerability Assessment Operators (VAO) and Vulnerability Remediation Operators (VRO) and were established by experience, policies, and procedures in weapon system manuals and other directives. Evaluators must realize that grading criteria contained herein cannot accommodate every situation. Written parameters must be tempered with mission objectives and, more importantly, mission/task accomplishment in the determination of overall cybercrew performance. Requirements for each evaluation are as follows:

2.2. Qualification Evaluations:

    2.2.1. Written Examination Requisites: See Table 1.1 **(T-3)**

    2.2.2. Emergency Procedures Evaluations: See paragraph 1.5.3. **(T-3)**

    2.2.3. Performance Phase: Required Areas 1 through 22 in Table 1.2 under CC, OC, BPO, CPO, DSO, IFO, MMO, SVO, VAO and VRO will be evaluated, unless not applicable as noted. **(T-3)**

2.3. Mission Certifications. Mission Certifications ensure individuals are capable of performing duties essential to the effective employment of the weapon system. Mission Certifications are accomplished IAW local training requirements and/or SQ/CC directions. Mission certification events are normally performed during Qualification evaluations, but may be performed on any mission/sortie with an instructor certified in that mission. **(T-3)**

2.4. General Crew Position Evaluation Criteria. The following general evaluation grading criteria are common to all crew positions unless indicated, regardless of special mission qualification(s) and additional certifications, and will be used for all applicable evaluations:

    2.4.1. AREA 1, Mission Planning (N)

        2.4.1.1. Q. Led or contributed to mission planning efforts IAW procedures prescribed in applicable guidance manuals, instructions and/or directives. Planning adequately addressed mission objectives and/or tasking. Planning adequately considered intelligence information, weapon system capability/operating status, and crew composition/ability to include a review of all Cybercrew Information File (CIF) Vol 1, Part B items with minor errors/deviations/omissions that did not impact mission effectiveness. **(T-3)**

        2.4.1.2. Q-. Errors/deviations/omissions had minor impact on mission effectiveness or efficiencies, but did not impact mission accomplishment or jeopardize mission success. **(T-3)**

2.4.1.3. U. Failed to adequately lead or contribute to the mission planning effort. Failure to comply with procedures prescribed in applicable guidance manuals, instructions, and/or directives contributed to significant deficiencies in mission execution/accomplishment. Failed to lead or participate in all required briefings and/or planning meetings without appropriate approval. Failed to review CIF. **(T-3)**

2.4.2. AREA 2, Systems and Equipment Knowledge (N)

2.4.2.1. Q. Demonstrated thorough knowledge of network traffic flow, architecture, system component(s)/equipment, limitations, performance characteristics and operating procedures. Correctly identified and located applicable components/equipment and determined operational status of system. Properly configured system components/equipment. Correctly identified and applied proper action(s) for system/equipment malfunctions. Followed all applicable system/equipment operating directives, guides, manuals etc. **(T-3)**

2.4.2.2. Q-. Minor deficiencies in demonstrating knowledge of network traffic flow, architecture, system component(s)/equipment, limitations, performance characteristics, or operating procedures but sufficient to perform the mission safely. Able to identify and locate components/equipment with minor errors. Slow to identify malfunctions and/or apply corrective actions with minor errors, omissions or deviations. Followed all system/equipment operating directives, guides, manuals, etc., with minor errors, omissions or deviations. Did not damage system/components/equipment or cause mission failure. **(T-3)**

2.4.2.3. U. Demonstrated severe lack of knowledge of network traffic flow, architecture system component(s)/equipment, limitations, performance characteristics, or operating procedures. Unable to identify or failed to locate essential components/equipment. Failed to identify malfunctions and/or apply corrective actions. Failed to follow system/equipment operating directives, guides, manuals, etc. resulting in unsatisfactory employment and/or mission failure. Poor procedures resulted in damage to system components/equipment. **(T-3)**

2.4.3. AREA 3, Briefing (N)

2.4.3.1. Q. Led or contributed to briefing effort as appropriate. Utilized/followed local briefing guides, manuals and/or instructions. Well organized and presented in a logical sequence, appropriate timeframe and professional manner. Effectively incorporated briefing/training aids where applicable and utilized effective techniques for accomplishing the mission. Briefed mission tasking/priorities, crew responsibilities/coordination, weapon system employment/sensor management, contract confliction, and mission package integration (as applicable). Accurately briefed the current situational awareness status. Crewmembers clearly understood roles, responsibilities, mission requirements and were prepared at briefing time. **(T-3)**

2.4.3.2. Q-. Led or contributed to briefing effort with minor errors/omissions/deviations. Utilized/followed local briefing guides, manuals and/or instructions with minor deviations. Briefing anomalies had minor impact on mission effectiveness but did not jeopardize mission success. **(T-3)**

2.4.3.3. U. Inadequate leadership or participation in briefing development and/or presentation. Did not utilize/follow local briefing guides, manuals and/or instructions. Disorganized and/or confusing presentation. Ineffective use of briefing/training aids. Failed to brief mission tasking/priorities, crew responsibilities/coordination, weapon system employment/sensor management, contract de-confliction , and mission package integration (as applicable). Failed to present major training events. Failed to present an accurate situational awareness picture. Was not prepared at briefing time. **(T-3)**

2.4.4. AREA 4, Positional Changeover Brief (N)

2.4.4.1. Q. Outgoing crewmember prepared and conducted a comprehensive positional changeover briefing with the oncoming crewmember IAW crew aid(s) and/or applicable directives. Reviewed factors, conditions, and the current operational/tactical situation for all missions, packages, sorties, etc., with the oncoming crewmember and ensured items necessary for the effective conduct of tasked missions were understood by the oncoming crewmember. Minor errors/omissions/deviations did not impact mission effectiveness. **(T-3)**

2.4.4.2. Q-. Outgoing crewmember prepared and conducted a positional changeover briefing with minor errors/omissions/deviations using crew aid(s) and applicable directives. Changeover briefing anomalies had minor impact on mission effectiveness but did not jeopardize mission success. **(T-3)**

2.4.4.3. U. Outgoing crewmember failed to prepare and conduct an effective positional changeover briefing with the oncoming crewmember and/or failed to use appropriate crew aid(s) and applicable directives. Changeover briefing contained errors/omissions/deviations that could have significantly detracted from mission effectiveness and/or jeopardized mission success. **(T-3)**

2.4.5. AREA 5, Operations Check Procedures (N)

2.4.5.1. Q. Performed all pre-mission/pre-operations checks as required IAW applicable guides and/or crew aids. Adequately ensured, determined and/or verified weapon system operational state and cybercrew readiness prior to on-watch period or entering tasked vulnerability period. Ensured crew understanding of most up-to-date tasking(s) prior to on-watch or vulnerability period execution. Deviated from crew aids and/or omitted steps only when appropriate and was able to substantiate justification. Minor errors/deviations/omissions did not detract from mission efficiencies nor jeopardize mission success. **(T-3)**

2.4.5.2. Q-. Minor errors/omissions occurred without justification but did not jeopardize overall mission success. **(T-3)**

2.4.5.3. U. Did not perform mission/operations checks. Failed to determine/verify weapon system operational state and cybercrew readiness prior to on-watch period or entering tasked vulnerability period. Did not utilize any crew aids and/or utilized wrong crew aids. Errors/deviations/omissions contributed to jeopardizing mission success. **(T-3)**

2.4.6. AREA 6, Situational Awareness (C)

2.4.6.1. Q. Conducted the mission with a sense of understanding/comprehension and in a timely, efficient manner. Anticipated situations, which would have adversely affected the mission and made appropriate decisions based on available information. Maintained overall good situational awareness. Recognized temporary loss of situational awareness in self or others and took appropriate action to regain awareness without detracting from mission accomplishment or jeopardizing safety. **(T-3)**

2.4.6.2. U. Decisions or lack thereof resulted in failure to accomplish the assigned mission. Demonstrated poor judgment or lost situational awareness. **(T-3)**

2.4.7. AREA 7, Safety (C)

2.4.7.1. Q. Aware of and complied with all factors required for safe operations and mission accomplishment. **(T-3)**

2.4.7.2. U. Was not aware of safety factors or disregarded procedures to safely operate the weapon system and/or conduct the mission. Conducted unsafe actions that jeopardized mission accomplishment and/or put crewmembers at risk of injury or death. Operated in a manner that could or did result in damage to the weapon system/equipment. **(T-3)**

2.4.8. AREA 8, Emergency Procedures (N)

2.4.8.1. Q. Recognized emergency situations or malfunctions and immediately demonstrated /explained appropriate response actions. Demonstrated/explained thorough knowledge of location and proper use of emergency equipment. Demonstrated/explained effective coordination of emergency actions with other crewmembers without delay or confusion. Followed appropriate crew aids as required. Minor errors did not impact efficiencies in addressing the emergency. (This area may be evaluated orally). **(T-3)**

2.4.8.2. Q-. Recognized emergency situations or malfunctions but slow to demonstrate/explain appropriate response actions. Minor errors and/or was slow to locate equipment and/or appropriate crew aids. **(T-3)**

2.4.8.3. U. Failed to recognize emergency situations or malfunctions. Failed to demonstrate/explain proper response actions. Failed to demonstrate/explain knowledge of location or proper use of emergency equipment or crew aids. Failed to demonstrate/explain coordination of emergency actions with other crewmembers. Crew aids errors/omissions/deviations contributed to ineffective actions or exacerbating an emergency situation and/or malfunction. **(T-3)**

2.4.9. AREA 9, Crew Discipline (C)

2.4.9.1. Q. Demonstrated professional crew discipline throughout all phases of the mission. Planned, briefed, executed and debriefed mission in accordance with applicable instructions and directives. **(T-3)**

2.4.9.2. U. Failed to demonstrate strict professional crew discipline throughout all phases of the mission. Violated or failed to comply with applicable instructions and directives, which could have jeopardized safety of crewmembers or mission accomplishment. **(T-3)**

2.4.10. AREA 10, Crew Coordination (N)

2.4.10.1. Q. Effectively coordinated with other crewmembers and/or teams during all phases of the mission enabling efficient, well-coordinated actions. Demonstrated knowledge of other crewmembers' duties and responsibilities. Proactively provided direction and/or information to the crew; communicated in a clear and effective manner, actively sought other crewmember opinions and/or ideas, and asked for or provided constructive feedback as necessary. **(T-3)**

2.4.10.2. Q-. There were some breakdowns in communication but they did not detract from overall mission success. Limited in knowledge of other crewmembers' duties/responsibilities. Unclear communication at times caused confusion and/or limited crew/team interaction. Some unnecessary prompting required from other crewmembers. **(T-3)**

2.4.10.3. U. Severe breakdowns in coordination caused or could have resulted in mission ineffectiveness, failure or jeopardized safety of crewmembers or teams. Lacked basic knowledge of other crewmembers' and/or teams' duties and responsibilities. Unclear/lack of communication or excessive prompting required by crewmembers or teams put mission and/or safety of others at risk. **(T-3)**

2.4.11. AREA 11, Communication (N)

2.4.11.1. Q. Timely and effective communication with external agencies and/or mission partners. Concise and accurate information exchanged using proper medium, terminology, format and/or brevity IAW applicable crew aids. Sound understanding and use of voice, email, chat and collaborative tools to communicate mission essential information. Demonstrated a thorough understanding of OPSEC procedures. **(T-3)**

2.4.11.2. Q-. Minor errors/deviations/omissions in communications with external agencies and/or mission partners that did not detract from overall mission accomplishment. Deviated from applicable crew aids but did not cause mission failure. **(T-3)**

2.4.11.3. U. Severe breakdowns in communication with external agencies and/or mission partners caused or could have resulted in mission ineffectiveness/failure or jeopardized safety of others. Significant OPSEC errors or deviations jeopardized mission accomplishment. Did not use crew aids. **(T-3)**

2.4.12. AREA 12, Task Management (N)

2.4.12.1. Q. Accurately identified, effectively prioritized and/or efficiently managed tasks based on existing and new information. Used available resources to manage workload, communicated task priorities to other crewmembers and/or internal teams. Recognized and requested assistance from other crewmembers when task-saturated. Gathered/crosschecked available data and effectively identified alternatives when necessary. **(T-3)**

2.4.12.2. Q-. Minor omissions and/or errors, which did not affect safety of crewmembers or effective mission accomplishment. Limited use of available resources to manage workload and/or did not completely communicate task priorities to other crewmembers and/or internal teams. Slow to recognize task saturation and/or request assistance from crewmembers. **(T-3)**

2.4.12.3. U. Failed to identify, prioritize or manage essential tasks leading to possible unsafe conditions or significant risk to mission accomplishment. Improperly or unable to identify contingencies, gather data, or communicate decisions putting mission accomplishment and/or safety of others at risk. Failed to recognize task overload or failed to seek assistance from other crewmembers, which put at risk mission accomplishment or safety of crewmembers. **(T-3)**

2.4.13. AREA 13, Reports, Logs and Forms (N)

2.4.13.1. Q. Recognized all situations meeting reporting criteria. When required, provided timely, accurate and correctly formatted reports Mission Reports (MISREPs) or inputs to mission-related information management portals/collaborative information sharing environments. All required logs [i.e., Master Station Log (MSL)], media and forms were complete, accurate, legible, and accomplished on time and IAW with applicable directives, tasking and policy. Information was provided in sufficient detail to allow accurate and timely analysis of associated data. Complied with security procedures and directives. **(T-3)**

2.4.13.2. Q-. Minor errors/deviations/omissions/latency on required reports, logs, media or forms led to minor inefficiencies but did not affect conduct of the mission. Complied with security procedures and directives. **(T-3)**

2.4.13.3. U. Failed to recognize situations meeting reporting criteria and/or failed to report events essential to mission accomplishment. Major errors/deviations/omissions/latency in accomplishing logs, reports/inputs, media, or forms precluded effective mission accomplishment or analysis of mission data. Failed to comply with security procedures and directives. **(T-3)**

2.4.14. AREA 14, Post Mission Activity (N)

2.4.14.1. Q. Accomplished and/or supervised timely post-mission checks, system shutdown procedures and workstation clean up IAW applicable checklists, guidance and directives. **(T-3)**

2.4.14.2. Q-. Minor deviations, omissions or errors but did not adversely impact mission effectiveness, cause damage to systems/equipment, or risk safety of others. **(T-3)**

2.4.14.3. U. Major deviations, omissions and/or errors which could have jeopardized mission effectiveness, caused equipment damage, or endangered others. **(T-3)**

2.4.15. AREA 15, Crew Debrief (N)

2.4.15.1. Q. Thoroughly debriefed the mission and/or contributed to the briefing content to ensure it included all pertinent items. Reconstructed operational events, compared results with initial objectives for the mission, debriefed deviations and provided individual crewmember feedback as appropriate. Organized IAW guidance/directives and professionally presented in a logical sequence using available briefing aids. Summarized lessons learned and ensured they were documented. Provided crew commander/operations controller with applicable input on all required mission/crew/system-related events, including mission log/report/database information for inclusion in the crew debrief. Used applicable crew aid(s) as required. Minor errors/ omissions/deviations did not impact debrief effectiveness or efficiencies. **(T-3)**

2.4.15.2. Q-. Led or contributed to debriefing effort with minor errors/omissions/deviations. Some events out of sequence with some unnecessary redundancy. **(T-3)**

2.4.15.3. U. Inadequate leadership or participation in debrief. Disorganized and/or confusing debriefing presentation. Ineffective use of briefing/training aids. Failed to reconstruct operational events, compare results with initial objectives for the mission, debrief deviations and/or offer corrective guidance as appropriate. Absent from debrief (whole or in-part) without appropriate supervisor approval. **(T-3)**

2.4.16. AREA 16, Composite Force / Mutual Support (N)

2.4.16.1. Q. Effectively planned and leveraged Composite Force (CF) support, Mutual Support (MS) agencies and/or internal/external teams when needed. **(T-3)**

2.4.16.2. Q-. Limited planning and/or leverage of CF support or MS agency support contributed to confusion among all or some agencies/teams. Less than optimum mission efficiency, however overall mission success was not jeopardized. **(T-3)**

2.4.16.3. U. Inadequate or incorrect planning/leverage of CF support, MS agency support and/or internal/external team support, resulted in mission failure. Did not leverage support when needed. **(T-3)**

2.4.17. AREA 17, Mission Management (N)

2.4.17.1. Q. Assured mission success by accurately identifying, effectively prioritizing, and efficiently managing mission tasks based on planned and updated information. Identified contingencies, gathered data, and formulated decisions. Clearly communicated task priorities and updates to crewmembers. Used available resources necessary to manage workload, monitor crew activity and aid in decision making. **(T-3)**

2.4.17.2. Q-. Minor omissions and/or errors, which did not affect safety of crewmembers or effective mission accomplishment. Limited use of available resources to aid decision making, manage workload and/or communicate task priorities/updates to other crewmembers. **(T-3)**

2.4.17.3. U. Failed to identify, prioritize or manage mission tasks leading to possible unsafe conditions or significant risk to mission accomplishment. Improperly or unable to identify contingencies, gather data, or communicate decisions putting mission accomplishment and/or safety of others at risk. Failed to communicate task priorities/updates to crewmembers or adequately monitor crew activity. **(T-3)**

2.4.18. AREA 18, Patrol Procedures (N)

2.4.18.1. Q. Effective and timely execution of dynamic targeting over target terrain. Demonstrated complete execution of entire targeting cycle (Find, Fix, Track, Target, Engage, and Assess [F2T2EA]) actions IAW the ROE, given restrictions or tactical situation. **(T-3)**

2.4.18.2. Q-. Remained IAW ROE, minor errors caused less than optimal dynamic targeting execution. Minor errors or delays in executing a component of the F2T2EA targeting cycle. **(T-3)**

2.4.18.3. U. Major errors delayed or prevented dynamic target execution. Major delay or inability to execute a component of the F2T2EA targeting cycle. Employment/engagement was outside the ROE, given restrictions, or tactical situation. **(T-3)**

2.4.19. AREA 19, Cyberspace Collection (N)

2.4.19.1. Q. Effective and timely execution resulted in prompt collection of relevant data and information from targeted terrain IAW tasking. **(T-3)**

2.4.19.2. Q-. Minor errors caused less than optimal data and information collection from the targeted terrain resulting in minor data loss. **(T-3)**

2.4.19.3. U. Major errors delayed or prevented data and information collection and/or resulted in data and information collection failure. Collected information was not related to targeted terrain and/or tasking. **(T-3)**

2.4.20. AREA 20, Cyberspace Strike (N)

2.4.20.1. Q. Effectively degraded, disrupted, denied or destroyed adversary activity in a timely and effective manner IAW all ROEs and restrictions. **(T-3)**

2.4.20.2. Q-. Minor errors in execution led to slower than desired performance in degrading, disrupting, denying or destroying adversary activity. **(T-3)**

2.4.20.3. U. Failed to degrade, disrupt, deny or destroy adversary activity in a timely and effective manner IAW all ROEs and given restrictions. Errors in execution caused a major delay in the mission execution window or prevented mission accomplishment. **(T-3)**

2.4.21. AREA 21, Cyberspace Control (N)

2.4.21.1. Q. Effective coordination with outside agency(s) and timely execution resulted in prompt access and/or network freedom of maneuver for supported cyberspace forces IAW tasking, ROEs and restrictions without errors. **(T-3)**

2.4.21.2. Q-. Complied with tasking but minor errors and/or less than optimal coordination with cyberspace partner(s) caused access and/or freedom of maneuver delays for supported cyberspace forces but did not cause mission failure. **(T-3)**

2.4.21.3. U. Major errors delayed or prevented execution, access or network freedom of maneuver. Employment/engagement was outside the tasking and/or caused mission failure. **(T-3)**

2.4.22. AREA 22, Secure Procedures (N)

2.4.22.1. Q. Effective use of tools and weapon system capabilities denied adversarial ability to exploit the targeted vulnerability IAW the ROE and applicable restrictions. **(T-3)**

2.4.22.2. Q-. While the targeted vulnerability was removed from assigned terrain IAW the ROE and other restrictions, end state was not achieved in a timely manner resulting in delayed mission completion. **(T-3)**

2.4.22.3. U. Major errors prevented the removal of targeted vulnerability in assigned terrain or caused significant delays in removal of vulnerability. Execution was outside of the ROE, given restrictions, or tactical situation. **(T-3)**

Chapter 3

INSTRUCTOR EVALUATIONS AND GRADING CRITERIA

3.1. General. The following grading criteria cannot address every situation. Written parameters must be tempered with sortie objectives, evaluator judgment and task accomplishment in the determination of overall cybercrew performance. **(T-2)**

3.2. Instructor Upgrade and Qualification Requisites. Prior to an initial Instructor Evaluation, Instructor examinees must complete all requisites for Instructor upgrade consideration, nomination and training IAW AFI 17-202 Vol 1, AFI 17-2CSCS Vol 1, and all applicable supplemental guidance. **(T-2)**

3.3. Instructor Qualification Evaluations. When possible, units should strive to combine instructor evaluations (initial and recurring/periodic) with periodic QUAL evaluations. Instructor evaluations can only be combined with QUAL evaluations when the examinee is in their periodic QUAL eligibility period. There is no eligibility period associated with an Instructor Qualification, however, Instructor qualifications will expire after the 17th month from the previous Instructor Qualification Evaluation. See paragraph 3.5 for documentation guidance. **(T-2)**

3.3.1. Initial Instructor evaluations should be conducted with a student occupying the applicable cybercrew position whenever possible. Recurring or periodic Instructor Evaluations may be conducted with the SEE role playing as the student.

3.3.2. The instructor examinee will monitor all phases of the mission from an advantageous position and be prepared to demonstrate or explain any area or procedure. The SEE will particularly note the instructor's ability to recognize student difficulties and provide effective, timely instruction and/or corrective action. The SEE should also evaluate the grade assigned and the completed grade sheet or event training form for the student on all initial instructor checks. **(T-2)**

3.3.3. The student will perform those duties prescribed by the instructor for the mission/sortie being accomplished. If an actual student is not available, the SEE will identify to the examinee (prior to the mission) the level of performance to be expected from the SEE acting as the student. If this option is utilized, at least one event or briefing must be instructed.

3.3.4. Periodic instructor evaluations may be administered in conjunction with required periodic qualification evaluations. The examinee must occupy the primary duty position for an adequate period to demonstrate proficiency in the crew position with required qualification evaluations. All instructor evaluations will include a pre-mission and post-mission briefing. **(T-2)**

3.3.5. Awarding a "U" in any of the Instructor Grading Criteria areas will result in a Q-3 for the overall instructor grade. The overall grade for the instructor portion of the evaluation will be no higher than the lowest overall grade awarded under QUAL. **(T-2)**

3.4. Instructor Evaluation Grading Criteria. All Instructor Evaluation Criteria must be observed and graded to ensure a complete evaluation. Specific requirements for each evaluation are as follows:

3.4.1. AREA 23, Instructional Ability (M)

3.4.1.1. Q. Demonstrated ability to effectively communicate weapon system capability, mission planning, briefing/debriefing, employment/TTP, and tasked mission areas to the student. Provided appropriate corrective guidance when necessary. Planned ahead and made timely decisions. Correctly analyzed student errors. **(T-2)**

3.4.1.2. Q-. Minor discrepancies in the above criteria that did not adversely impact student progress. **(T-2)**

3.4.1.3. U. Unable to effectively communicate with the student. Did not provide corrective action where necessary. Did not plan ahead or anticipate student problems. Incorrectly analyzed student errors. Adversely impacted student progress. **(T-2)**

3.4.2. AREA 24, Instructional Briefings/Critique (M)

3.4.2.1. Q. Briefings were well organized, accurate and thorough. Reviewed student's present level of training and defined mission events to be performed. Demonstrated ability during critique to reconstruct the mission/sortie, offer mission analysis, and provide corrective guidance where appropriate. Completed all training documents according to prescribed directives. Appropriate grades awarded. **(T-2)**

3.4.2.2. Q-. As above but with minor errors or omissions in briefings, critique, or training documents that did not adversely impact student progress. **(T-2)**

3.4.2.3. U. Pre-mission or post-mission briefings were marginal or nonexistent. Did not review student's training folder or past performance. Failed to adequately critique student or conducted an incomplete mission analysis, which compromised learning. Student strengths or weaknesses were not identified. Adversely impacted student progress. Inappropriate grades awarded. Overlooked or omitted major discrepancies. **(T-2)**

3.4.3. AREA 25, Demonstration and Performance (M)

3.4.3.1. Q. Effectively demonstrated procedures and techniques. Demonstrated thorough knowledge of weapon system/components, procedures, and all applicable publications and regulations. **(T-2)**

3.4.3.2. Q-. Minor discrepancies in the above criteria that did not adversely impact student progress. **(T-2)**

3.4.3.3. U. Did not demonstrate correct procedure or technique. Insufficient depth of knowledge about weapon system/components, procedures or proper source material. Adversely impacted student progress. **(T-2)**

3.5. Instructor Evaluation Documentation.

3.5.1. Instructor Qualification Evaluations will be documented as a SPOT evaluation on the AF Form 4418 and AF Form 4420, *Individual's Record of Duties and Qualifications*, and maintained in the member's cybercrew qualification folder IAW AFI 17-202 Vol 2, applicable higher headquarters supplements and local supplemental guidance. **(T-2)** Additional Instructor Evaluation documentation is as follows:

3.5.2. Initial Instructor Qualification Evaluation.

3.5.2.1. If conducted in conjunction with the Instructor Examinee's periodic QUAL evaluation, the Instructor Qualification Evaluation will be documented on the same AF Form 4418, placing SPOT in the second "Evaluation Type" block of Section II Qualification below annotating QUAL. Place a statement in Section V Comments that the QUAL evaluation was in conjunction with an Initial Instructor Qualification Evaluation. Place any comments specific to the Instructor portion of the evaluation separately from the QUAL portion of the evaluation. **(T-2)**

3.5.2.2. If the Instructor Qualification Evaluation is not in conjunction with a periodic QUAL evaluation, document the evaluation as a SPOT in the first "Evaluation Type" block of Section II Qualification and place a statement in Section V Comments that the evaluation was an Initial Instructor Qualification Evaluation. Place any comments regarding commendable performance and/or discrepancies for the instructor evaluation in Section V Comments. **(T-2)**

3.5.2.3. Upon completion of the AF Form 4418, place the appropriate corresponding entry onto the AF Form 4420. **(T-2)**

3.5.3. Recurring/Periodic Instructor Qualification Evaluation.

3.5.3.1. If conducted in conjunction with the Instructor Examinee's periodic QUAL evaluation, the Instructor Qualification Evaluation will be documented on the same AF Form 4418, placing SPOT in the second "Evaluation Type" block of Section II Qualification below annotating QUAL. Place a statement in Section V Comments that the evaluation was a periodic QUAL evaluation in conjunction with periodic or recurring Instructor Qualification Evaluation. Place any comments specific to the Instructor portion of the evaluation separately from the QUAL portion of the evaluation. **(T-2)**

3.5.3.2. If the Instructor Qualification Evaluation is not in conjunction with a periodic QUAL evaluation, document the evaluation as a SPOT in the first "Evaluation Type" block of Section II Qualification and place a statement in Section V Comments that the evaluation was recurring or periodic Instructor Qualification Evaluation. Place any comments regarding commendable performance and/or discrepancies for the instructor evaluation in Section V Comments. **(T-2)**

3.5.3.3. Upon completion of the AF Form 4418, place the appropriate corresponding entry onto the AF Form 4420. **(T-2)**

3.5.4. Letter of Certification (Letter of Xs).

3.5.4.1. Upon the successful completion of an Instructor Qualification Evaluation, units will ensure the crewmembers instructor status is reflected on the Letter of Xs. **(T-2)**

3.5.4.2. Upon the expiration of a qualification or failure of an Instructor Qualification Evaluation, units will ensure the crewmembers instructor status is reflected on the Letter of Xs. **(T-2)**

Chapter 4

SEE OBJECTIVITY EVALUATIONS AND GRADING CRITERIA

4.1. General. SEE Objectivity Evaluations are a vehicle for commanders to upgrade crewmembers for SEE qualification and a tool to monitor the evaluator crew force's adherence to Stan/Eval directives. Grading criteria contained herein cannot accommodate every situation. Written parameters must be tempered with sortie objectives, evaluator judgment and task accomplishment in the determination of overall examinee performance. The criteria contained in this chapter are established by experience, policies, and procedures set forth in weapon system manuals and other directives. The criteria contained in this chapter are applicable to all SEE Objectivity Evaluations for CSCS crewmembers. **(T-2)**

4.2. Evaluator Upgrade and Qualification Requisites. Evaluator upgrade candidates will be selected from the most qualified and competent instructors. **(T-2)**

4.2.1. Wing/Group/Squadron. SEE Upgrade candidate nominations will be approved by the OG/CC in writing. Once approved, candidates must complete all SEE training IAW AFI 17-202 Vol 2, this instruction and all applicable supplemental guidance. **(T-2)** As a minimum, SEE training will consist of:

4.2.1.1. Local SEE academics/instruction covering all Stan/Eval programs and procedures. Training completion should be documented on a locally developed OG/CC crew aids along with a signed certificate from the OG/CC or OG/CD. Both crew aids and certificate will be maintained in the unit Stan/Eval office. **(T-2)**

4.2.1.2. The candidate observing one entire evaluation performed by a qualified SEE. NOTE: To the maximum extent possible, SEE Upgrade candidates should observe evaluations conducted within the weapon system for which they are qualified, however when not practical, the observed evaluation may be conducted with a qualified SEE within in the same Group regardless of weapon system or crew position. Training completion should be documented on a locally developed OG/CC crew aids and maintained in the unit Stan/Eval office. **(T-2)**

4.2.1.3. Completion of a SEE Objectivity Evaluation under the supervision of a qualified SEE. NOTE: The SEE Objectivity will be conducted within the weapon system and crew position for which the SEE Upgrade candidate (SEE Examinee) maintains qualification. See paragraph 4.5 for SEE Objectivity Evaluation (AF Form 4418) documentation guidance. **(T-2)**

4.2.2. MAJCOM/NAF. MAJCOM and NAF appointed CSCS evaluators will be qualified in the CSCS weapon system and maintain at a minimum Basic Mission Capable (BMC) currency/proficiency status IAW AFI 17-2CSCS Vol 1 and all applicable supplemental guidance. Additionally, MAJCOM and NAF evaluators for the CSCS weapon system will have had previous SEE experience at the wing, group or squadron level in the CSCS WS. **(T-2)**

4.3. SEE Objectivity Evaluations. There is no eligibility period or expiration date associated with a SEE Objectivity Evaluation. Once obtained, crewmembers maintain SEE qualification unless they fail a QUAL evaluation, fail an Instructor evaluation, fail a SEE Objectivity Evaluation, their weapon system QUAL expires, or upon their SEE appointment being revoked/rescinded by the appointing official. See paragraph 4.5. for SEE Objectivity Evaluation documentation guidance. **(T-2)**

4.3.1. Only a qualified cyberspace weapon system SEE may administer a SEE Objectivity Evaluation to a cyberspace SEE examinee. SEE Objectivity Evaluations may be administered by SEE Examiners that are qualified in a different cyberspace weapon system type or crew position from the SEE examinee. NOTE: This is common when the SEE Objectivity Evaluation is in conjunction with a higher headquarters inspection. **(T-2)**

4.3.2. SEE Objectivity Evaluations will not be combined with any other type evaluation. **(T-2)**

4.3.3. SEE Objectivity Evaluations will ensure the SEE examinee (for example in the case of a SEE Objectivity conducted as part of a higher headquarters inspection) observes and grades the entire mission activity of the QUAL examinee. Mission activity is defined as all mission planning, briefing, execution, and debrief activities for the mission/sortie. **(T-2)**

4.3.4. The SEE Upgrade candidate or SEE Examinee will brief the qualified SEE Examiner on all observations, grades, commendable/discrepancies (if any), recommended additional training, and other mission related debrief topics prior to debriefing the QUAL examinee and/or examinee's supervisor. **(T-2)**

4.3.5. The SEE Upgrade candidate or SEE Examinee will complete the AF Form 4418 and have the SEE Examiner review it for completeness and accuracy. The SEE Examiner's signature block and signature (not signature/block of the SEE Upgrade candidate or SEE Examinee) will be entered on the AF Form 4418. **(T-2)**

4.3.6. The SEE Examiner will administer a pre-brief and debrief to the SEE Examinee. **(T-2)**

4.3.7. For SEE Upgrade candidates, SEE Objectivity evaluations will only be administered for observed INIT QUAL or periodic QUAL evaluations. Additionally, the QUAL evaluation may not be combined with an Instructor Evaluation. **(T-2)**

4.4. SEE Objectivity Evaluation Grading Criteria. All SEE Objectivity Evaluation Criteria must be observed and graded to ensure a complete evaluation. The following grading criteria will be used by SEE's when conducting SEE Objectivity Evaluations. A grade of Q- or U will require additional training. **(T-2)** Specific requirements for each evaluation are as follows:

4.4.1. AREA 26, Compliance with Directives (M)

4.4.1.1. Q. Complied with all operational directives and guidance. Complied with all directives pertaining to the administration of a positional and/or instructor evaluation. **(T-2)**

4.4.1.2. Q-. Complied with most directives. Deviations did not jeopardize the mission, the effectiveness of the evaluation, or crew safety. **(T-2)**

4.4.1.3. U. Failure to comply with directives jeopardized mission effectiveness, effectiveness of the evaluation, and/or crew safety. **(T-2)**

4.4.2. AREA 27, Stan/Eval Examiner (SEE) Briefing (M)

4.4.2.1. Q. Thoroughly briefed the examinee on the conduct of the evaluation, mission requirements, responsibilities, grading criteria and examiner actions/position during the evaluation. **(T-2)**

4.4.2.2. Q-. Items were omitted during the briefing causing minor confusion. Did not fully brief the examinee as to the conduct and purpose of the evaluation. **(T-2)**

4.4.2.3. U. Examiner failed to adequately brief the examinee. **(T-2)**

4.4.3. AREA 28, Performance Assessment and Grading (M)

4.4.3.1. Q. Identified all discrepancies and assigned proper area grade. Awarded the appropriate overall grade based on the examinee's performance. **(T-2)**

4.4.3.2. Q-. Most discrepancies were identified. Failed to assign Q- grade when appropriate. Assigned discrepancies for performance, which was within standards. Awarded an overall grade without consideration of cumulative deviations in the examinee's performance. **(T-2)**

4.4.3.3. U. Failed to identify most discrepancies. Did not award a grade commensurate with overall performance. Failed to assign additional training when warranted. **(T-2)**

4.4.4. AREA 29, Additional Training Assignment (M)

4.4.4.1. Q. Assigned proper additional training when warranted. NOTE: If the QUAL Examinee's performance (i.e. Q1) does not warrant the assignment of additional training, the SEE Examinee will verbally explain to the SEE Examiner the proper procedures for assigning additional training. This may be accomplished as part of the SEE Objectivity pre-brief or debrief. **(T-2)**

4.4.4.2. Q-. Additional training assigned was insufficient to ensure the examinee would achieve proper level of qualification. SEE Examinee's discrepancy or omission was correctable prior to QUAL Examinee debrief and in the SEE Objectivity debrief. **(T-2)**

4.4.4.3. U. Failed to assign additional training when warranted. **(T-2)**

4.4.5. AREA 30, Examinee Critique / Debrief (M)

4.4.5.1. Q. Thoroughly debriefed the examinee on all aspects of the evaluation. Reconstructed and debriefed all key mission events, providing instruction and references to directives and guidance when applicable. **(T-2)**

4.4.5.2. Q-. Some errors/omissions in reconstructing key mission events, in discussing deviations/discrepancies, referencing directives/guidance and debriefing of assigned grades. Did not advise the examinee of all additional training when warranted. Errors/omissions did not adversely affect overall evaluation effectiveness. **(T-2)**

4.4.5.3. U. Failed to discuss any assigned area grades or the overall rating. Changed grades without briefing the examinee and/or supervisor. Did not debrief key mission events and/or provide appropriate instruction during critique. **(T-2)**

4.4.6. AREA 31, Supervisor Debrief (M)

4.4.6.1. Q. Thoroughly debriefed the QUAL Examinees. Reconstructed and debriefed all key mission events pertinent to the QUAL Examinee's performance, citing references to directives and guidance when applicable. Briefed the supervisor on all discrepancies requiring additional training, downgraded areas and the overall qualification rating being assigned to the QUAL Examinee. NOTE: If the QUAL Examinee's performance (i.e. Q1) does not warrant a supervisor debrief, the SEE Examinee will verbally explain to the SEE Examiner the proper procedures for conducting a supervisor debriefing. This may be accomplished as part of the SEE Objectivity pre-brief or debrief. **(T-2)**

4.4.6.2. Q-. Some errors/omissions in reconstructing key mission events, discussing deviations/discrepancies, referencing directives/guidance, debriefing of assigned additional training, and assigning of QUAL Examinee grades/ratings with the supervisor. Errors/omissions did not adversely affect overall evaluation effectiveness. **(T-2)**

4.4.6.3. U. Failed to discuss any observed discrepancies, assigned area downgrades or the overall rating with the supervisor. Changed grades without briefing the examinee and/or supervisor. Did not debrief key mission events contributing to the QUAL examinees overall performance and assigned qualification rating. **(T-2)**

4.4.7. AREA 32, SEE Performance and Evaluation Documentation (M)

4.4.7.1. Q. SEE Examinee performed as briefed and ensured a thorough evaluation of the QUAL and/or Instructor (INSTR) evaluation examinee. SEE Examinee correctly documented the QUAL or INSTR Examinee's performance on the AF Form 4418. **(T-2)**

4.4.7.2. Q-. Minor errors or discrepancies during the mission did not impact or detract from the QUAL or INSTR Examinees' performance. Minor errors/discrepancies in accomplishing documentation. **(T-2)**

4.4.7.3. U. Major errors/disruptions impacted or detracted from the QUAL or INSTR Examinee's performance and/or prevented a thorough evaluation. Failure or major errors/discrepancies in accomplishing documentation. **(T-2)**

4.5. SEE Objectivity Evaluation Documentation. SEE Objectivity Evaluations will be documented as a SPOT evaluation on the AF Form 4418 and AF Form 4420 and maintained in the member's cyber crew qualification folder IAW AFI 17-202 Vol 2 and applicable higher headquarters/local supplemental guidance. **(T-2)**

4.5.1. Letter of Certification (Letter of Xs).

4.5.1.1. Upon the successful completion of a SEE Objectivity Evaluation, units will ensure the crewmembers SEE status is reflected on the Letter of Xs. **(T-2)**

4.5.1.2. Upon the decertification or loss of SEE qualification, units will ensure the Letter of Xs appropriately reflects the crewmember's status. **(T-2)**

WILLIAM J. BENDER, Lt Gen, USAF
Chief, Information Dominance and Chief
Information Officer

Attachment 1

GLOSSARY OF REFERENCES AND SUPPORTING INFORMATION

References

AFPD 17-2, *Cyberspace Operations*, 12 April 2016

AFI 17-202 Volume 1, *Cybercrew Training*, 2 April 2014

AFI 17-202 Volume 2, *Cybercrew Standardization and Evaluation Program*, 15 October 2014

AFI 17-202 Volume 3, *Cyberspace Operations and Procedures*, 6 May 2015

AFI 17-2CSCS Volume 1, *Cyberspace Security and Control System (CSCS) Cybercrew Training*

AFI 33-360, *Publications and Forms Management*, 1 December 2015

AFMAN 33-363, *Management of Records*, 1 March 2008

Prescribed Forms

None

Adopted Forms

AF Form 4418, *Certificate of Cybercrew Qualification*

AF Form 4420, *Individual's Record of Duties and Qualifications*

AF Form 847, *Recommendation for Change of Publication*

Abbreviations and Acronyms

AFI—Air Force Instruction

AFIN—Air Force Intranet

AFMAN—Air Force Manual

AFSPC—Air Force Space Command

ANG—Air National Guard

BPO—Boundary Protection Operator

CC—Crew Commander

CPO—Client End Point Protection Operator

CRM—Crew Resource Management

CSCS—Cyberspace Security and Control System

CTD—Cybercrew Training Device

DSO—Directory Services Operator

EPE—Emergency Procedure Evaluation

HQ—Headquarters

IAW—In Accordance With

IFO—Infrastructure Operator

INSTR—Instructor

LEP—List of Effective Pages

MAJCOM—Major Command

MMO—Monitoring Management Operator

MSN—Mission Qualification

NAF—Numbered Air Force

N/N—No-notice

OC—Operations Controller

OG—Operations Group

OG/CC—Operations Group Commander

OGV—Operations Group Standardization/Evaluation

OPR—Office of Primary Responsibility

QUAL—Qualification

SEE—Stan/Eval Examiner

SPOT—Spot Evaluation

SQ—Squadron

SQ/CC—Squadron Commander

SVO—Storage and Virtualization Operator

VAO—Vulnerability Assessment Operator

VRO—Vulnerability Remediation Operator

Terms

Airmanship—A crewmember's continuous perception of self and weapon system/mission equipment in relation to the dynamic environment of operations, threats, and tasking, and the ability to forecast and execute tasks based on that perception.

Boundary Protection Operator (CSCS—BPO) – Allows/denies/redirects/logs network traffic in, though, and from base firewalls and proxies. Additionally, evaluates, detects, prevents and implements counter-measures to protect network hosts, data, voice and key mission systems from unauthorized network activity.

Client End Point Protection Operator (CSCS—CPO) – Remediates vulnerabilities and weaknesses identified in cyberspace terrain and associated software suites utilized by Air Force Information Systems and net-centric capabilities.

Commendable—An observed exemplary demonstration of knowledge and/or or noteworthy ability to perform by the examinee in a particular graded area/subarea, tactic, technique, procedure, and/or task.

Crew Commander (CC)—Cyberspace operator qualified to perform crew commander duties.

Cyberspace Training Devices—All trainers, computer assisted instruction, sound-on-slide programs, videos, and mockups designed to prepare students for operations training or augment prescribed continuation training.

Deficiency—Demonstrated level of knowledge or ability to perform is inadequate, insufficient, or short of meeting required or expected proficiency.

Deviation—Performing an action not in sequence with current procedures, directives or regulations. Performing action(s) out of sequence due to unusual or extenuating circumstances is not considered a deviation. In some cases, momentary deviations may be acceptable; however, cumulative deviations will be considered in determining the overall qualification level.

Directory Services Operator (CSCS-DSO)—Provides authentication and accessibility to clients in the Air Force Network domain.

Discrepancy—Any observed deviations/errors/omissions, individually or cumulative, that detracts from the examinee's performance in obtaining a Q for a particular grading area/subarea.

Error—Departure from standard procedure. Performing incorrect actions or recording inaccurate information.

Inadequate—Lack or underutilization of available crew aids or resources to effectively/efficiently make operational and tactical decisions, gain/maintain situational awareness, or accomplish a task.

Inappropriate—Excessive reliance on crew aids/other resources or utilizing a crew aid/ resource outside its intended use.

Infrastructure Operator (CSCS-IFO)—Employs both configuration and security policies on network components to enforce policies and techniques that effectively and securely route network traffic.

Instructor—Crewmember trained, qualified and certified by the squadron commander as an instructor to perform both ground and in-flight training.

Instructor Supervision—When a current instructor, who is qualified in the same crew position, supervises a maneuver or training event.

Major (deviation/error/omission)—Detracted from task accomplishment, adversely affected use of equipment, or violated safety.

Minor (deviation/error/omission)—Did not detract from task accomplishment, adversely affect use of equipment or violate safety.

Monitoring Management Operator (CSCS-MMO)—Provides situational awareness of cyberspace terrain and weapons system component health monitoring solutions for the CSCS.

Omission—To leave out a required action or annotation.

Operations Controller (OC)—Cyberspace operator qualified to perform operations controller duties.

Stan/Eval Examiner (SEE)—A crewmember designated to administer evaluations.

Storage and Virtualization Operator (CSCS-SVO)—Performs backup, recovery, and archiving via storage area networks (SAN).

Supervised Training Status—Crew member will perform weapon system duties under instructor supervision as designated by the squadron commander or evaluator.

Vulnerability Assessment Operator (CSCS—VAO) – Identifies vulnerabilities within cyberspace terrain and associated software suites utilized by Air Force Information systems and net-centric capabilities. In addition, identifies and assesses the weaknesses in cyberspace terrain that adversaries may gain/maintain access to the AFNet.

Vulnerability Remediation Operator (CSCS—VRO) – Remediates vulnerabilities within cyberspace terrain and associated software suites utilized by Air Force Information systems and net-centric capabilities.

BY ORDER OF THE SECRETARY
OF THE AIR FORCE

AIR FORCE INSTRUCTION 17-2CSCS,
VOLUME 3

16 MAY 2017

Cyberspace

CYBERSPACE SECURITY AND
CONTROL SYSTEM (CSCS)
OPERATIONS AND PROCEDURES

COMPLIANCE WITH THIS PUBLICATION IS MANDATORY

ACCESSIBILITY: Publications and forms are available for downloading or ordering on the e- Publishing website at **www.e-Publishing.af.mil**

RELEASABILITY: There are no releasability restrictions on this publication

OPR: HQ USAF/A3CX/A6CX

Certified by: HQ USAF/A3C/A6C
(Brig Gen Kevin B. Kennedy)
Pages: 25

This volume implements Air Force (AF) Policy Directive (AFPD) 17-2, *Cyberspace Operations*, and references AFI 17-202 Volume 3, *Cyberspace Operations and Procedures.* It applies to all Cyber Security and Control System (CSCS) units. This publication applies to all military and civilian AF personnel, members of the AF Reserve Command (AFRC), Air National Guard (ANG), and contractor support personnel in accordance with appropriate provisions contained in memoranda support agreements and AF contracts. This publication requires the collection and or maintenance of information protected by the Privacy Act (PA) of 1947. The authorities to collect and maintain the records prescribed in this publication are Title 10 United States Code, **Chapter 857** and Executive Order 9397, Numbering System for Federal Accounts Relating to Individual Persons, 30 November 1943, as amended by Executive Order 13478, Amendments to Executive Order 9397 Relating to Federal Agency Use of Social Security Numbers, November 18, 2008.

The authorities to waive wing/unit level requirements in this publication are identified with a Tier ("T-0, T-1, T-2, T-3") number following the compliance statement. See AFI 33-360, *Publications and Forms Management*, Table 1.1, for a description of the authorities associated with the Tier numbers. Submit requests for waivers through the chain of command to the appropriate Tier waiver approval authority, or alternately, to the publication OPR for non-tiered compliance items. Refer recommended changes and questions about this publication to the Office of Primary Responsibility (OPR) using AF Form 847, *Recommendation for Change of Publication*; route AF Forms 847 from the field through Major Command (MAJCOM) publications/forms managers to AF/A3C/A6C. Ensure all records created as a result of processes prescribed in this publication are maintained in accordance with AF Manual (AFMAN) 33-363, *Management of Records*, and disposed of in accordance with (IAW) the AF Records Disposition Schedule (RDS) located in the AF Records Management Information System (AFRIMS). The RDS is located on the AF Portal **https://www.my.af.mil/afrims/afrims/afrims/rims.cfm**.

Chapter 1

GENERAL GUIDANCE

1.1. References, Abbreviations, Acronyms and Terms. See Attachment 1

1.2. General. This volume, in conjunction with other governing directives, prescribes procedures for operating the CSCS weapon system under most circumstances. It is not a substitute for sound judgment or common sense. Procedures not specifically addressed may be accomplished if they enhance safe and effective mission accomplishment.

1.3. Waivers. Unless another approval authority is cited ("T-0, T-1, T-2, T-3"), waiver authority for this volume is the MAJCOM/A3 (or equivalent). Submit requests for waivers using AF Form 679, *Air Force Publication Compliance Item Waiver Request/Approval*, through the chain of command to the appropriate Tier waiver approval authority. If approved, waivers remain in effect for the life of the published guidance, unless the waiver authority specifies a shorter period of time, cancels in writing, or issues a change that alters the basis for the waiver.

1.4. Deviations. In the case of an urgent requirement or emergency, the Crew Commander will take appropriate action(s) to ensure safe operations. **(T-3)**

1.5. Processing Changes. Submit recommended changes and questions about this publication through MAJCOM channels. **(T-2)**

1.5.1. Send recommended changes or comments to HQ USAF/A3CX/A6CX, 1480 Air Force Pentagon, Washington, DC, 20330-1480, through appropriate channels, using AF Form 847, *Recommendation for Change of Publication.*

1.5.2. The submitting MAJCOM will forward information copies of AF Forms 847 to all other MAJCOMS that use this publication. Using MAJCOMs will forward comments on AF Forms 847 to the OPR. **(T-2)**

1.5.3. OPR will:

1.5.3.1. Coordinate all changes to the basic instruction with affected MAJCOM/A3s. **(T-2)**

1.5.3.2. Forward change recommendations to MAJCOM/A3 for staffing and AF/A3 approval. **(T-2)**

1.6. Supplements. Guidance for supplementing this publication is contained in AFI 33-360. Supplements will not duplicate, alter, amend or be less restrictive than the provisions of this instruction. **(T-2)**

Chapter 2

MISSION PLANNING

2.1. Responsibilities. Individual crews, unit operations and intelligence functions jointly share responsibility for mission planning. The Crew Commander is ultimately responsible for ensuring all aspects of mission planning, to include complying with command guidance, is accomplished. Unit commanders may supplement mission planning requirements but will ensure an appropriate level of mission planning is conducted prior to each mission. All missions and/or events will be planned, briefed and debriefed. **(T-3)**

2.2. Mission Planning Guidelines.

2.2.1. Effective mission accomplishment requires thorough mission planning and preparation. Specific mission planning elements are addressed in Air Force Tactics, Techniques, and Procedures (AFTTP) 3-1.General Planning, AFTTP 3-1.CSCS, 24 Air Force, AFCYBER & Joint Forces Headquarters-Cyber (JFHQ-C) AFCYBER Tactical Mission Planning, Briefing and Debriefing Guide, 24 AF Defensive Cyberspace Operations Concept of Employment, and any local crew aids. While not directive, these manuals are authoritative and useful in ensuring adequate mission planning and employment. **(T-3)**

2.2.2. Standard Operating Procedures (SOP). The squadron commander (SQ/CC) is the approval authority for squadron standards. Operations group commander (OG/CC) may publish and approve group standards. The operations group Standardization and Evaluation office (OGV) will review all standards for compliance with this AFI and all other applicable guidance. **(T-3)**

2.2.3. Commanders will provide adequate time and facilities for mission planning. Crews will accomplish sufficient planning to ensure successful mission accomplishment. Units will maintain facilities where all information and materials required for mission planning are available. **(T-3)**

2.2.4. Commanders will ensure other activities, such as recurring academic training, training device periods, additional duties, etc., do not interfere with time allotted for mission planning and crew mission briefing. **(T-3)**

2.2.5. The following mission planning areas will be considered prior to execution: Mission, Environment, Enemy, Effects, Capabilities, Plan, Phasing, Contracts or Contingencies (ME3C-[PC]2). The following mission information should be addressed during mission planning:

2.2.5.1. Tasking Order and line number (if applicable) **(T-3)**

2.2.5.2. Minimum forces **(T-3)**

2.2.5.3. Terrain **(T-3)**

2.2.5.4. Communication plan **(T-3)**

2.2.5.5. Vulnerability/operating window **(T-3)**

2.2.5.6. Deconfliction plan (if applicable) **(T-3)**

2.2.5.7. Abort criteria and contingency plan **(T-3)**

2.2.5.8. Weapon system health/status **(T-3)**

2.2.6. As a result of this planning, a Mission Data Card (MDC) will be created as an aid for execution. These should, at a minimum, include the Tasking Order and line number, Crew line-up and Package Leads, Callsign, the Area of Operation/Terrain, Communication plan, Vulnerability/operating window, and Deconfliction plan. **(T-3)**

2.3. Briefings.

2.3.1. The Crew Commander is responsible for presenting a logical briefing to promote a safe and effective mission(s). All crewmembers will attend the mission brief unless previously coordinated with the squadron director of operations (SQ/DO) or designated representative. **(T-3)**

2.3.2. The Crew Commander will plan adequate time to discuss required briefing items commensurate with the complexity of the mission and operator capabilities. Any item published in MAJCOM/Numbered Air Force (NAF)/wing/group/squadron standards or AFIs that is understood by all participants may be briefed as "standard." **(T-3)**

2.3.3. Briefings will conclude no later than 15 minutes prior to scheduled sortie.

2.3.4. Briefing Guides. Briefing guides will be used by the lead briefer with a reference list of items, which may apply to specific missions. An example briefing guide is in Attachment 2. Units may augment these guides as necessary. Items may be briefed in any sequence, provided all minimum requirements listed in this AFI and other local directives and guidance are addressed. **(T-3)**

2.3.5. All briefings will include the following Mission Planning Considerations:

2.3.5.1. Risk Management **(T-3)**

2.3.5.2. Mission and crew Go/No-Go status **(T-3)**

2.3.5.3. Mission priorities and objectives **(T-3)**

2.3.5.4. Crew Line-up **(T-3)**

2.3.5.5. Rollback, Contingency Plans (Abort Criteria) **(T-3)**

2.3.5.6. Push times, Route, Deconfliction, Environment, Time Over Target/Terrain (TOT/T), & Re-attacks **(T-3)**

2.3.5.7. Significant rules (e.g., Special Instructions (SPINs), Training rules, ROE) **(T-3)**

2.3.5.8. Contracts, roles, and responsibilities of each crewmember **(T-3)**

2.3.5.9. Weapon system status, facility status **(T-3)**

2.3.5.10. Intel support will brief the intelligence portion **(T-3)**

2.3.6. Anyone not attending the mission brief will receive, at a minimum, an overview of the mission objectives, their roles and responsibilities and emergency procedures (EP) prior to becoming actively involved in crew operations. **(T-3)**

2.3.7. Positional Changeover Brief. For operational needs, crews may be required to brief oncoming crewmembers. These will be delivered IAW checklist(s) and applicable directives. **(T-3)**

2.3.8. Alternate Missions. Alternate missions will be briefed in case the originally planned and briefed mission is cancelled/aborted. **(T-3)**

2.3.8.1. If the alternate mission parallels the planned mission, brief the specific mission elements that are different. **(T-3)**

2.3.8.2. Mission elements may be modified and briefed after start of execution as long as mission safety is not compromised. Crew Commanders will ensure changes are acknowledged by all crewmembers. **(T-3)**

Chapter 3

NORMAL OPERATING PROCEDURES

3.1. Pre-Mission Arrival Times. The SQ/DO may adjust crew report time to meet mission requirements. Crew report times will allow sufficient time to accomplish all pre-mission activities. **(T-3)**

3.2. Pre-Mission Duties. Prior to mission execution, crewmembers should only be scheduled for duties related to the scheduled mission. **(T-3)**

3.2.1. Example: Crewmember is scheduled for a sortie from 8 am – 12 pm; crewmember duty day is scheduled from 7 am – 3 pm. Prior to mission execution, crewmember performs pre-mission duties (e.g., planning, briefing, etc.). After the mission debrief, crew is released to perform other/additional duties. **(T-3)**

3.3. Go/No Go. The SQ/CC will implement the Go/No-Go program to ensure individual crewmembers are current, qualified and/or adequately supervised to perform operations and have reviewed Crew Information File (CIF) Volume 1, Part B, prior to conducting operations. Crewmembers will not operate on the weapon system until the Go/No-Go is accomplished and verified. **(T-3)**

3.3.1. The SQ/CC will designate in writing those individuals who are responsible for accomplishing the daily Go/No-Go verification for all crewmembers performing mission duties for that day. Note: Those designated to accomplish the Go/No-Go will not include individuals performing crew mission duties for that day. **(T-3)**

3.3.2. Designated individuals will verify, document, and sign off on the Go/No-Go status prior to releasing crewmembers for any mission execution. Go/No-Go accomplishment is an essential item in the mission pre-brief. Record the Go/No-Go accomplishment and verification in the MAJCOM approved automated system. The unit will maintain these records for one year. **(T-3)**

3.3.3. If automated functionality exists to accomplish the Go/No-Go verification, unit operating instructions will include backup procedures to permit Go/No-Go verification when the relevant information system is unavailable. **(T-3)**

3.3.4. The unit Go/No-Go process will verify the following minimum items for all crew members scheduled to perform crew duties:

3.3.4.1. Qualification/certification IAW AFI 17-2CSCS Volume 1, *Cyberspace Security and Control System (CSCS) Cybercrew Training*, and AFI 17-2CSCS Volume 2, *Cyberspace Security and Control System (CSCS) Standardization and Evaluations*, for the crew position, mission, and duties they are scheduled to perform. Note: Crewmembers not qualified/certified and in training status will require instructor or evaluator supervision to conduct crew duties. **(T-3)**

3.3.4.2. Currency IAW AFI 17-2CSCS Volume 1, *Cyberspace Security and Control System (CSCS) Cybercrew Training*, for the crew position, mission, and duties they are scheduled to perform. Note: Crewmembers not current in the crew position and/or mission will require instructor supervision to conduct crew duties until regaining currency. **(T-3)**

3.3.4.3. Documented review by each crewmember of all CIF Volume 1, Part B, read file items. Note: An initial review and certification of all volumes will be accomplished prior to an individual's first training or operational mission. Assigned or attached crewmembers on extensive absence from conducting missions (90 days or more) will accomplish a complete review of all volumes prior to operations. **(T-3)**

3.4. Crew Information File (CIF)/Crew Bulletins (CB). The SQ/CC will ensure accurate CIF/CBs are available for crewmembers. Crewmembers will review CIF/CBs before all missions, and update the CIF record with the latest CIF item number, date and crewmember's initials. **(T-3)**

3.4.1. Electronic signatures or sign-off may be used on CIFs. **(T-3)**

3.4.2. Crewmembers delinquent in CIF review or joining a mission enroute will receive a CIF update from a primary crewmember counterpart on the mission. **(T-3)**

3.4.3. Items in the CB may include interim local procedures and policies concerning equipment and personnel generally not found in any other publications. **(T-3)**

3.5. Unit-Developed Checklist/Local Crew Aids.

3.5.1. Locally developed checklists and crew aids may be used and will, at a minimum, include the following:

3.5.1.1. Emergency action checklists and communication-out information. **(T-3)**

3.5.1.2. Other information as deemed necessary by the units (e.g., local mission planning guides, briefing/debriefing guides, reference data sheets, local training diagrams, and local area maps of sufficient detail to provide situational awareness on area boundaries). **(T-3)**

3.5.2. Unit Stan/Eval will maintain in the CIF library the list of current and authorized checklists, crew aids and other information as necessary. **(T-3)**

3.6. Forms and Logs. The Master Station Log (MSL) is the unit's official record of events that occurred during operations or training. The purpose is to maintain an accurate and detailed record of all significant events pertaining to operations occurring during each sortie. The Crew Commander is responsible for documenting significant events/crew actions required for the MSL. The Crew Commander is responsible for content, accuracy and timeliness of all inputs to mission-related information management portals/collaborative information sharing environments IAW with applicable directives, tasking and policy. **(T-3)**

3.7. Required Equipment/Publications. Crewmembers will have all equipment and publications required for mission execution. These may be maintained and carried electronically provided operable viewing and printing capability exists throughout mission execution. OGV will maintain the list of required equipment/publication items. **(T-3)**

3.7.1. Required equipment includes, but is not limited to, personal accounts, passwords, password grids, all required logins and orders. **(T-3)**

3.7.2. The Crew Commander is responsible for ensuring contents, mission readiness and availability of the Deployment Case, Password Binder, and other critical documentation required for mission execution. **(T-3)**

3.8. Operations Check (Ops Check).

3.8.1. Crew members will perform Ops Checks at initial check-in, during times of authentication, and as required during sortie period based on mission triggers and requirements. **(T-3)**

3.8.2. Crews will, at a minimum, check the following items during Ops Checks: route, environment, verification of access, and terrain. **(T-3)**

3.9. On Station/Off Station. Crews will be prepared for mission execution and are expected to be on station at the beginning of the TOT/T, and will be off station by the end of the TOT/T, unless circumstances occur which are beyond crew control. **(T-3)**

3.10. Vulnerability (VUL) Window. Crews are bounded by the vulnerability (VUL) window. Deviations from the assigned VUL window will be coordinated through the Crew Commander and approved by the tasking authority. **(T-3)**

3.11. Abort/Knock-it-off. A tactical commander may declare a knock-it-off (training use only) or abort (cease action/event/mission). **(T-3)**

3.12. Dynamic Targeting. Ad hoc and/or emerging target tasking can occur. During tasked missions, an operator may identify and report something that may require ad hoc or dynamic targeting/re-tasking. Dynamic re-tasking allows modification of the mission to support changing mission objectives. This includes everything from re-tasking the operator within the mission requirements to an entirely new mission that is added to the current tasking order. **(T-3)**

3.13. Communications and Crew Coordination. Recorded crew communications represent official communications, and crewmembers should be aware they have no expectation of privacy. Crews will use brevity codes as defined in SPINS to the maximum extent possible **(T-3)**.

3.14. Communications.

3.14.1. Mission execution requires at least one method of communication for all operations. **(T-3)**

3.14.2. The Crew Commander is responsible for developing and briefing the communication plan. Communications planning is performed to determine who should talk, when, and via what medium. An Example Communications Planning Guide can be found in Attachment 4. **(T-3)**

3.14.3. The Crew Commander will ensure a designated crewmember will monitor all primary communications, unless otherwise directed, during all phases of operations. **(T-3)**

3.15. Mission Report (MISREP). Tasking authorities, future missions and debriefs rely on timely, accurate MISREPs. All MISREPs will be completed prior to debrief. **(T-3)**

3.15.1. The Crew Commander is responsible for providing timely, accurate and correctly formatted reports to the tasking authority. **(T-3)**

3.15.2. A MISREP will be accomplished once the cybercrew completes a mission or particular phase of the mission IAW guidance/tasking. **(T-3)**

3.15.3. The Crew Commander will review the MISREP for accuracy and completeness, and submit to the tasking authority. **(T-3)**

3.15.4. Each crewmember is responsible for providing the appropriate data regarding their mission area for the MISREP per local guidance. **(T-3)**

3.15.5. Local procedures/templates may be developed to ensure standardization of reporting. **(T-3)**

3.16. Crew Changeover. Crewmembers from the off-going and on-coming sorties during a multi-sortie day will participate in a crew changeover briefing. Direct crew changeover only applies if crews are performing 24/7 operations. If 24/7 operations are not occurring, crew changeover briefings will be incorporated into the next pre-mission briefing. At a minimum, the changeover will include all items previously identified for the pre-mission briefing. **(T-3)**

3.17. Debriefing.

3.17.1. All missions will be debriefed. **(T-3)**

3.17.2. The Crew Commander is responsible for leading the crew debrief **(T-3)**.

3.17.3. Debriefs will address all aspects of the mission (planning, briefing and execution) and ensure all participants receive feedback through the development of Lessons Learned (LL) and Learning Points (LP). LL and LP should be applied as soon as operationally feasible (i.e. implemented in training, resulted in process changes, update checklists, etc.). SQ/DO will determine a tracking process to insure LL and LP are implemented. **(T-3)**

3.17.4. Debrief will address crewmember responsibilities, de-confliction contracts, tactical employment priorities, and task management. **(T-3)**

3.17.5. The Crew Commander will review the record of all tactical portions of the sortie to assess member effectiveness. **(T-3)**

3.17.6. The debriefing should occur at multiple levels (e.g., crew debrief and team debrief) depending on the mission type (i.e., single ship, large force employment). The debriefing guide is in Attachment 3.3.17.7. **(T-3)**

Chapter 4

CREW DUTIES, RESPONSIBILITIES AND PROCEDURES

4.1. CSCS Crew Requirement. The CSCS Crew will consist of expertise from each component of the weapon system (see AFTTP 3-1, CSCS Crew Construct). This enables the CSCS Crew to employ all aspects of the CSCS Weapon System and support all CSCS mission types. In some cases, there may be personnel with expertise that may support multiple crews. **(T-3)**

4.2. Crew Commander Responsibilities. The Crew Commander is responsible for each sortie. The Crew Commander is responsible for the safe, effective conduct of operations. Crew Commander responsibilities and/or authority include:

4.2.1. Managing crew resources and safe mission accomplishment. **(T-3)**

4.2.2. Welfare of the crew. **(T-3)**

4.2.3. Ensuring that any portion of the operation affecting the accomplishment of the mission is coordinated with the tasking authority. **(T-3)**

4.2.4. Ensuring risk management decision matrix is performed through all phases of the mission. **(T-3)**

4.3. Crew Stations. Crewmembers will be on the operations floor during the critical trigger points/phases of execution. Crewmembers will notify the Crew Commander prior to departing their assigned primary duty station. **(T-3)**

4.4. Crew Duties. Crews are responsible to the Crew Commander for the safe, effective use of the weapon system and mission accomplishment. A crew brief will be accomplished before each mission execution to ensure an understanding of all aspects of the mission. **(T-3)**

4.5. Crew Positions.

4.5.1. Crew Commander (CSCS-CC). Serves as the command authority for CSCS crew operations and provides command oversight for operations crew personnel. The CSCS-CC is also responsible for the management of crewmembers' execution of assigned missions as well as enforcing policies and procedures to ensure successful mission accomplishment.

4.5.2. Operations Controller (CSCS-OC). Responsible for management of operations, execution of assigned missions and reporting their status to Crew Commander.

4.5.3. Operations Crew Personnel. Operate one or more components of the CSCS Weapon System executing operations as tasked by the Crew Commander to support friendly forces and accomplish mission objectives in assigned terrains as outlined in assigned mission plans. CSCS Operator positions include:

4.5.3.1. Boundary Protection Operator (CSCS-BPO). Allows/denies/redirects/logs network traffic in, through, and from base firewalls and proxies. Additionally, evaluates, detects, prevents and implements counter-measures to protect network hosts, data, voice and key mission systems from unauthorized network activity.

4.5.3.2. Client End Point Protection Operator (CSCS-CPO). Remediates vulnerabilities and weaknesses identified in cyberspace terrain and associated software suites utilized by Air Force Information Systems and net-centric capabilities.

4.5.3.3. Directory Services Operator (CSCS-DSO). Provides authentication and accessibility to clients in the Air Force Network domain.

4.5.3.4. Infrastructure Operator (CSCS-IFO). Employs both configuration and security policies on network components to enforce policies and techniques that effectively and securely route network traffic.

4.5.3.5. Monitoring Management Operator (CSCS-MMO). Provides situational awareness of cyberspace terrain and weapons system component health monitoring solutions for the CSCS.

4.5.3.6. Storage and Virtualization Operator (CSCS-SVO). Performs backup, recovery and archiving via storage area networks (SAN).

4.5.3.7. Vulnerability Assessment Operator (CSCS-VAO). Identifies vulnerabilities within cyberspace terrain and associated software suites utilized by Air Force Information systems and net-centric capabilities. In addition, identifies and assesses the weaknesses in cyberspace terrain that adversaries may exploit to gain/maintain AFNet access.

4.5.3.8. Vulnerability Remediation Operator (CSCS-VRO). Remediates vulnerabilities within cyberspace terrain and associated software suites utilized by Air Force Information systems and net-centric capabilities.

4.6. Crew Construct. A standard full complement CSCS Crew consists of 10 (ten) personnel. One (1) Crew Commander, One (1) Operations Controller and One (1) Operations Crewmember from each of the components of the weapon system. Crew construct may vary based on the type of mission; SQ/DO may tailor crew manning to meet operational requirements. CSCS operating units that cannot field a full complement crew are required to identify their crew construct to OGV. See Figure 4.1 for full complement crew construct positional requirements. **(T-3)**

4.6.1. CSCS operating units may field multiple crews to support multiple missions. **(T-3)**

4.6.2. Each CSCS crew equates to a tail number. **(T-3)**

4.6.2.1. Example: 83 may field up to two (2) CSCS crews. o Tail numbers include: #83A, #83B

Figure 4.1. Standard Full Complement CSCS Crew Construct.

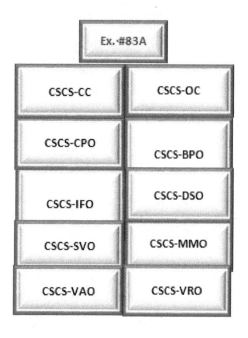

4.7. Maximum Load out per CSCS Crew per Sortie for missions. (T-3)

4.7.1. CSCS crews may only be tasked to support a single Line of Effort per sortie **(T-3)**

4.7.1.1. Ex. "#83A tasked to support DCO missions for CTO day 15-AA"

4.7.1.2. Ex. "#83B tasked to support DoDIN missions for CTO day 15-AA"

4.7.2. Limitations based on capacity and mission types will be identified by HHQs mission planning based on the number of CSCS Crews (tails) available for tasking. **(T-3)**

4.7.2.1. Due to the varying scope of missions, SQ/DOs and CSCS Crews will coordinate with HHQ's to identify additional CSCS Crew ops capacity during mission planning. **(T-3)**

4.7.2.2. Mission planning should identify capacity constraints, restraints, and minimum forces required. **(T-3)**

4.8. Crew Qualification. Each person assigned as a primary crewmember will be current and qualified in that crew position, mission and weapon system, or in a training status under the supervision of a qualified instructor. **(T-3)**

4.8.1. Basic Cybercrew Qualified (BCQ) crewmembers may perform primary crew duties on any training sortie to include joint training and exercises when receiving MQT or evaluations. BCQ crewmembers executing training sorties must be under the supervision of a qualified instructor/evaluator in their respective crew position. **(T-3)**

4.8.2. Basic Mission Capable (BMC) crewmembers may perform primary crew duties on any training mission. The unit commander will determine the readiness of each BMC crewmember to perform primary crew duties. **(T-3)**

4.8.3. Mission Ready (MR) crewmembers may perform primary crew duties in any position in which they maintain qualification, certification, currency and proficiency. **(T-3)**

4.8.4. Non-current or Unqualified crewmembers may perform crew duties only on designated training or evaluation missions under the supervision of a qualified instructor/evaluator. **(T-3)**

4.9. New/Modified Equipment and/or Capabilities. Crewmembers not qualified and/or certified in the operation of new or modified equipment and/or weapon system capabilities will not operate that equipment or perform any duties associated with that weapon system capability unless under the supervision of a current and qualified instructor of like specialty or unless otherwise specified by MAJCOM guidance. **(T-3)**

4.10. Crew Rest/Duty Period/Sortie Duration. Crew rest, crew duty period and crew augmentation will be IAW all applicable guidance with the following additional guidance:

4.10.1. Crew Rest. Commanders will ensure crews are afforded a 12-hour non-duty period before the duty period begins to ensure the crewmember is provided adequate time to rest before performing a mission or mission-related duties. Crew rest is free time, and includes time for meals, transportation and eight hours uninterrupted sleep. Rest is defined as a condition that allows an individual the opportunity to sleep. Each crewmember is individually responsible for ensuring they obtain sufficient rest during crew rest periods. **(T-3)**

4.10.2. Exceptions to the 12-Hour Minimum Crew Rest Period. Crew rest may be reduced to a minimum of 10 hours with COG/CC approval. **(T-3)**

4.10.2.1. Continuous operations mean three or more consecutive sorties of at least 12 hours duration separated by minimum crew rest. **(T-3)**

4.10.2.2. The crew rest exception shall only be used for contingency/surge operations and not for scheduling conveniences. **(T-3)**

4.10.2.3. The Crew Commander will ensure any reduction in the crew rest period that was approved by the SQ/CC or COG/CC is annotated in the MISREP. **(T-3)**

4.10.3. Duty Period. The crew duty period will not exceed twelve (12) hours, which includes planning, briefing and debriefing. The SQ/DO must approve any requests for a crewmember to perform or attend non-mission related duties or events during a phase of the PBED. **(T-3)**

4.10.4. Sortie. For planning purposes, the average sortie duration (ASD) is 6 hours. **(T-3)**

4.10.5. Crew Scheduling. Mission crew scheduling will be accomplished IAW crew rest limitations in para 4.10. Units will publish, post, and monitor schedules for the crew force and initiate changes to the schedules based on proper tracking of qualifications, certifications, restrictions and other factors as required to meet mission objectives. **(T-3)**

4.10.5.1. Commanders will ensure a crewmember on leave or temporary duty (TDY) is notified if an event is altered in any way or added to the crewmember's schedule within the first 72 hours of their scheduled return. **(T-3)**

4.10.5.2. Notifications will be made immediately after the change is official, not later than 12 hours prior to the scheduled event time. Units will ensure that oncoming crewmembers will be capable of meeting crew risk management requirements in addition to ensuring that crewmembers do not consume alcohol within 12 hours of mission planning/execution. **(T-3)**

WILLIAM J. BENDER, Lt Gen, USAF
Chief of Information Dominance and Chief
Information Officer

Attachment 1

GLOSSARY OF REFERENCES AND SUPPORTING INFORMATION

References

AFPD 17-2, *Cyberspace Operations*, 12 April 2016

AFI 33-360, *Publications and Forms Management*, 1 December 2015

AFI 17-2CSCS Volume 1, *Cyberspace Security and Control System (CSCS) Cybercrew Training*

AFI 17-2CSCS Volume 2, *Cyberspace Security and Control System (CSCS) Standardization and Evaluations*

AFI 17-202 Volume 3, *Cyberspace Operations and Procedures*, 6 May 2015

AFMAN 33-363, *Management of Records*, 1 March 2008

AFTTP 3-1.CSCS Crew Construct

AFTTP 3-1.General Planning

AFTTP 3-1.Threat Guide Chapter 13

24 Air Force (24 AF), AFCYBER & JFHQ-C AFCYBER Tactical Mission Planning, Briefing and Debriefing Guide

24 AF Defensive Cyberspace Operations Concept of Employment

MULTI-SERVICE BREVITY CODES, AFTTP 3-2.5, September 2014

FB 12-12, *Defensive Cyberspace Operations-Tactical Coordinator*

FB 14-19, *Defensive Cyber Operations Large Force Employment Considerations*

Adopted Forms

AF Form 679, *Air Force Publication Compliance Item Waiver Request/Approval*

AF Form 847, *Recommendation for Change of Publication*

Abbreviations and Acronyms

AFCYBER—Air Forces Cyber

AFPD—Air Force Policy Directive

AFI—Air Force Instruction

AFMAN—Air Force Manual

AFRC—Air Force Reserve Command

AFRIMS—Air Force Records Information Management System

AFTTP—Air Force Tactics, Techniques and Procedures

ANG—Air National Guard

ASD—Average Sortie Duration

BCQ—Basic Cybercrew Qualification

BMC—Basic Mission Capable

CB—Crew Bulletin

CC—Commander

CIF—Crew Information File

CSCS—Cyberspace Security and Control System

CSCS-BPO—CSCS Boundary Protection Operator

CSCS-CC—CSCS Crew Commander

CSCS-CPO—CSCS Client End Point Protection Operator

CSCS-DSO—CSCS Directory Services Operator

CSCS-IFO—CSCS Infrastructure Operator

CSCS-MMO—CSCS Monitoring Management Operator

CSCS-OC—CSCS Operations Controller

CSCS-SVO—CSCS Storage and Virtualization Operator

CSCS-VAO—CSCS Vulnerability Assessment Operator

CSCS-VRO—CSCS Vulnerability Remediation Operator

CT—Continuation Training

DO—Director of Operations

EP—Emergency Procedures

IAW—In Accordance With

JFHQ-C -Joint Forces Headquarters-Cyber

LL—Lesson Learned

LP—Learning Point

MAJCOM—Major Command

MDC—Mission Data Card

MISREP—Mission Report

MR—Mission Ready

MSL—Master Station Log

NAF—Numbered Air Force

NC—Non-current

OG—Operations Group

OGV—Standardization and Evaluation

OPR—Office of Primary Responsibility

ROE—Rules of Engagement

SOP—Standard Operating Procedures

SPINS—Special Instructions

SQ—Squadron

TOT/T—Time over Target/Terrain

USAF—United States Air Force

Average Sortie Duration (ASD) – ASD is used to convert sorties to operating/execution hours and vice versa. MAJCOM/A3TB uses the unit's last programmed ASD when initially determining execution/operating hours programs for the current and future years. Units will update ASD annually to reflect the unit's best estimate of the optimum sortie duration after considering historical experiences, changes in missions, deployments, etc. The formula to calculate ASD is ASD=# of weapon system hours employed divided by number of sorties.

Basic Cybercrew Qualification (BCQ) – A cybercrew member who satisfactorily completed IQT. The crewmember will carry BCQ only until completion of MQT. BCQ crewmembers will not perform RCP-tasked events or sorties without instructor crewmembers.

Basic Mission Capable (BMC) – The status of a crewmember who satisfactorily completed IQT and MQT to perform the unit's basic operational missions, but does not maintain MR/CMR status. Crewmember accomplishes training required to remain familiarized in all and may be qualified and proficient in some of the primary missions of their weapon system BMC requirements.

Boundary Protection Operator (CSCS—BPO) – Allows/denies/redirects/logs network traffic in, though, and from base firewalls and proxies. Additionally, evaluates, detects, prevents and implements counter-measures to protect network hosts, data, voice and key mission systems from unauthorized network activity.

Campaign – A series of related major operations aimed at achieving strategic and operational objectives within a given time and space.

Certification – Designation of an individual by the certifying official as having completed required training and/or evaluation and being capable of performing a specific duty.

Client End Point Protection Operator (CSCS—CPO) – Remediates vulnerabilities and weaknesses identified in cyberspace terrain and associated software suites utilized by Air Force Information Systems and net-centric capabilities.

Composite Force Training (CFT) – Scenarios employing multiple units of the same or different weapon systems types, each under the direction of its own package leader, performing the same or different roles. Only one event may be logged per mission.

Continuation Training (CT) – Training, which provides crewmembers with the volume, frequency and mix of training necessary to maintain currency and proficiency in the assigned qualification level.

Core Mission – Core Missions are operational mission actions or training scenario profiles that relate to the unit's DOC statement requirements. The base mechanism used to achieve missions is sorties.

Core Mission Sortie – Core Mission Sorties are operational mission actions or training scenario profiles that relate to the unit's DOC statement requirements—.

Crew – Also referred to as crewmembers, consist of individuals who conduct cyberspace operations or computer network exploitation and are typically assigned to a specific weapon system.

Crew Commander—Serves as the command authority for CSCS crew operations and provides command oversight for operations floor personnel as well as enforcing policies and procedures to ensure successful mission accomplishment.

Crew Information File (CIF) – A collection of publications and material determined by the MAJCOM and unit as necessary for day-to-day operations.

Currency – A measure of how frequently and/or recently a task is completed. Currency requirements should ensure the average crewmember maintains a minimum level of proficiency in a given event.

Cyber (adj.)—Of or pertaining to the cyberspace environment, capabilities, plans or operations.

Cyberspace – A global domain within the information environment consisting of the interdependent network of information technology infrastructures and resident data, including the Internet, telecommunications networks, computer systems, and embedded processors and controllers.

Cyberspace Operations (CO) – The employment of cyberspace capabilities where the primary purpose is to achieve objectives in or through cyberspace.

Deviation – Performing action(s) not in sequence with current procedures, directives or regulations. Performing action(s) out of sequence due to unusual or extenuating circumstances is not considered a deviation. In some cases, momentary deviations may be acceptable; however, cumulative deviations will be considered in determining the overall qualification level—.

Directory Services Operator (CSCS—DSO) – Provides authentication and accessibility to clients in the Air Force Network domain.

Event – An item that occurs or is encountered that initiates a process requiring a set of tasks to be accomplished. Multiple events may be completed and logged during a sortie (be it operational sortie or a training sortie) unless specifically excluded elsewhere in this instruction.

Experienced Crewmember (EXP)—Crewmember that meets the hours requirement in Vol 1.

Incident Response (IR)—Executes surveillance missions after the detection of an emerging target to characterize target(s); confirming or invalidating target(s) providing amplifying targeting information for follow-on forces.

Infrastructure Operator (CSCS—IFO) – Employs both configuration and security policies on network components to enforce policies and techniques that effectively and securely route network traffic.

Mission—Missions are operations conducted with an intended purpose. Missions are conducted by a unit and/or units with relevant capability and preponderance of capacity. The base mechanism used to achieve mission objectives are sorties. Missions may require multiple sorties from multiple units to accomplish the mission's objectives.

Mission Ready (MR)—A crewmember who satisfactorily completed IQT and MQT, and maintains certification, currency and proficiency in the command or unit mission.

Monitoring Management Operator (CSCS—MMO) – Provides situational awareness of cyberspace terrain and weapons system component health monitoring solutions for the CSCS.

Non—current (NC) or Unqualified (UNQ) – Crew may perform crew duties only on designated training or evaluation missions under the supervision of a qualified instructor/examiner.

Off Station—Off Station is when a force package maneuvers off the assigned task and is no longer assigned to the terrain/target. Egress may be required to leave tasked terrain and/or targets. Indicates that crewmember(s) is not in position or no longer performing assigned tasks.

On Station—On Station is when the cyberspace operation commences on tasked terrain and targets. Ingress/Enroute may be required to reach tasked terrain and/or targets. Plan accordingly for mission execution success. On station indicates crew has reached assigned TOT/T.

Qualification—Qualifies a crewmember to perform the duties of a particular crew position in the specified weapon system. Requires AF Form 8/8a documentation.

Ready Cybercrew Program (RCP) – RCP is the formal continuation training (CT) program that provides the baseline for squadrons to use in developing a realistic training program to meet all DOC statement tasked requirements as well as specific NAF mission prioritization. RCP defines the minimum required mix of annual sorties, simulator missions, and training events crew will accomplish to sustain mission readiness. These programs have clearly defined objectives and minimum standards that enhance mission accomplishment and safety. RCP sorties are tracked. In order to be effective, each mission will successfully complete a sufficient number of events applicable to that mission type, as determined by the Squadron Commander. With completion of IQT and MQT, a crewmember is trained in all the basic missions of a specific unit, unless a specific exception is provided in the WS-specific Vol1. RCP applies to CMR/MR and BMC positions.

Sortie – The actions an individual weapon system takes to accomplish a mission and/or mission objective(s) within a defined start and stop period.

Storage and Virtualization Operator (CSCS—SVO) – Performs backup, recovery, and archiving via storage area networks (SAN).

Target—An entity or object that performs a function for the adversary considered for possible engagement or other action.

Task – A clearly defined action or activity specifically assigned to an individual or organization that will be done as it is imposed by an appropriate authority.

Terrain – The cyberspace area of operations where a force package is directed to conduct a sortie. Terrain is defined as Internet Protocol (IP) address, domain, or transport space within the DoDIN or AF enclave (commonly referred to as "blue" space), or commercial, contractor-owned

, mission partner-owned ("grey" space) host, server, and network devices that enable C2, communication, sensing, and access capabilities.

Time Over Target/Terrain (TOT/T) – The exact timing requested by the tactical commander, directed by the tasking authority or specified in the tasking order to prosecute a mission. The TOT/T is based on the available vulnerability window (can be an enduring or time-sensitive requirement) and will be executed within the vulnerability window; authorization for a TOT/T outside a vulnerability window can only be authorized by the tasking authority.

Total ASD Time – Total time for all sorties completed in military service to include student time. Time accumulated will be in the crewmember's current rating.

Upgrade Training – Training needed to qualify to a crew position of additional responsibility for a specific weapon system (e.g., special mission qualifications).

Vulnerability Assessment Operator (CSCS—VAO) – Identifies vulnerabilities within cyberspace terrain and associated software suites utilized by Air Force Information systems and net-centric capabilities. In addition, identifies and assesses the weaknesses in cyberspace terrain that adversaries may gain/maintain access to the AFNet.

Vulnerability Remediation Operator (CSCS—VRO) – Remediates vulnerabilities within cyberspace terrain and associated software suites utilized by Air Force Information systems and net-centric capabilities.

Vulnerability (VUL) Window – This is a window of opportunity and direction for a tactical commander to conduct operations. A VUL Window is bounded (start by/finish by) to give a tactical commander the authorized and suspensed timing available to plan and prosecute mission. Deviations from the assigned VUL Window must be approved by the tasking authority.

Weapon System—A combination of one or more weapons with all related equipment, materials, services, personnel, and means of delivery and deployment (if applicable) required for self-sufficiency.

Attachment 2

EXAMPLE BRIEFING GUIDE

A2.1. This attachment provides guidance and consideration for developing unit briefing guides. Additional guidance and information can be found in the Air Force Tactics, Techniques, and Procedures (AFTTP) 3-1.General Planning, AFTTP 3-1.CSCS, 24 AF, AFCYBER & JFHQ-C AFCYBER Tactical Mission Planning, Briefing and Debriefing Guide, and others. These manuals are authoritative, not directive, and should be considered when developing unit specific guides.

Figure A2.1. Example Briefing Guide.

NOTE: This layout can be used for multiple briefs; however, the focus areas and emphasis items will be different as the audiences are different.
☐ Timehack
☐ Administration
☐ Roll call
☐ Classification
☐ Mission Assignments
☐ Mission/Tasking
☐ Environment
☐ Enemy
☐ Effects
☐ Capabilities
☐ Plan
☐ Phasing
☐ Contracts
☐ Contingencies
☐ Comm Plan / C2 Plan
☐ Reporting
☐ Alternate Mission
☐ Questions / Comments

Attachment 3

EXAMPLE DEBRIEFING GUIDE

Figure A3.1. Example Debriefing Guide.

Debrief Presentation Format:
☐ Classification
☐ ROE
☐ Admin/Alibis
☐ Objectives
☐ Planning
☐ Execution
☐ Big Rocks
☐ Debrief Focus Points
☐ Lessons Learned
☐ Assessments

Attachment 4

EXAMPLE COMMUNICATIONS PLANNING GUIDE

Figure A4.1. Example Communications Planning Guide.

OBJECTIVE: Develop a simple plan to specify who should talk, when, and via what medium.
☐ Check orders and SPINs, ROEs, preapproved actions, etc. for applicable:
o Comm standards
o Check-in procedures
o Code words and Brevity terms
o Authentication
o Other comm procedures applicable to the mission
☐ Comm plan specifics:
o Weapon system/location operations
o Sortie period/timing
o Chat rooms/channels (i.e. single chat room vs multiple chat rooms)
☐ Specific server names/URLs/IPs as needed
☐ Chat room assignments
☐ Room purposes (execution vs planning)
o Multi-level security considerations
o Triggers/contracts for transitioning between primary and backup comm
☐ Ensure the COMM plan is delivered to all mission partners via Coord Card
o Maintain version control (e.g. "Current as of DATE/TIME")

BY ORDER OF THE
SECRETARY OF THE AIR FORCE

AIR FORCE MANUAL 17-1301

10 FEBRUARY 2017

Cyberspace

COMPUTER SECURITY (COMPUSEC)

COMPLIANCE WITH THIS PUBLICATION IS MANDATORY

ACCESSIBILITY: Publications and forms are available for downloading or ordering on the e-Publishing website at www.e-publishing.af.mil.

RELEASABILITY: There are no releasability restrictions on this publication.

OPR: SAF/CIO A6CS

Certified by: SAF/CIO A6S
(Brigader General Patrick Higby)

Supersedes: AFMAN33-282, 28 March 2012

Pages: 69

This Air Force Manual (AFMAN) implements Computer Security in support of Air Force Policy Directive (AFPD) 17-1, *Information Dominance Governance and Management,* and Air Force Instruction (AFI) 17-130, *Air Force Cybersecurity Program Management.* Computer Security (COMPUSEC) is identified as a cybersecurity discipline in AFI 17-130 and defined within this document. This instruction applies to all AF military, civilian, and contractor personnel under contract by DoD, regardless of Air Force Specialty Code (AFSC), who develop, acquire, deliver, use, operate, or manage COMPUSEC for Air Force (AF) organizations. This instruction applies to the Air National Guard (ANG) and Air Force Reserve Command (AFRC). The term major command (MAJCOM), when used in this publication, includes field operating agencies (FOA) and direct reporting units (DRU). Additional instructions and manuals are listed on the AF Publishing Website at http://www.e-publishing.af.mil under "Electronics Publications." Direct questions, recommended changes, or conflicts to this publication through command channels using the AF Form 847, *Recommendation for Change of Publication*, to SAF/CIO A6. Send any supplements to this publication to SAF/CIO A6 for review, coordination, and approval prior to publication. Unless otherwise noted, the SAF/CIO A6 is the waiver approving authority to policies contained in this publication. The authorities to waive wing/unit level requirements in this publication are identified with a Tier number ("T-0, T-1, T-2, and T-3") following the compliance statement. See AFI 33-360, *Publications and Forms Management*, Table 1.1, for a description of the authorities associated with the Tier numbers. Submit requests for waivers through the chain of command to the appropriate Tier waiver approval authority, or alternately, to the Publication OPR for non-tiered compliance items. Ensure that all records created as a result of processes prescribed in this publication are maintained in accordance with (IAW) AFMAN 33-363, *Management of Records*, and disposed IAW AF Records Disposition Schedule (RDS) located in the Air Force Records Information Management System (AFRIMS). The use of the name or mark of any specific manufacturer, commercial product, commodity, or service in this publication does not imply endorsement by the AF.

SUMMARY OF CHANGES

This document is substantially changed, updating Public Key Infrastructure (PKI) policy, incident management, and access control as a result of a DoD and AF policy directive updates. Review this manual in its entirety.

Chapter 1

INTRODUCTION

1.1. Introduction. Computer Security (COMPUSEC) is a cybersecurity discipline identified in AFI 17-130. Compliance ensures appropriate implementation of measures to protect all AF Information System (IS) resources and information.

The COMPUSEC objective is to employ countermeasures designed for the protection of confidentiality, integrity, availability, authentication, and non-repudiation of United States (US) government information processed by AF ISs.

1.2. Applicability. This publication applies to all AF ISs and devices used to process, store, display, transmit, or protect AF information, regardless of classification or sensitivity, unless exempted.

1.2.1. This publication is binding on all military, civilian and contract employees, who develop, acquire, deliver, use, operate, or manage AF Information Technology (IT). This publication applies to all AF IT used to receive, process, store, display, transmit, or protect AF information, regardless of classification or sensitivity. AF IT includes but is not limited to ISs (major applications and enclaves), Platform Information Technology (PIT) and PIT systems, IT services (internal and external), standalone systems, and IT products (software, hardware, and applications).

1.2.2. More restrictive Federal, DoD, AF guidance take precedence over this publication.

1.2.3. This publication and implementation guidance identified within is not applicable to Special Access Programs or Intelligence Community (IC) ISs to include Sensitive Compartmented Information (SCI) ISs. Refer to the IC Directive (ICD) 503, *Intelligence Community Information Technology Systems Security Risk Management, Certification and Accreditation*, and AFI 16-701, *Management, Administration and Oversight of Special Access Programs*.

1.3. Exceptions. Document exceptions and deviations to guidance in this publication affecting ISs as part of the applicable IS security authorization package, IAW AFI 17-101, *The Risk Management Framework (RMF) for Air Force Information Technology (IT)*. Submit modifications, exceptions, and deviations through the system/enclave change management process.

1.3.1. Process equipment acquisition waiver requests IAW AFMAN 17-1203, *Information Technology (IT) Asset Management (ITAM)*.

1.3.2. See AFI 17-100, *Air Force Information Technology (IT) Service Management*, for Commercial Internet Service Provider (CISP) waiver guidance.

1.3.3. See AFMAN 17-1303, *Cybersecurity Workforce Improvement Program*, for certification requirement waiver guidance.

Chapter 2

ROLES AND RESPONSIBILITIES

2.1. AFSPC Cyberspace Support Squadron (AFSPC CYSS). Provides cyber networking expertise to HQ AFSPC for COMPUSEC activities and functions.

2.1.1. Provides COMPUSEC policy and technical subject matter expertise for the AF Enterprise.

2.1.2. Provides field support and program management for COMPUSEC to SAF CIO/A6, AFSPC, and all MAJCOMs/FOAs/DRUs. Supports SAF/CIO A6 and AFSPC cybersecurity initiatives. Reviews, evaluates, and interprets AF COMPUSEC doctrine, policy, and procedures. Develops/coordinates recommendations on implementation of the doctrine, policy, and procedures to AFSPC A2/3/6.

2.1.3. Coordinates with the AFSPC Cybersecurity Division as required and accomplishes other roles and responsibilities as directed by HQ AFSPC.

2.2. Air Force Life Cycle Management Center (AFLCMC), Cryptologic and Cyber Systems Division, Responsive Cyber Acquisition Branch, Information Assurance Section(AFLCMC/HNCYP). AF Public Key Infrastructure (PKI) System Program Office (SPO). Manages the AF PKI and carries out tasks/actions as the SAF/CIO A6 PKI Management Authority (PMA) and/or the pertinent DoD organizations direct. This includes the implementation, operation, and sustainment of PKIs and all associated enabling efforts.

2.2.1. Identifies all PKI requirements to SAF/CIO A6.

2.2.2. Integrates PKI into existing ISs as identified in the PKI implementation and program plans. Ensures future IS programs are fully compatible and interoperable with the DoD PKI, as required by DoD and Air Force policy.

2.2.3. Assists the MAJCOMs and supported Combatant Commands (COCOMs) with PK Enablement (PKE) of systems.

2.2.4. Provides PKI Helpdesk and field support to the AF.

2.2.5. Develops and sustains new PKI capabilities for the Air Force and/or for DoD.

2.2.6. Maintains and enforces the integrity of the PKI and its use.

2.3. Wing Cybersecurity Office (WCO). The WCO addresses all COMPUSEC requirements on the base, including those of tenant units (i.e., FOAs, DRUs, and other MAJCOM units), unless formal agreements exist IAW AFI 17-130. Personnel assigned to the WCO will:

2.3.1. Evaluate modifications, exceptions, and deviations to ISs for accuracy and completeness before forwarding to the appropriate agency; see Chapter 1. **(T-1).**

2.3.2. Train designated representatives of the Commanders Support Staff (CSS) on Air Force Network (AFNet) account management and COMPUSEC administrative processes and procedures; conduct annual or "as needed" refresher training; see Chapter 3. **(T-1).**

2.3.3. Consult with host or MAJCOM Foreign Disclosure Office (FDO) before authorizing Foreign National/Local National (FN/LN) access to ISs; see Chapter 4. **(T-1).**

2.3.4. Conduct COMPUSEC assessments; see Chapter 7. **(T-1).**

2.3.5. Assist with assessment or analysis supporting Vulnerability Management; see Chapter 3 and AFI 17-100. **(T-1).**

2.3.6. Coordinate with the system/enclave ISSO/ISSM before deciding whether to sanitize media for reuse or disposal; see Chapter 6. **(T-0).**

2.4. Organizational Commander (or Equivalent). Maintains the COMPUSEC program IAW this publication, ensuring AF ISs operate effectively by protecting and maintaining the confidentiality, integrity, and availability of IS resources and information processed throughout the system's life cycle. Organizational commanders will:

2.4.1. Suspend access to unclassified and classified ISs when actions threaten or damage AF ISs; see Chapter 4. **(T-0).**

2.4.2. Ensure proper procedures are followed in response to classified information spillages affecting AF ISs; see Chapter 5. **(T-0).**

2.4.3. Review all approved removable media waivers semi-annually to ensure continuous validation of mission requirements; see Chapter 5. **(T-0).**

2.4.4. Endorse follow-up COMPUSEC assessment reports validating the status of open findings; see Chapter 7. **(T-1).**

2.5. Information System Security Manager (ISSM). An ISSM (formerly an Information Assurance Manager [IAM]) is responsible for the cybersecurity of a program, organization, system, or enclave and provides direction to the Information System Security Officer (ISSO) (formerly a system Information Assurance Officer [IAO]). Duties of the ISSM are outlined in DoDI 8500.01, *Cybersecurity,* AFI 17-130, and AFI 17-101. ISSMs will:

2.5.1. Obtain required training and maintain applicable cybersecurity workforce certification; see Chapter 3. **(T-0).**

2.5.2. Perform risk identification and assessment activities supporting the change management activities for the system/enclave; see Chapter 3. **(T-0).**

2.5.3. Maintain approval and inventory documentation for Authorizing Official (AO)-authorized personally-owned hardware and software; see Chapter 5. **(T-1).**

2.5.4. Process removable media waivers; see Chapter 5. **(T-1).**

2.5.5. Protect collaborative computing devices used in classified environments; see Chapter 5. **(T-0).**

2.5.6. Participate in remanence security (REMSEC) risk management processes; see Chapter 6. **(T-1).**

2.5.7. Conduct annual unit/organization COMPUSEC self-assessments using the AFMAN 17-1301 COMPUSEC Self-Assessment Communicator (SAC) located in the AF Inspector General (IG) Management Internal Control Toolset (MICT). **(T-1).**

2.5.8. Assist with AFMAN 17-1301 COMPUSEC SAC review and remediation activities; see Chapter 7. **(T-1).**

2.5.9. FNs/LNs are not authorized to hold ISSM positions IAW DoD 8570.01-M, *IA Workforce Improvement Program*. **(T-0).**

2.6. Information System Security Officer (ISSO). An ISSO (formerly a system IAO) is responsible for the technical implementation of a cybersecurity program. When circumstances warrant, a single individual may fulfill both the ISSM and the ISSO roles. DoDI 8500.01, AFI 17-130, and AFI 17-101 outline the duties of the ISSO. ISSOs will:

2.6.1. Provide protection from threats through implementation of technical and physical security mechanisms; see **Chapter 5**. **(T-0).**

2.6.2. Maintain approval and inventory documentation for AO-authorized personally-owned hardware and software; see **Chapter 5**. **(T-1).**

2.6.3. Participate in REMSEC risk management processes; see **Chapter 6**. **(T-1).**

2.6.4. Execute procedures that identify the residual risk and risk tolerance; see **Chapter 6**. **(T-0).**

2.6.5. Conduct annual COMPUSEC self-assessments using the AFMAN 17-1301 COMPUSEC SAC located in the IG MICT; see **Chapter 7**. **(T-1).**

2.6.6. Assist with AFMAN 17-1301 COMPUSEC SAC review and remediation activities; see **Chapter 7**. **(T-1).**

2.6.7. FNs/LNs are not authorized to hold ISSO positions IAW DoDI 8500.01. **(T-0).**

2.7. Commanders Support Staff (CSS). Organizations implement and enforce AFNet account management and COMPUSEC administrative processes and procedures using the guidance within this instruction IAW AFI 17-130. Personnel performing administrative cybersecurity functions will:

2.7.1. Verify user compliance with annual CyberAwareness Challenge training; see **Chapter 4**. **(T-0).**

2.7.2. Maintain AFNet network access documentation; see **Chapter 4**. **(T-0).**

2.7.3. Assist the WCO with administrative cybersecurity functions (administrative tasking orders, in/out-processing checklists, distribute user training materials, etc.); see **Chapter 5**. **(T-0).**

2.7.4. Conduct annual unit/organization self-assessments using the AFMAN 17-1301 COMPUSEC SAC located in the IG MICT; see **Chapter 7**. **(T-1).**

Chapter 3

TRAINING AND RESOURCES

3.1. General. COMPUSEC includes all measures to safeguard ISs and information against sabotage, tampering, denial of service, espionage, fraud, misappropriation, misuse, or release to unauthorized persons. Successful implementation of COMPUSEC requires adequate training and proper application of cybersecurity/IA resources.

3.2. COMPUSEC Training Requirements

3.2.1. Military personnel in the 3D0X3 career field attend technical school training in the following courses. Upon successful completion of the final course, trainees are awarded a 3-skill level and a DoD 8570.01-M certification as an IA Management (IAM) Level I/IA Technical (IAT) Level II. . Current course identification, status, length, and prerequisite information may be found at the Education and Training Course Announcements website at **https://etca.randolph.af.mil/default1.asp** under "AETC."

3.2.1.1. E3AQR3D033, *IT Fundamentals Basic*, at Keesler AFB.

3.2.1.2. E3AQR3D033, *Cyber Surety*, at Keesler AFB.

3.2.1.3. E3ABR3D033, *Cyber Surety Security+ Certification*, at Keesler AFB.

3.2.2. All civilian, military, and contractor personnel performing ISSM duties:

3.2.2.1. Attend the Air Education and Training Command (AETC)- formal training course E3AZR3D053, *Information System Security Manager (ISSM)* at Keesler AFB within 6 months of assuming ISSM duties.

3.2.2.2. Complete the Air Force Qualification Training Package (AFQTP) 3D0X3-211RA, *Information Assurance Manager Handbook.* Use the AFQTP:

3.2.2.2.1. As an interim training measure while an individual waits for a class date for the ISSM course.

3.2.2.2.2. As refresher training for individuals that have ISSM experience but have not performed duties as an ISSM within 3 years.

3.2.2.2.3. Contractor personnel may substitute the AFQTP when contract limitations do not allow ISSM course attendance.

3.2.2.3. Follow the Cybersecurity workforce security certification requirements relative to the function, category (technical or managerial), and level of the position as specified in AFMAN 17-1303, DoD Directive (DoDD) 8140.01, *Cyberspace Workforce Management,* and DoD 8570.01-M, *Information Assurance Workforce Improvement Program.* Additional training and/or certifications may be necessary depending on specific requirements of the ISSM position. More information on DoD-approved 8570 baseline certifications is available in an extension to Appendix 3 of DoD 8570.01-M on the Defense Information Systems Agency (DISA) Information Assurance Support Environment (IASE) website (**http://iase.disa.mil/iawip/Pages/iabaseline.aspx**).

3.2.3. Cybersecurity Workforce. Training and certification of cybersecurity personnel depend upon the types of tasks assigned by the organizational commander. Determine the tasks performed and consult DoD 8570.01-M and AFMAN 17-1303 for training and certification requirements.

> 3.2.3.1. Cybersecurity Workforce categories are IAT and IAM. Specialties are Computer Network Defense Service Providers (CND-SPs) and IA System Architects and Engineers (IASAEs).

> 3.2.3.2. Cybersecurity Workforce personnel performing IAT/IAM level tasks require the appropriate certifications.

3.2.4. CSS Training. The WCO provides direction, oversight, and annual training for designated representatives of the CSS. The WCO locally develops the CSS cybersecurity training programs and includes the following COMPUSEC-specific items:

> 3.2.4.1. Authorized users, access requirements, and access documentation.

> 3.2.4.2. Account management and trouble reporting functions (including IAO Express/Enterprise Service Desk [ESD]).

> 3.2.4.3. SIPRNet token recovery actions.

3.3. Information Assurance Collaborative Environment (IACE). The AF IACE serves as the primary cybersecurity/IA support resource for WCO and managers, providing a collaborative one-stop-shop for cybersecurity/IA ideas, questions, discussions, and hosts dynamic content for information sharing (**https://cs.eis.af.mil/sites/10060**).

For classified content, the IACE- Secret Internet Protocol Router Network (SIPRNet) (IACE-S) is available at http://intelshare.intelink.sgov.gov/sites/af_cybersecurity/SitePages/Home.aspx.

3.4. Methods and Procedures Technical Orders (MPTO). MPTOs provide procedural guidance to the cybersecurity workforce to implement and manage methods and processes pertaining to COMPUSEC policy. Specific COMPUSEC-related MPTOs are MPTO 00-33B-5004, *Access Control for Information Systems;* MPTO 00-33B-5006, *End Point Security for Information Systems;* and MPTO 00-33B-5008, *Remanence Security for Information Systems.* Obtain MPTOs via the organizational Technical Order Distribution Account (TODA) on Enhanced Technical Information Management System (ETIMS) **https://www.my.af.mil/etims/ETIMS/index.jsp**).

3.5. Information Technology Asset Procurement. Comply with evaluation and validation requirements in DoDI 8500.01 for all IT services, hardware, firmware, software components, or products incorporated into DoD ISs.

> 3.5.1. Follow the guidance in AFMAN 17-1203 and the AF Information Technology Commodity Council (ITCC) guidance available on the AF Portal or AFWAY (**https://www.afway.af.mil/**) for procurement activities of all IT hardware, cellular, and peripheral devices (e.g., desktops, laptops, servers, commercial mobile devices [CMDs], multifunction devices [MFDs] printers, scanners, and wireless peripheral devices).

> 3.5.2. Comply with the evaluation and validation requirements of Committee on National Security Systems Policy (CNSSP) 11, *National Policy Governing the Acquisition of*

Information Assurance (IA) and IA-Enabled Information Technology Products, for all IA and IA-enabled products.

3.5.3. Life Cycle Management.   Procure products and adopt risk-based program management IAW AFI 63-101/20-101, *Integrated Life Cycle Management.*

3.5.4. Unified Capabilities (UC).   Modernizing IT capabilities while aligning with joint solutions remain two of the AF's key goals. AFMAN 17-1202, *Collaboration Services and Voice Systems Management,* and DoDI 8100.04, *DoD Unified Capabilities (UC),* provide guidance related to Voice and Video over Internet Protocol (VVoIP), Video Teleconferencing (VTC), and interoperability.

3.5.4.1. In accordance with DoDI 8100.04, use/obtain UC products certified by the DISA Joint Interoperability Test Command (JITC), JITC certifies interoperability and the UC-implementing DoD component AO or the DISA Certifying Authority (CA) certifies for Cybersecurity under RMF. Approved products are listed on the DISA UC Approved Products List (APL) (**https://aplits.disa.mil/processAPList.action**) and should be added to the enclave security authorization package and assessed for Cybersecurity through the RMF process.

3.5.4.2. As a general rule, Section 508-compatible Voice over Internet Protocol (VoIP) devices are not listed on the DISA UC APL unless the vendor has included the assistive technology (AT) end device as part of the VoIP system's evaluation package. Organizations may request that the vendor add the product to the current UC APL certification package and request a "desktop review" from the DISA Unified Capabilities Certification Office (UCCO). The DISA UCCO (Email: **disa.meade.ns.list.unified-capabilities-certification-office@mail.mil**) has a listing of all product representatives. This review ensures the product operates with the current fielded VoIP system. If the vendor is unable or unwilling to add the AT product to the UC APL certification, identify compliance with AFMAN 17-1202 in the enclave/IS security authorization package.

3.5.4.3. All Air Force VTC suites are transitioning off the Integrated Services Digital Network (ISDN)-based Defense Information System Network (DISN) Video Service-Global (DVS-G) to Global Video Services (GVS), IAW Maintenance Tasking Order (MTO) 2014-295-001. AF organizations should not expend funds on the upgrade, replacement, and acquisition of voice, video, and/or data services equipment outside of the GVS program.

3.5.5. Cloud Services.   Acquire and implement private and/or public cloud computing services in support of the Air Force Information Network (AFIN) IAW AFI 17-100.

3.5.6. Foreign produced products. Under Title 10, United States Code (U.S.C.), Section 2533a (*Requirement to Buy Certain Articles from American Sources; Exceptions*) and reflected in Federal Acquisition Regulation (FAR) Subpart 25.1, *Buy American – Supplies, 25.103 Exceptions*, and Defense Federal Acquisition Regulation Supplement (DFARS) Part 225 – *Foreign Acquisition, Subpart 225.1, Buy American – Supplies, 225.103 Exceptions,* there are exceptions allowing the purchase of foreign-made commercial technology. For guidance go to **https://www.acquisition.gov/** to access the FAR and DFARS (under "Supplemental Regulations").

3.5.6.1. Use an approved importer or through a World Trade Organization Government Procurement Agreement (WTO GPA) country. AFWay, ITCC, and General Services Administration (GSA) offer foreign-made products secured from an approved importer or WTO GPA.

3.5.6.2. Countries barred from providing products and services are listed on the "Domestic Preference Restrictions" table available at the *Defense Procurement and Acquisition Policy* website under the "Restrictions on Purchasing from Non-U.S. Sources" area (**http://www.acq.osd.mil/dpap/cpic/ic/restrictions_on_purchases_from_non-us_sources.html**).

3.6. Configuration Management Resources. Securely configure and implement all IT products. Cybersecurity/IA reference documents, such as National Institute of Standards and Technology (NIST) Special Publications (SP), DISA Security Technical Implementation Guides (STIGs), DISA Security Requirements Guides (SRGs), National Security Agency (NSA) Security Configuration Guides, AF Technical Orders (TOs), and other specialized publications are used for the security configuration and implementation guidance. Apply these reference documents IAW DoDI 85xx.xx series, AFI 33-xxx series, and AFI 17-xxx series publications to establish and maintain a minimum baseline security configuration and posture. Document all configuration changes with the enclave/system ISSM in the IS security authorization package IAW AFI 17-101 and the system change management process.

Chapter 4

INFORMATION SYSTEM ACCESS CONTROL

4.1. Introduction. AF ISs connect to the DoD Information Network (DoDIN) subnetworks (e.g., SIPRNet, Non-classified Internet Protocol Router Network [NIPRNet], GVS, etc.) IAW Chairman of the Joint Chiefs of Staff Instruction (CJCSI) 6211.02, *Defense Information Systems Network (DISN) Responsibilities.* Every individual who has access to standalone systems, specialized/functional ISs, enterprise ISs, and/or mission systems is an IS user.

4.1.1. Access to AF ISs is a revocable privilege and is granted to individuals based on need to know and IAW National Security Telecommunications and Information Systems Security Policy (NSTISSP) No. 200, *National Policy on Controlled Access Protection;* DoD 5200.2-R, *Personnel Security Program*; and CJCSI 6510.01, *Information Assurance (IA) and Support to Computer Network Defense (CND).* Follow procedural guidance in MPTO 00-33B-5004.

4.1.2. The Information System Owner (ISO) ensures methods are in place to verify user access requests before granting IS access. Address delegation of authority for specific system/enclave access in the system authorization package.

4.2. Authorized Users. An authorized user is any appropriately cleared individual required to access a DoD IS to carry out or assist in a lawful and authorized governmental function. Configure authorized user account creation and administration using role-based access schemes; see AFMAN 17-1201, *User Responsibilities and Guidance for Information Systems.* Consult AFI 31-501, *Personnel Security Program Management,* for investigation requirements for access to an Automated Information System (AIS) position, as outlined in DoD 5200.2-R, Appendix 10.

4.2.1. All authorized users (e.g., military, civilian, contractor, temporary employees, volunteers, interns, key spouses, and American Red Cross personnel) will complete CyberAwareness Challenge training prior to being granted access to an IS. **(T-0).** Users annually re-accomplish CyberAwareness Challenge training; organizations maintain compliance IAW DoD 8570.01-M. Authorized user access to unclassified and classified ISs based on the assigned duties and the Automated Data Processing (ADP) position categories identified in DoD 5200.2-R, Appendix 10: Category ADP-III (also referred to as IT-III) are nonsensitive positions.

4.2.1.1. CyberAwareness Challenge training is located on the Advanced Distributed Learning Service (ADLS) accessible via the AF Portal.

4.2.1.2. A publically accessible version of the CyberAwareness Challenge training is located on the DISA website (**http://iase.disa.mil**). Users without an ADLS account may substitute this training for initial network access.

4.2.1.3. When a user requires a new/modification to his/her account (due to change of station or assignment, Temporary Duty [TDY], etc.), the gaining CSS verifies the user meets access requirements before granting access to the IS. Users are not required to retake the CyberAwareness Challenge training provided the user has a valid and current (within a year) course completion record. Verification of completion may be accomplished using the printed or electronic copy of CyberAwareness Challenge training certificate from DISA or ADLS or confirmation by the CSS.

4.2.1.4. System access by authorized users requires PKI access methods as specified in DoDI 8520.03, *Identity Authentication for Information Systems,* and CJCSI 6510.01.

4.2.2. Privileged User. Grant privileged access to unclassified and classified ISs based on the assigned duties and the ADP position categories identified in DoD 5200.2-R, Appendix 10: Category ADP-I (also referred to as IT-I) are Privileged positions and Category ADP-II (also referred to as IT-II) are Limited Privileged positions.

4.2.2.1. Administrative and privileged accounts require PKI user authentication IAW United States Cyber Command (USCYBERCOM) Tasking Order (TASKORD) 2015-0102, *Implementation and Reporting of DoD Public Key Infrastructure (PKI) System Administrator and Privileged User Authentication.*

4.2.2.2. Privileged users should meet all the requirements of an authorized user as specified in AFMAN 17-1303 and paragraph 4.2.1.

4.2.2.3. Privileged users are established and administered with a role-based access scheme IAW the system policy and **Chapter 3** of DoD 5200.2-R and AFMAN 17-1303.

4.2.2.4. System access requires PKI access methods as specified in DoDI 8520.03 and CJCSI 6510.01.

4.2.2.5. Privileged users access only data, control information, software, hardware, and firmware that they are authorized access and fulfills the "need to know" requirement.

4.2.2.6. To maintain separation of duties and least privilege, users maintain separate accounts, a user account for day-to-day or "non-privileged" functions, and a privileged account for administrative functions IAW DoD 8570.01-M.

4.2.2.7. Prohibit sharing of privileged user accounts and credentials between users.

4.2.2.8. Configure privileged user remote access IAW the applicable DISA STIGs (i.e., Enclave, Operating System, Remote Access, Directory Services Domain, etc.) and the selected security controls within the RMF package.

4.2.2.9. Privileged users are position-certified IAW DoD 8570.01-M and qualified IAW AFMAN 17-1303.

4.2.2.10. Privileged users complete an *Information System Privileged Access Agreement and Acknowledgement of Responsibilities* IAW DoD 8570.01-M (Appendix 4).

4.2.3. Foreign Nationals/Local Nationals. A FN/LN user is anyone who is not a US citizen or permanent resident, IAW Title 8, Code of Federal Regulations, *Aliens and Nationality.*

4.2.3.1. The MAJCOM FDO determines authorized and privileged "need to know" for the administrative access and control of information, software, hardware and firmware to include controlled unclassified information (CUI) and classified information, IAW DoD Manual (DoDM) 5200.01, Volume 4, DoD *Information Security Program: Controlled Unclassified Information (CUI).*

4.2.3.1.1. WCOs consult the Host or MAJCOM FDO and applicable ISSM before authorizing access by FN/LN users to ISs processing, storing, or transmitting classified and CUI. Note: Specific FN/LN access guidance can be found in the following publications: MPTO 00-33A-1301, *Foreign National NIPRNet Access Core Services*; MPTO 00-33B-5004; MPTO 00-33B-5006; MPTO 00-33A-1202, *Air Force Network Account Management*; MPTO 00-33D-2001, *AFNET Enterprise Services Naming Conventions*; AFI 16-107, *Military Personnel Exchange Program*; AFI 16-201, *Air Force Foreign Disclosure and Technology Transfer Program*; DoDD 5230.25, *Withholding of Unclassified Technical Data from Public Disclosure*; DoDD 5400.7, *DoD Freedom of Information Act (FOIA) Program*; DoD 5400.7-R_AFMAN 33-302, *Freedom of Information Act Program*; AFI 33-332, *Air Force Privacy and Civil Liberties Program*; DoDD 5230.11, *Disclosure of Classified Military Information to Foreign Governments and International Organizations*; and DoDD 5230.20, *Visits and Assignments of Foreign Nationals*.

4.2.3.1.2. Pursuant to applicable host-nation agreements, FN/LN privileged users are certified to baseline computing environment (CE) IAW DoD 8570.01-M. If privileged access is required to an IS, restrict FN/LN user access to IAT I/II level positions and only under the immediate supervision of a US citizen. Furthermore, document access in the IS security assessment package.

4.2.3.1.3. At the discretion of the ISO, FN/LN system access requires PKI access methods as specified in **Chapter 8**.

4.2.3.1.4. Sanitize or configure classified ISs to restrict access by FN/LNs to only classified information authorized for disclosure to the FN/LNs government or coalition, as necessary to fulfill the terms of their assignments IAW applicable host MAJCOM FDO requirements.

4.2.3.1.5. Other Considerations. Non-US citizens who are permanent legal residents are required to meet the same requirements of any US citizen for access to the unclassified network or system, as outlined in paragraph 4.2.1.

4.2.3.2. Before authorizing FN/LN access to unclassified ISs, the ISO ensures compliance with the IS access requirements in MPTO 00-33A-1301.

4.2.4. Group Accounts. The Enterprise AO (or applicable AO if entirely within their boundary) is the approving authority for group accounts and may require a Defense Information Assurance Security Accreditation Working Group (DSAWG) waiver IAW CJCSI 6510.01 and DoDI 8520.02, *Public Key Infrastructure (PKI) and Public Key (PK) Enabling*. Document authorization in the system/enclave authorization package.

4.2.4.1. Requests for group accounts using individual/unique authentication should be submitted via email to AFSPC CYSS/CYZ PKI (**afspc.cyss.cys.2@us.af.mil**).

4.2.4.2. Group accounts that do not use an individual/unique authenticator require DSAWG approval. To submit requests to the DSAWG for approval, contact AFSPC CYSS/CYZ PKI (**afspc.cyss.cys.2@us.af.mil**).

4.2.5. Temporary and Volunteer Accounts. Grant only unclassified IS access to temporary employees and volunteer personnel in support of their assigned duties.

4.2.5.1. A volunteer is any individual (including key spouses) authorized to be DoD volunteers as defined in DoDI 1100.21, *Voluntary Services in the Department of Defense*. Restrict volunteers to ADP-III/IT-III level positions IAW DoDI 5200.2-R, Appendix 10.

4.2.5.2. Temporary employees and volunteers are required to meet the requirements as specified in paragraph 4.2.1.

4.2.5.3. Temporary employees and volunteers require PKI access as outlined in Chapter 8.

4.3. Required Account Access Documentation

4.3.1. When required by the ISO for IS access, the CSS or ISSO ensures the DD Form 2875, *System Authorization Access Request (SAAR)*, is completed and signed. Document access requests, Annual Information Awareness (CyberAwareness Challenge) training completion, and justification for access and clearance/background investigation verification as referenced by DoD 5200.2-R and AFI 31-501. DD Form 2875 signatures can be "wet" or digitally signed. Do not combine multiple system access requests on the same DD Form 2875.

4.3.1.1. CSSs/ISSOs, in coordination with the organizational security manager, verify user background investigation requirements IAW DoD 5200.2-R.

4.3.1.2. The ISSO/ISSM (referred to as the "Information Assurance Officer" on the DD Form 2875) retains the DD Form 2875 IAW instructions outlined on the form for non-AFNet ISs. The CSS retains the DD Form 2875 according to the instructions on the form for AFNet ISs.

4.3.1.2.1. Original DD Form 2875s for unprivileged AFNet accounts may be transferred when duty assignments change; the gaining unit's CSS may use local methods to update duty information in the "IAO Express" tool and shared drive access requirements. The losing unit's CSS ensures termination of shared drive access prior to users out-processing. Changes to privileged account access requirements require a new DD Form 2875.

4.3.1.2.2. Re-accomplish DD Form 2875s for AFNet-SIPRNet (AFNet-S) accounts when access requirements change.

4.3.2. In accordance with AFMAN 17-1201, users of all authorized IS devices (to include Mobile Computing Devices) sign the standardized AF Form 4394, *Air Force User Agreement Statement-Notice and Consent Provision*, prior to initial IS access. For wireless devices, users complete the standardized AF Form 4433, *US Air Force Unclassified Wireless Mobile Device User Agreement*. Maintain copies of signed AF Forms 4433 within the CSS.

4.3.3. Access to classified ISs also requires a Standard Form (SF) 312, *Nondisclosure Agreement*, IAW AFI 16-1404, *Air Force Information Security Program*.

4.4. Token Access. IAW DoDI 8520.02 and DoDI 8520.03, users authenticating to DoD networks require the use of a hardware token. Follow guidance in Chapter 8 to obtain a hardware token prior to being granted access to AFNet and AFNet-S Directory Services Domains and authenticating to NIPRNet or SIPRNet PK-Enabled websites.

4.5. Loss of Access. Access to an AF IS is a privilege and continued access is contingent on personnel actions, changes in need to know, or operational necessity; see AFMAN 17-1201. The ISO has the authority to re-instate users who have lost access.

4.5.1. Specific procedural information for account disabling is located in MPTO 00-33B-5004.

4.5.2. Failure to complete annual CyberAwareness Challenge training results in immediate suspension of access to unclassified and classified ISs.

4.5.3. Actions that threaten or damage AF ISs may result in immediate suspension of access to unclassified and classified ISs IAW CJCSI 6510.01 and DoD 5200.2-R. Deliberate inappropriate use of user accounts or systems may result in administrative disciplinary action IAW AFMAN 17-1201.

4.5.3.1. If an individual's clearance is suspended, denied, or revoked, immediately suspend access to classified ISs. Commanders should review circumstances surrounding the suspension, denial, or revocation to determine if continued access to unclassified systems is warranted and if revocation of the hardware token is required. Commanders may provide recommendations regarding user access to the ISO.

4.5.3.2. If an individual violates the IS terms of use, commanders should consider suspending access pending re-accomplishment of CyberAwareness Challenge training. Additional restrictions on reinstatements for classified ISs are determined locally and should follow the guidelines of DoD 5200.2-R.

4.6. Account Management. AF direction is to use PKI-based identification and authentication IAW DoDI 8520.02, DoDI 8520.03 and the USCYBERCOM Communications Tasking Order (CTO) 07-015, *Public Key Infrastructure (PKI) Implementation, Phase 2* (**https://www.cybercom.mil/J3/orders/Pages/CTOs.aspx**). Manage all user accounts using applicable system configuration guidance; follow TOs published by AFSPC (e.g., MPTO 00-33B-5004, MPTO 00-33A-1202 [for AFNet accounts], and the applicable DISA STIGs [enclave, application security, operating system, database, etc.]).

4.6.1. ISSM/ISSOs implement automated IS controls to check and disable IS user accounts that have been dormant more than 30 days IAW CJCSI 6510.01.

4.6.1.1. AF CIO Exception: Disable National Guard and Reserve member IS user accounts only after 90 days of inactivity.

4.6.1.2. Document system specific IS user account disabling requirements after periods of inactivity in the IS security authorization package.

4.6.1.3. ISSMs provide a monthly list of disabled SIPRNet accounts to the base Local Registration Authority (LRA) for SIPRNet hardware token recovery actions; see **Chapter 8**.

4.6.2. Delete unnecessary (to include service accounts) and/or default accounts and change all factory default or user-generated passwords included in a newly acquired system (software or hardware) IAW the configuration information in the IS security authorization package before allowing any user access to the system.

4.6.2.1. Rename default accounts that cannot be deleted, IAW applicable DISA STIGs.

4.6.2.2. Do not execute root-level access in IS applications.

4.6.2.3. Disable/deactivate user accounts (do not delete/deprovision) when users are unable to remotely access their accounts due to an extended absence or when a user is suspended from work, IS access is revoked for any reason, or the security clearance is suspended as specified in paragraph 4.5.3.

Chapter 5

END POINT SECURITY

5.1. Introduction. End point security provides the basis for overall protection of AF-controlled IT assets. Follow CJCSI 6510.01 on the use of DoD-provided, enterprise-wide automated tools/solutions (e.g., Host Based Security System [HBSS]) to ensure interoperability with DoD and AF provided enterprise-wide solutions for remediation of vulnerabilities for endpoint devices.

5.2. General Protection. All authorized users should protect networked and/or standalone ISs against tampering, theft, and loss. Protect ISs from insider and outsider threats by controlling physical access to the facilities and data by implementing procedures identified in Joint, DoD, AF publications, and organizationally created procedures. See AFI 31-101, *Integrated Defense*, for physical access security guidance. End point security procedures are located in MPTO 00-33B-5006.

5.2.1. Identify and authenticate users before gaining access to any government IS IAW guidance in **Chapter 4**.

5.2.2. ISSM/ISSO provide protection from threats by ensuring proper configuration of technical security mechanisms and establishing physical controls for the removal and secure storage of information from unattended ISs (e.g., Common Access Card [CAC] removal lock feature, keyboard locks, secure screen savers, add-on security software). This is done IAW the DISA Operating Systems STIGs and the system security plan (SSP) (found in the system authorization package in the Enterprise Mission Assurance Support Service [eMASS]). See NIST SP 800-53, Revision 4, *Security and Privacy Controls for Federal Information Systems and Organizations,* for more information about SSPs.

5.2.3. Treat devices released to or potentially accessed by unauthorized personnel (outside DoD control) as an untrusted device until IS security policy requirements are re-established and validated IAW the DISA *Removable Media Storage and External Connections* STIG.

5.2.4. Protect devices at the applicable security classification of the information stored in the device IAW CJCSI 6510.01 and this publication.

5.2.5. Protect display devices to prevent inadvertent viewing of classified and controlled or sensitive information by unauthorized users (e.g., away from windows, doorways, public areas); for more information see the DISA *Traditional Security Checklist*.

5.2.6. Control viewing of US-Only ISs and equipment by FNs/LNs IAW CJCSI 6510.01; see the DISA *Traditional Security Checklist*.

5.2.7. Ensure transmission of sensitive information is encrypted using NIST-certified cryptography at a minimum IAW CJCSI 6510.01.

5.2.8. Ensure the transmission of classified information is encrypted using NSA-approved cryptography IAW AFMAN 17-1302, *Communications Security (COMSEC) Operations,* and CJCSI 6510.01.

5.2.9. In areas where classified information is processed, ensure ISs meet TEMPEST requirements IAW Air Force Systems Security Instruction (AFSSI) 7700, *Emission Security* (to become AFMAN 17-1305).

5.2.10. Appropriately mark and label IT devices IAW the highest level of classification processed or displayed on the device IAW DoDM 5200.01, Volume 2 *DoD Information Security Program: Marking of Classified Information*, and DoD 5220.22-M, *National Industrial Security Program Operating Manual (NISPOM)*, if appropriate.

5.2.10.1. Display/peripheral devices (e.g., monitors, projectors, televisions) are required to be either physically marked or technically configured to display the classification banner.

5.2.10.1.1. Display devices located within the same classification environment or mixed environments attached to approved Keyboard, Video, Monitor (KVM) device are not required to be physically labeled if the desktop backgrounds are configured through the IS to identify the classification level.

5.2.10.1.2. Mark and label all KVM switches (regardless of classification environment) to identify the switch position and the associated classification of the connected systems IAW the DISA *Keyboard, Video, Mouse Switch Security* STIG.

5.2.10.2. Physically mark and label all mobile computing devices with the potential to be located/used in mixed environments or publically accessible areas with the highest classification level of the information approved to be processed by the device. If necessary due to mission or operating environment requirements, coordinate with WCO and Wing Information Protection (IP) Office in developing alternate marking and labeling methods.

5.2.11. Contact the organizational security manager for devices involved in data spillage or security incidents IAW AFI 16-1404. For REMSEC guidance, see Chapter 6.

5.3. Software Security. The ISSM ensures all software is included in the IS security authorization package IAW AFI 17-101 and CJCSI 6510.01. Comply with AFMAN 17-1203 for software accountability guidance.

5.3.1. Freeware, public domain software, shareware originating from questionable or unknown sources (e.g., World Wide Websites), and Peer-to-Peer file sharing software are highly susceptible to malicious logic and can only be used after a risk assessment (see AFI 17-101) has been conducted.

5.3.2. Prohibit use of trial or demonstration software due to its unreliability and potential source-code flaws.

5.4. Malicious Logic Protection. Protect ISs from malicious logic (e.g., virus, worm, Trojan horse) attacks by applying a mix of human and technological preventative measures IAW the DISA STIGs and CJCSI 6510.01.

5.4.1. Implement antivirus software with current signature files IAW DoD Antivirus Security Guidance (**http://www.disa.mil/cybersecurity/network-defense/antivirus**). The ISSM documents a process for updating devices that are not able to receive automatic updates (i.e., standalone systems, TDY laptops, etc.) in the SSP IAW with the NIST SP 800-53.

5.4.2. Use only security patches and antivirus tools/signature files/data files obtained from the Defense Asset Distribution Systems (DADS) hosted at the DoD Patch Repository at **https://patches.csd.disa.mil/**.

5.4.3. Configure virus scanning frequency and real-time protection IAW the applicable DISA STIG; document scanning frequency in the SSP IAW NIST SP 800-53.

5.4.4. Using additional antivirus software may be approved through the security authorization process; any additional antivirus software should be used in conjunction with DoD-approved antivirus software (**http://www.disa.mil/cybersecurity/network-defense/antivirus**).

5.4.5. Users report malicious logic intrusions or any other deviation and misconfiguration IAW AFI 16-1404.

5.4.6. Implement malicious logic protection for Mobile Code Technologies IAW the DISA *Application Security and Development* STIG and the DoD Policy Memorandum, *Mobile Code Technologies Risk Category List Update* (**http://iase.disa.mil/policy-guidance/Pages/index.aspx**).

5.5. Data Spillage/Classified Message Incidents (CMIs). Data spillage incidents occur when a higher classification level of data is placed on a lower classification level system/device (including CMDs) IAW the Committee on National Security Systems (CNSS) *Glossary 4009*. When classified information is processed or maintained on an unclassified IS, the individual discovering the incident initiates security incident procedures IAW DoDM 5200.01, Volume 3, *DoD Information Security Program: Protection of Classified Information,* and AFI 16-1404.

5.6. Telework . Criteria for determining eligibility for telework are identified in DoDI 1035.01, *Telework Policy,* and AFI 36-816, *Civilian Telework Program.* See DoD Administration Instruction (AI) 117, *Telework Program*, for implementation guidance (**http://www.dtic.mil/whs/directives/index.html**). For detailed information on telework methods reference NIST SP 800-46, *Guide to Enterprise Telework and Remote Access Security* (**http://csrc.nist.gov/publications/PubsSPs.html**).

5.6.1. Configure all teleworking government furnished equipment (GFE) for remote access with an approved encryption solution (e.g., virtual private network [VPN], transport layer security [TLS]) IAW DISA *Remote Access Policy, Remote Endpoint,* and *Remote Access VPN* STIGs.

5.6.2. GFE, software, and communications with appropriate security measures are required for any telework arrangement that involves CUI data. See DoDI 1035.01, Enclosure 3 for additional restrictions for CUI and Personally Identifiable Information (PII) data (**http://www.dtic.mil/whs/directives/index.html**).

5.6.3. Each approved telework worksite (either the teleworker's home or a Telework Center) requires a DD Form 2946, *Department of Defense Telework Agreement.* If an alternative telework worksite is used due to a lack of resources (i.e., no electricity, ISP outage, etc.), complete a DD Form 2946 and secure the worksite IAW the DISA *Remote Access Policy* STIG.

5.7. Data Encryption.   Encrypt sensitive information (e.g., CUI, For Official Use Only [FOUO], PII, Health Insurance Portability and Accountability Act [HIPAA], Privacy Act, Proprietary).   Validate IA/IA-enabled products providing encryption through the Common Criteria Evaluation and Validation Scheme (CCEVS), Common Criteria Portal, or the cryptographic modules and algorithms evaluated IAW the NIST Cryptographic Algorithm Validation Program (CAVP) and of Cryptographic Module Validation Program (CMVP).   The CAVP provides validation testing of Federal Information Protection Standards (FIPS)-approved and NIST-recommended cryptographic algorithms and their individual components, such as compliance with FIPS 180-4, *Secure Hash Standard (SHS),* for implementing Secure Hash Algorithm (SHA) 256, FIPS 197*, Advanced Encryption Standard (AES),* and other FIPS. Cryptographic algorithm validation is a prerequisite of the CMVP.   The CMVP validates cryptographic modules to FIPS 140-2, *Security Requirements for Cryptographic Modules.* Under the *Federal Information Security Modernization Act of 2014* (Public Law 113-283), compliance with FIPS is mandatory for non-national security systems and may not be waived.

Follow additional guidance in USCYBERCOM CTO 08-001, *Encryption of Sensitive Unclassified Data at Rest (DAR) on Mobile Computing Devices and Removable Storage Media Used Within the Department of Defense (DoD)*, and the CNSSP No. 15, *National Information Assurance Policy on the Use of Public Standards for the Secure Sharing of Information Among National Security Systems.*

5.7.1. DAR and data in transit protection requires FIPS 140-2 validated cryptographic modules for securing CUI and PII and NSA approved cryptographic systems for classified data IAW CJCSI 6510.01.

5.7.1.1. Comply with any approved Enterprise DAR solution(s) for AFNet systems.

5.7.1.2. Use CCEVS-validated products or NIST-evaluated cryptographic modules that provide the minimum FIPS 140-2 validated cryptographic module implementing SHA-256 for DAR for non-Windows platform operating systems.

5.7.2. Classified Data At Rest (CDAR).   Protect classified national security information at rest IAW CJCSI 6510.01 using NSA-approved cryptographic and key management systems offering appropriate protection levels and approved for protecting CDAR or approved physical security measures as identified in DoDM 5200.01, Volume 3.   AFSPC CYSS Cryptographic Modernization Office (**CYSS.CYS.AFCOMSEC-CryptoMod@us.af.mil**) is the designated lead for all AF CDAR encryption use cases.

5.8. Personally -Owned Hardware and Software.   Personally-owned hardware and software used to process DoD information requires mission critical justification and AO approval.   The ISSO/ISSM maintains approval and inventory documentation between the user and government organization in IS security authorization package.

5.8.1. The introduction of personally-owned hardware and/or software to an IS may be a violation of the IS user agreement and subject to repercussions outlined in the IS SSP, and may result in loss of user access, see paragraph 4.5.

5.8.2. Do not introduce personally-owned/developed software or connect personally-owned media or peripheral devices with volatile or non-volatile memory (including, but not limited to, music/video Compact Disk (CD)/Digital Versatile Disk (DVD), commercial MP3 players, and Universal Serial Bus [USB] drives) to AF ISs and/or GFE.

5.8.3. Comply with TEMPEST and physical security requirements, and ensure approval for personally-owned devices prior to introduction into classified processing areas. This applies to fitness monitors, wearable smart technology devices, tablets, e-readers, recording devices (audio, video, etc.), Bluetooth, and near field communication. See paragraph 5.11.4 for more information.

5.9. Wireless Services. Comply with DoDI 8500.01 and DoDD 8100.02, *Use of Commercial Wireless Devices, Services, and Technologies in the Department of Defense (DoD) Global Information Grid (GIG),* for wireless services (radio frequency [RF] and infrared [IR]) integrated with or connected to AF ISs.

5.9.1. Implement wireless peripheral devices, to include keyboard/mouse/pointer devices, IAW requirements outlined in the Wireless STIGs, the National Information Assurance Partnership (NIAP) *Mobile Device Fundamentals Protection Profile, DoD Annex* (**https://www.niap-ccevs.org/pp/**). Acquire wireless peripheral devices IAW AFMAN 17-1203.

5.9.2. Follow applicable TEMPEST guidance for all wireless capabilities. Wireless capabilities are prohibited in areas where classified information is discussed or processed without written approval from the Enterprise AO (or applicable AO if classified wireless capabilities fall entirely within their boundary and do not touch the AFIN) and the Air Force Certified TEMPEST Technical Authority (AF CTTA) IAW DoDD 8100.02.

5.9.3. Configure wireless network solutions IAW the DISA Wireless STIGs and CJCSI 6510.01; document wireless configurations in the IS security authorization package for Enterprise AO (or applicable AO if the wireless capabilities fall entirely within their boundary and do not touch the AFIN) approval IAW DoDD 8100.02. Configure mobile device wireless network solutions IAW the applicable DISA Mobility STIGs and SRGs as applicable.

5.9.4. Configure all unclassified wireless peripheral devices (e.g., keyboards, mice, pointers/forwarders, etc.) with FIPS 140-2 validated encryption modules IAW CJCSI 6510.

5.9.4.1. Implement end-to-end data encryption for unclassified information over an assured channel, and certify under the NIST CMVP to meet requirements of FIPS 140-2 IAW DoDD 8100.02. Secure classified information within NSA-approved encryption solutions IAW CJCSI 6510.

5.9.4.1.1. Individual exceptions to unclassified wireless encryption may be granted on a case-by-case basis IAW DoDD 8100.02 and this publication after a risk assessment and approval by the Enterprise AO (or applicable AO if the wireless capabilities fall entirely within their boundary and do not touch the AFIN); see boundary specific appointment letters (**https://cs1.eis.af.mil/sites/SAFCIOA6/A6S/afcks/AFAAP/Lists/DAA_Program/ AO_Public.aspx**).

5.9.4.1.2. The AF Enterprise AO has accepted the risk for not implementing FIPS 140-2 validated cryptographic modules on Bluetooth keyboard, mouse, and pointing devices used on the unclassified AFNet. Risk acceptance does not extend to non-AFNet systems/enclaves. All HIPAA-compliant medical Bluetooth devices determined to be medically necessary or beneficial to patient care are authorized for use with AFNet and CMD with or without FIPS 140-2 certification.

5.9.4.1.3. Bluetooth headsets designed for IP-based telephones on the unclassified network do not require FIPS 140-2 validated encryption. These devices are prohibited on classified networks. Bluetooth headsets are approved for unclassified voice communication with AF-authorized mobile devices while driving a motor vehicle and for on base and mission-required communications, including VoIP headsets in unclassified work environments.

5.9.4.1.4. Bluetooth single point headsets used with UC soft phones on an unclassified network do not require FIPS 140-2 validated encryption; ISSM/ISSO annotate approval for use in the system authorization package. Multipoint headsets that allow simultaneous multiple pairing (headset-computer and headset-CMD) are prohibited.

5.9.4.2. IR wireless mice/pointers and keyboards require AO approval; for use in classified processing areas implement applicable TEMPEST countermeasures.

5.10. Mobile Computing Devices. Mobile computing devices are IS devices such as portable electronic devices (PEDs), CMDs (including enterprise activated CMDs), laptops, and other handheld devices that can store data locally and access AF-managed networks through mobile access capabilities.

5.10.1. Configure and handle all devices IAW applicable DISA Mobility STIGs, *Mobile Policy* SRG, any updated/newly released mobile operating system STIG (e.g., Apple, Android, Windows Phone), and CJCSI 6510.01. Obtain Enterprise AO approval for all non-compliant STIG configuration standards.

5.10.2. Prior to issuance of each CMD, the CSS verifies user compliance with the DISA Smartphone and Tablet training (**http://iase.disa.mil/eta/Pages/index.aspx**). CMD users complete annual training IAW DISA *CMD Policy* STIG.

5.10.3. Government-owned mobile devices connecting to DoD systems require proper approval and documentation in the IS security authorization package. The AF Enterprise AO is the approving authority for use of PKI software certificates on enterprise activated CMDs. Enterprise AO approval is required prior to provisioning CMDs with DoD PKI digital certificates as outlined in paragraph 8.13. Submit requests to AFSPC CYSS/CYZ PKI (**afspc.cyss.cys.2@us.af.mil**).

5.10.4. Prohibit the introduction of government or personal cellular/personal communications system and/or RF, IR wireless devices, and other devices such as cell phones and tablets, and devices that have photographic or audio recording capabilities into areas (e.g., rooms, offices) where classified information is processed and discussed. Exceptions to this policy requires adherence to TEMPEST requirements IAW DoDD 8100.02, written approval by the AF CTTA IAW AFI 16-1404, NIST SP 800-53A Revision 4, *Assessing Security and Privacy Controls in Federal Information Systems and Organizations, Building Effective Security Assessment Plans*, and the Enterprise AO (or applicable AO if the wireless capabilities fall entirely within their boundary and do not touch the AFIN); see boundary specific appointment letters (**https://cs1.eis.af.mil/sites/SAFCIOA6/A6S/afcks/AFAAP/Lists/DAA_Program/AO_Pu blic.aspx**).

5.10.4.1. Approval by the AO is based upon the ISSM risk assessment and AF CTTA recommendation.

5.10.4.1.1. Telehealth monitoring devices (i.e., pacemakers, implanted medical devices, personal life support systems, etc.) or assistive devices (e.g., hearing aids) with Bluetooth/RF capabilities are exempt from this requirement IAW AFI 16-1404 and DoDD 8100.02.

5.10.4.1.2. Supplemental devices designed to interconnect wirelessly between telehealth/assistive devices to a VoIP handset, CMD, or similar communications device require a TEMPEST countermeasure review, AF CTTA recommendation, and AO approval prior to use in a classified area.

5.10.4.2. If approved, document AO approval within the IS security authorization package and address countermeasures in the TEMPEST assessment for classified processing areas.

5.10.5. Use only approved secure (classified) mobile computing (e.g., DoD Mobility Classified Capability-Secret [DMCC-S] replacement for Secure Mobile Environment [SME] PED) wireless devices for storing, processing, and transmitting classified information.

5.10.5.1. Encrypt classified data stored on secure (classified) mobile computing wireless devices using NSA-approved cryptographic and key management systems IAW CJCSI 6510.01.

5.10.5.2. Configure secure (classified) mobile computing wireless devices IAW the appropriate DISA Mobility STIG (e.g., SME-PED or its replacement, DMCC-S).

5.10.6. All users issued a mobile device sign a mobile device user agreement IAW AFI 10-712, *Cyberspace Defense Analysis (CDA) Operations and Notice and Consent Process,* using the AF Form 4433.

5.10.6.1. For all CMDs (to include Non-Enterprise Activated [NEA] CMDs), document approved changes to baseline configurations (to include software, security settings, applications) on the AF Form 4433, Part II, Block 12, *Remarks as Needed.* Annotate the date the user completed the DISA Smartphone and Tablet (**http://iase.disa.mil**) training in Block 12 of the form.

5.10.6.2. The AF Enterprise AO is the approval authority for all optional or undesignated security settings for all AF enterprise activated CMDs as defined in the appropriate DISA STIGs Configuration Tables (**http://iase.disa.mil**).

5.10.6.3. Organizations that have migrated to the Defense Enterprise Email (DEE) – NIPRNet defer to the service level agreement (SLA) with the DoD Mobility Unclassified Capability (DMUC) leased service.

5.10.7. ISSMs ensure mobile devices comply with the DAR/DIT requirements in paragraph 5.8.

5.10.8. Users immediately report any lost or stolen device to the issuing organization and system ISSO IAW AFMAN 17-1203.

5.10.8.1. Remotely wipe lost or stolen CMDs (through previously installed wiping application or by cellular carrier) and suspend the corresponding service plan, if applicable.

5.10.9. Maintain positive control over all hardware peripheral devices (i.e., portable printer devices, removable media (USB storage devices, optical media, external hard drives, power accessories, etc.) that may accompany the mobile computing device.

5.10.10. NEA CMD acquired through the AF ITCC are approved for use within the AF for any non-sensitive unclassified DoD tasks. NEA CMDs are only authorized to process/store publically available information (e.g., conducting training, monitoring meteorological data, viewing flight maps, and recruiting activities).

5.10.10.1. Prohibit NEA CMD devices from storing and/or processing classified information, CUI, HIPAA information, and other sensitive information.

5.10.10.2. Configure government-owned NEA CMDs IAW the current DISA STIG.

5.10.10.3. Track and manage all government-owned NEA CMDs IAW AFI 17-210, *Radio Management,* and AFMAN 17-1203.

5.10.10.4. Limit personal use of government-owned NEA CMDs with government-paid cellular plans to prevent excessive data charges over monthly limits (see AFMAN 17-1203).

5.10.10.5. All NEA CMDs are required to use hardware tokens via CAC readers and access any public facing DoD PKI-enabled websites; DoD-issued software certificates are not authorized for use with NEA CMDs IAW the DISA *Mobile Policy* SRG.

5.10.10.6. For purchasing NEA CMD applications, obtain licenses per the vendor's software licensing agreement. Organizations track licenses to ensure fiscal responsibility and prevent duplicate purchases IAW AFMAN 17-1203.

5.10.11. Commanders and users follow NSA Guidance, NSA MIT-005FS-2014, *Mitigations for Spillage of Classified Information onto Unclassified Mobile Devices* (www.iad.gov under "IA Advisories and Alerts"), for handling CMD spillages.

5.10.11.1. AF-owned NEA CMDs contaminated with CUI, PII, HIPAA, and other sensitive unclassified data may be cleared following the procedures outlined in NSA MIT-005FS-2014. Contact HQ AFSPC A2/3/6, DSN 692-9582, afspc.a6s@us.af.mil for CMD spillage questions.

5.10.11.2. In the event there is CUI and/or HIPAA data discovered on a personally-owned CMD, the owner of the device assumes liability for the data breach.

5.11. Peripheral Devices. A computer peripheral is any external device that provides input and output for the computer (e.g., mouse, scanners, smart boards, pointers, and keyboard devices are input devices, etc.). Output devices receive data from the desktop or laptop providing a display or printed product (e.g., monitors, projectors, printers, and MFDs).

5.11.1. Use of basic peripherals such as headsets, mice, and keyboards do not require individual authorization (i.e., in the system authorization package) as long as they are not programmable, do not contain persistent storage capabilities, or require additional software (excluding device drivers).

5.11.2. Web cam usage on any IS requires documentation in the SSP. Use of web cams in classified environments requires physical security and/or TEMPEST countermeasures.

5.11.3. Assistive Technology (AT) (Section 508). AT refers to a service or device that is used to increase, maintain, or improve functional capabilities of individuals with disabilities. AT can refer to an item, piece of equipment, software, or system that has been acquired commercially.   AT solutions may include compact keyboards, breath-controlled keyboard/mouse devices, alternative pointing devices, assistive listening devices (wired, FM, and Bluetooth), video phones, screen reader software, screen magnification software, voice recognition software, etc. For more information, see AFI 33-393, *Electronic and Information Technology Accessible to Individuals with Disabilities Section 508.*

5.11.3.1. Wounded Warrior Program.   The Computer/Electronic Accommodations Program (CAP) conducts needs assessments, procures and delivers AT to Medical Treatment Facilities (MTFs) or wounded warrior program, and provides training. The MTFs record the needs assessment and document on a DD Form 2987, *CAP Accommodation Request.* DoDI 6025.22, *Assistive Technology (AT) for Wounded, Ill, and Injured Service Members,* outlines the roles and processes but does not include the local supporting communications unit.

5.11.3.1.1. DoDI 6025.22 does require that all CAP activities meet applicable acquisition, confidentiality, privacy, security, and disclosure requirements IAW DoDD 5400.11, *DoD Privacy Program,* and DoD 5400.11-R, *Department of Defense Privacy Program.* For more information, see the CAP document, *Handbook for Providing Assistive Technology to Wounded Service Members* (**http://www.cap.mil**).

5.11.3.1.2. Organizations conduct or request an assessment from the local communications unit to ensure the end point device operates properly. CAP staff members can work with the communications unit or designated assessor by discussing specific assistive technologies. Equipment can only be delivered to a Federal government facility and installed by the local communications support activity. The CAP is not responsible for the installation of AT. The enclave or system ISSM may submit any non-IA/IA-enabled software to Air Force Network Integration Center (AFNIC)/NTS for certification. Once certified (or if there is no software to certify), the ISSM conducts a risk assessment to determine the overall impact to the enclave/system security posture and adds it to the IS/enclave security authorization package.

5.11.3.2. In accordance with Public Law 109-364, Title V, Section 561, *Military Personnel Policy,* the AT is authorized by law to become the property of the wounded service member at his or her separation from active service. Therefore, the AT can and should remain with the service members as they transition to other locations or leave the military. While the service member remains on active duty, review/assess any software upgrades on a case-by-case basis.

5.11.3.3. When CAP purchases AT for a DoD civilian employee, the equipment becomes the property of the employee's organization. The individual organizations have the freedom to decide if equipment should go with the employee if they change federal jobs or stay with the agency. CAP strongly encourages organizations to transfer the AT with the federal employee to another federal job, reducing the time waiting for replacement equipment for the employee, ensuring reuse of the technology, and saving federal funds.

5.11.4. Regardless of the classification, configure and handle peripheral devices IAW the DISA *Removable Storage and External Connections* STIG and identify in the IS security authorization package.

5.11.5. Any deviation to the configuration specified in the DISA *Removable Storage and External Connections* STIG requires approval by the AO, to include classified networks and systems.

5.11.6. Configure MFDs and networked printers IAW the *Multifunction Device and Network Printers* STIG. Only use Common Criteria-certified MFDs IAW CNSSP No. 11 and DoDI 8500.01.

   5.11.6.1. Acquire all MFDs through AFWay using an ITCC blanket purchase agreement (BPA). The acquisition of any MFD device outside of the AFWay process requires MAJCOM approval. If the device is not listed on AFWay, obtain a waiver through AFWay to purchase the desired device. Guidance for obtaining a waiver may be pursued through the "Request for Quote" process at the AFWay website (**https://www.afway.af.mil/**). See AFMAN 17-1203 for more information.

   5.11.6.2. Document MFDs utilizing IA-enabled functions (e.g., scan to email) in the IS security authorization package for approval by the AO IAW the DISA *Multifunction Device and Network Printers* STIG.

5.11.7. At the end-of-life, handle peripheral devices containing non-volatile memory IAW **Chapter 6.**

5.12. Removable Media. Removable media is any type of storage media designed to be removed from a computer (e.g., external hard drives, flash, USB devices, optical media, etc.).

5.12.1. Scan approved removable media devices for viruses before use.

5.12.2. Configure and handle all approved removable media devices IAW all applicable DISA STIGs and CJCSI 6510.01.

5.12.3. Protect removable media containing PII and CUI taken outside organizational networks IAW CJCSI 6510.01 and DODM 5200.01, Volume 4.

   5.12.3.1. The ISSO/ISSM informs users on DAR requirements, ensuring stored information on removable media complies with the requirements outlined in paragraph 5.8 and configured IAW the DISA *Removable Storage and External Connections* STIG.

   5.12.3.2. USB approved external or optical media devices should be approved by the ISO IAW AFI 33-332 prior to storing PII electronic records assigned as High or Moderate Impact.

   5.12.3.3. Report any lost or stolen removable media containing CUI or PII to the privacy monitor immediately, IAW AFI 33-332.

5.12.4. Ensure the safeguarding, marking, and labeling of all media IAW the requirements for the highest level of information ever contained on the media IAW DoDM 5200.01, Volume 2.

5.12.4.1. Ensure proper classification, marking, storing, transportation, and destruction of removable flash media devices IAW DoDM 5200.01, Volumes 2 and 3, and remanence security guidelines; see **Chapter 6**.

5.12.4.2. Unless an AF Enterprise AO-approved write protection mechanism or write protection process (COMPUSEC Toolbox and/or NSA's File Sanitization Tool [FiST][or replacement tool]) is used, unclassified media introduced into a classified IS becomes classified IAW CJCSI 6510.01 and the AF Enterprise AO (AFSPC/A6) Memorandum, *Guidance for Manual Data Transfers Across Security Domains.*

5.12.4.3. Disable "write" mechanisms for all forms of removable media on SIPRNet ISs IAW USCYBERCOM CTO, *Protection of Classified Information on Department of Defense (DoD) Secret Internet Protocols Router Network (SIPRNet)* 10-133 (**https://www.cybercom.mil/default.aspx**).

5.12.4.4. Organizations with a mission requirement to write to removable media submits requests for a waiver to the AO or alternate approving authority (e.g., Group Commander) IAW the *AF DAA Combined Implementation Guidance for USCYBERCOM CTO 10-084 and CTO 10-133 Memorandum* located at (**https://cs3.eis.af.mil/sites/afao/cto10133/default.aspx**).

5.12.4.5. WCOs verify that organization commanders review all approved waivers semi-annually to validate the mission requirement. If no longer required due to a change in mission, role, or assignment, the system ISSM submits a request to remove the device/user account from the waiver and disable the USB ports/CD Drives.

5.12.4.6. Users are required to notify the approving waiver authority if the waiver requirement is no longer needed.

5.12.4.7. System ISSMs validate the approved waivers against the HBSS whitelist semi-annually, verifying the removed devices/user accounts. For systems unable to implement HBSS, manually verify the removal of write capabilities on each device.

5.12.5. Prohibit the use of removable media devices disguised to look like common items (e.g., pens, bracelets, erasers) in areas where DoD ISs are present.

5.12.6. The ISSO/ISSM ensures the proper handling of storage devices that contain classified information IAW **Chapter 6**.

5.12.7. Whitelist all external storage media (to include memory sticks, thumb drives, camera memory cards, digital cameras, smart phones, media players, external storage devices, flash media, and similar technologies) connected via USB ports to AFIN systems. Submit the whitelist waiver IAW the current TASKORD and/or MTO.

5.12.8. Removable flash media use is prohibited until organizations have identified procedures, put appropriate technologies in place, and have received approval from the AO or alternate approving authority (e.g., O-6 Group Commander or equivalent) IAW the *AF DAA Combined Implementation Guidance for USCYBERCOM CTO 10-084 and 10-133* memorandum. Only USB removable flash media (USB thumb drives) devices that have FIPS 140-2 certification under the NIST CMVP for encryption are authorized for purchase and use on the AFIN. View the vendor information at http://csrc.nist.gov/groups/STM/cmvp/index.html under the "Module Validation Lists" hyperlink.

5.12.9. Account for all removable media devices in the Asset Inventory Management system or the most current, mandated AF IT inventory control system.

5.12.9.1. Report the loss of any removable media device that is whitelisted immediately to the WCO for whitelist removal actions IAW the current MTO. Treat recovered removable media devices as untrusted.

5.12.9.2. Report the loss of any removable media device containing PII to the organizational privacy monitor immediately.

5.13. Collaborative Computing. Collaborative computing provides an opportunity for a group of individuals and/or organizations to share and relay information in such a way that cultivates team review and interaction in the accomplishment of duties and attainment of mission accomplishment. Configure and control collaborative computing technologies (e.g., Defense Collaboration Services [DCS], MilSuite, SharePoint, etc.) to prevent unauthorized users from seeing and/or hearing national security information and material at another user's workstation area.

5.13.1. Follow information in paragraph 3.5.5 for cloud based collaborative computing.

5.13.2. The system ISSM ensures the use of cameras/microphones in unclassified and/or classified environments are documented and approved in the IS security authorization package. Protect collaborative computing devices used in classified environments, see paragraph 5.2.

5.13.3. Configure webcams, attached microphones, and control the projection of information viewable by webcams IAW the DISA *Voice and Video over IP (VVoIP)* and Video Services Policy STIGs. Collaborative computing mechanisms that provide video and/or audio conference capabilities need to provide a clear visible indication that video and/or audio mechanisms are operating to alert personnel when recording or transmitting IAW the DISA *VVoIP Overview* STIG.

5.14. Contractor-Owned Information Systems. Contractor-owned or operated ISs need to meet all security requirements for connection to the AFIN IAW CJCSI 6211.02, AFI 17-100, and AFI 16-1404. Interconnection with the AFIN is accomplished IAW DoDI 8510.01, *Risk Management Framework (RMF) for DoD Information Technology (IT),* and configured IAW the appropriate DISA *Network* STIGs.

5.14.1. Authorize externally-owned IS and PIT systems that are dedicated to DoD processing and are effectively under DoD configuration control IAW DoDI 8510.01.

5.14.2. Off-base, non-DoD owned facilities require Defense Security Service (DSS) approval to process classified DoD information IAW DoD 5220.22-M.

5.14.3. On base contractors within AF-controlled facilities comply with the FAR, DFARS, and DoDI 4161.02, *Accountability and Management of Government Contract Property,* as required by contract.

5.14.4. Enclave/system ISSOs/ISSMs/CSSs maintain a listing of all contractor-owned or operated IS equipment within AF facilities.

5.14.5. Any system configuration outside the normal baseline client image requires documentation in the IS security authorization package and program contract.

5.15. Foreign-Owned Information Systems. Do not use foreign-owned or -operated (e.g., joint/coalition) IS hardware or software to process US sensitive or classified information for critical processing, unless required by international treaties or security agreements. See CJCSI 6211.02, CJCSI 6510.01, and DoDD 5230.11 for more information.

5.16. Other Service or Agency Owned Information Systems. Other service/agency-owned and operated ISs (i.e., Army, Navy, State Department, etc.) should meet all security requirements for connection to the AFIN as defined in AFI 17-101 and DoDI 8510.01. Follow reciprocity and reuse procedures IAW DoDI 8510.01.

Chapter 6

REMANENCE SECURITY

6.1. Introduction . Remanence is the residual information remaining on storage media. REMSEC actions are taken to protect the confidentiality of information on ISs (to include infrastructure devices such as routers and switches). See the IS security authorization package for system specific incident response and REMSEC procedures. Exercise risk management procedures IAW DoDI 8500.01, CJCSI 6510.01, and NIST SP 800-88, *Guidelines for Media Sanitization.*

AF policy is to safeguard classified and sensitive information, no matter what the media. Safeguarding classified and sensitive information in computer memory and media is particularly important during routine maintenance, product end of life, and reuse. ISOs, privileged users, ISSMs, ISSOs, WCOs, operations personnel, and other responsible people should know the risk factors before sanitizing ISs media and releasing them from the controlled environment. To protect against compromise allow only authorized and properly cleared persons with a need to know access to media containing classified and sensitive information.

6.1.1. Risk Assessment. Balance risk management decisions on information sensitivity, threats and vulnerabilities, and the effectiveness and potential impact of the decided action.

6.1.1.1. When assessing the risk of releasing ISs media from DoD control, the ISSO should develop procedures that identify the residual risk and risk tolerance (the acceptable level of risk as determined by the ISO). Follow the guidance in MPTO 00-33B-5008, Appendix C, and NIST SP 800-30, Revision 1, *Guide for Risk Assessments*.

6.1.1.2. The ISSO, assisted by the WCO, assesses the risks in consultation with the Wing IP Office before deciding whether to sanitize for reuse or disposal.

6.1.1.3. The ISO considers the full range of vulnerabilities and security implications to include the actual loss if an unauthorized entity extracts the residual information, the threat directed against this information, the threat of recovery, and the potential for damage. See MPTO 00-33B-5008 for risk management guidance.

6.1.2. Risk Management. Utilizing REMSEC within an organization is a risk management process that involves the information owner, ISO, ISSM, ISSO, and security manager to make a determination of potential impact prior to sanitizing media or devices for reuse or disposal. The decision is based on a complete risk analysis that involves the identification of organizational mission, mission impacts, threats, and possible compromise to the IS or information. A thorough cost benefit analysis coupled with mission priorities provides the framework for this decision.

6.1.2.1. Once the risk analysis has been completed, document the mitigations and any residual risk in the IS security authorization package SSP and Plan of Actions and Milestones (POA&M).

6.1.2.2. As the monetary cost of media decreases, the cost of sanitizing media may become impractical and destruction may become more cost effective. Costs to be considered in the sanitization and destruction decision include purchase price of sanitization software and degaussing/destruction equipment, periodic recertification of equipment, cost of outsourcing, and time required for verification, documentation, and tracking of sanitized media.

6.2. Sanitization. REMSEC actions to sanitize medium (smartphone, Flash, random access memory [RAM] and read only memory [ROM], optical disks, solid state drives [SSDs], magnetic disks, hard disk drives [HDD], etc.) is dependent upon classification of data contained within the device.

6.2.1. Sanitization of unclassified devices follows NIST SP 800-88. The term "sanitization" is defined in SP 800-88 as a process to render access to target data on the media infeasible for a given level of effort. Clear, purge, and destroy are actions that can be taken to sanitize media.

6.2.1.1. Clear – A method of sanitization that applies logical techniques to sanitize data in all user-addressable storage locations for protection against simple non-invasive data recovery techniques; typically applied through the standard Read and Write commands to the storage device, such as by rewriting with a new value or using a menu option to reset the device to the factory state (where rewriting is not supported).

6.2.1.2. Purge – A method of sanitization that applies physical or logical techniques that render target data recovery infeasible using state of the art laboratory techniques.

6.2.1.3. Destroy – Renders target data recovery infeasible using state of the art laboratory techniques and results in the subsequent inability to use the media for storage of data.

6.2.2. Sanitization of classified devices follows the NSA/Central Security Service (CSS) Policy Manual 9-12, *NSA/CSS Storage Device Sanitization Manual,* and involves the destruction of the media and/or data via degaussing, incineration, disintegration, shredding, embossing/knurling, chopping/pulverizing/wet pulping (paper), grinding, strip shredding/cutting, or power removal (dynamic random-access memory [DRAM], static random-access memory [SRAM], volatile Field Programmable Gate Array [FPGA]). Only products listed on the NSA Evaluated Products List (EPL) or received approval from NSA may be used to destroy classified information (to include media and devices) per NSA/CSS Policy Manual 9-12. Contact the NSA/CSS System and Network Analysis Center (SNAC) at (410) 854-6358 or via email at SNAC@radium.ncsc.mil, to obtain technical guidance concerning appropriate methods, equipment, and standards for destroying classified electronic media, IT equipment, electronic components, and other similar or associated materials.

6.2.2.1. Degauss (HDD/Diskettes) – Process for reducing the magnetization of a storage device to zero by applying a reverse (coercive) magnetizing force, rendering any previously stored data unreadable and unintelligible, and ensuring that it cannot be recovered by any technology known to exist. Classified IT storage media cannot be declassified by overwriting per DoDM 5200.01, Volume 3.

6.2.2.2. Embossing/Knurling (CDs/DVDs) – One or two rotating knurled shafts press down on the surface, elongating the focal point and making all information unreadable and inaccessible.

6.2.2.3. Grinding (CDs) – Sanitize by destroying the surface of the optical storage media; DVDs and Blu-Ray disks have information layers in the middle of the disk, making grinding ineffective for sanitization.

6.2.2.4. Disintegration (HDD/Diskettes/CDs/DVDs/SSDs) – Reduces the storage media into small fragments of a specific size, depending upon the type, using a knife mill.

6.2.2.5. Incinerate (HDD/Diskettes/CD/DVD/BluRay Disks/SSD) – Destruction using high heat/temperatures to reduce the media into ash.

6.2.2.6. Shredding (Diskettes/CD/DVD) – Physical shredding of media into small strips using two interlocking patterned drums that rotate in opposing directions.

6.2.2.7. Power Removal (DRAM/SRAM/volatile FPGA) – Clearing of volatile memory by removing power source for a specific duration.

6.2.2.8. Strip Shredding or Cutting (smart cards only) – Destruction of smart cards by cutting or shredding in small pieces.

6.2.3. When sanitization cannot be accomplished (e.g., inoperable disk), destroy the media IAW DoDM 5200.01, Volume 3.

6.2.4. Before media can be reused in a classified environment or released from organizational control, complete a separate administrative procedure for declassification. To determine the classification of the data, consult the applicable system classification guide. The Defense Technical Information Center (DTIC) maintains a repository and index of security classification guides IAW DoDM 5200.01, Volume 1, *DoD Information Security Program: Overview, Classification, and Declassification,* or contact the system/enclave ISSM for a copy.

6.3. Media Reuse. Sanitize media to ensure that no data or information remains on operable media that are to be reused within the DoD.

6.3.1. Clear unclassified media before reuse; purge media containing sensitive data (e.g., PII) prior to reuse. Reference NIST SP 800-88.

6.3.2. Clear classified media before reuse and reuse only in a classified environment IAW CJCSI 6510.01.

6.4. Disposal. Disposal is the process of reutilizing, transferring, donating, selling, destroying, or other final removal of media from service. Disposal of government hardware and software is governed by DoDM 4160.21, Volume 4, *Defense Materiel Disposition Manual: Instructions for Hazardous Property and Other Special Processing Materiel,* and DoDM 4160.21, Volume 2, *Defense Materiel Disposition Manual: Property Disposal and Reclamation.*

6.4.1. Purge or destroy all unclassified IS storage media before leaving the control of the DoD, IAW NIST SP 800-88.

6.4.1.1. Dispose of unclassified electronic media IAW NIST SP 800-88. Dispose of unclassified computing systems and hard drives IAW DoDM 5200.01, Volume 3, Enclosure 7. When no longer needed, unclassified computer systems and hard drives may be disposed of outside the DoD. In some circumstances, the equipment may be provided to non-government entities for reutilization.

6.4.1.2. The Defense Logistics Agency Disposition Services (DLADS) disposes of excess property received from the military services. Turned in property is first offered for reutilization within the DoD, then transfer to other federal agencies, or donation to state/local governments and other qualified organizations. The demanufacture (DEMAN) program is the resource recovery and recycling program designed to reclaim precious metals and recycle scrap for equipment that is not usable (end of lifecycle, destroyed, etc.). For more information about the DLADS, see http://www.dispositionservices.dla.mil.

6.4.1.3. Track and dispose of unclassified IS storage media previously contaminated with classified data as classified media IAW CJCSI 6510.01. Reference DoDM 5200.01, Volume 3, Enclosure 3 for disposal and destruction of classified hard drives, electronic media, processing equipment components, etc. Destroy and declassify IAW NSA/CSS Policy Manual 9-12. Document destruction using guidance IAW MPTO 00-33B-5008.

6.4.2. Destroy all classified IS storage media unless being used in an IS environment at the same or higher classification level. Reuse of classified IS storage media in unclassified environments is prohibited. At the end of life, destroy IAW CJSCI 6510.01 and the sanitization/declassification procedures of NSA/CSS Policy Manual 9-12. For installations without the means to sanitize or verify sanitization, NSA does accept and destroy some classified media. Follow the guidance on the NSA Classified Materiel Conversion (CMC) for packaging, documenting, and shipping devices at https://www.nsa.gov/cmc/. Direct questions to the CMC Customer Service Office at 301-688-6672 or via email at cmc@nsa.gov.

6.5. Mixed Media Devices. Determine the sanitization requirements of mixed media devices, following MPTO 00-33B-5008, NSA/CSS Policy Manual 9-12, and NIST SP 800-88. Sanitization is complete by appropriately sanitizing all the media contained within the device. Hardware such as routers, switches, MFDs, etc., may contain multiple types of media and the sanitization methods are based on the type of media and the classification of the operational environment. Most network architecture devices have solid-state storage devices such as RAM, ROM, FPGA, smart cards, and Flash Memory. DRAM, SRAM, Ferroelectric RAM (FRAM), Magnetic RAM (MRAM), Erasable Programmable Read Only Memory (EPROM), Ultra-Violet EPROM (UVEPROM), and Electrically EPROM (EEPROM) have specific sanitization requirements.

Chapter 7

COMPUSEC ASSESSMENTS

7.1. Purpose . The COMPUSEC Assessment is designed to provide Cybersecurity personnel assistance with implementing and maintaining a cybersecurity program.

7.2. Objective . The COMPUSEC Assessment is a "find and fix" program review, essentially functioning as a staff assistance visit and therefore, the COMPUSEC Assessment is not intended to replace, but rather augment, the Air Force Inspection System (AFIS) and strengthen the AF cybersecurity program IAW AFI 17-130 and AFI 90-201, *The Air Force Inspection System.*

7.2.1. In instances where local inspection authorities (e.g., Wing Inspection Teams) are already performing inspection activities in partnership with the WCO, conduct a separate annual COMPUSEC assessment at the discretion of the WCO and organizational commander.

7.2.2. WCO assessments may be combined with MAJCOM IG inspections that assess COMPUSEC criteria.

7.2.3. Results of these inspections satisfy annual COMPUSEC assessment reporting requirements in paragraph 7.4.

7.3. Assessment Process . WCO will perform annual assessments of all units utilizing IT under the control of the base communications unit, including IT of tenant units (i.e. FOAs, DRUs, and other service units) unless formal agreements exist. **(T-1).** For Joint bases, the AF is responsible for all AF-owned IT and infrastructure. The annual period is defined as the 12-month timeframe since either the last WCO Assessment or MAJCOM IG Inspection.

7.3.1. Assessments consist of an interview and site visit with the applicable ISSO/ISSM/CSS. During the interview, the WCO reviews all responses annotated on the AFMAN 17-1301 COMPUSEC MICT SAC (**https://mict.us.af.mil/**) provided by the ISSO/ISSM/CSS during the last self-assessment. As part of the site visit, the WCO may assess organizational compliance with any COMPUSEC criteria as outlined in this manual. Sample assessment items may be found on the IACE. Additional areas for review are at the discretion of the WCO.

7.3.1.1. For geographically separated units (GSUs), remote interviews (i.e., over the phone) are acceptable in lieu of a site visit when travel costs are a concern.

7.3.1.2. In-brief, out-brief, and other formalization of assessment processes are at the discretion of the WCO and the assessed unit.

7.3.2. Assessments are not graded, but should instead provide organizational commanders an accurate COMPUSEC posture indication by itemizing the deficient COMPUSEC items and summarizing additional observations, recommendations, and best practices.

7.4. Reports. COMPUSEC Assessment Reports provide a narrative description of the deficiencies and significant trends identified during the annual COMPUSEC Assessment. Reports consist of detailed unit reports, follow-up reports, and annual executive summaries.

7.4.1. Detailed unit reports include a narrative of deficient COMPUSEC items, impacts if deficiencies are not corrected, additional areas assessed, assistance provided, recommendations, and best practices. **(T-1)**. Generate and provide detailed unit reports to organizational Commanders (or equivalent) no later than (NLT) 10 days after the COMPUSEC Assessment is completed. **(T-1)**.

7.4.2. Follow-up reports addressing any open findings will be completed by the assessed unit every 30 days, endorsed by the organizational commander (or equivalent), and sent to the WCO for review. **(T-1)**. Findings remain open until considered closed by the WCO that performed the assessment.

7.4.3. Annual executive summary reports reflect the status of the COMPUSEC posture of the Wing (or equivalent) and include a summary of deficient COMPUSEC items, impact if deficiencies are not corrected, assistance provided, and recommendations. **(T-1)**. WCOs will generate and provide annual executive summary reports to the Wing Commander (or equivalent) NLT 31 January of each year. **(T-1)**. No reply or follow-up is required on executive summary reports.

Chapter 8

PUBLIC KEY INFRASTRUCTURE

8.1. Introduction. A vital element of the DoD defense-in-depth strategy is the use of a common, integrated DoD PKI to enable network security services throughout the enterprise. PKI includes a combination of hardware, software, policies, and procedures, as well as, the ability to authenticate, protect, digitally sign, and when necessary, encrypt electronic mail (email) and documents. PKI verifies identities using digital signatures and certificates.

Implementation of PKI through PK enabling is required on all IT IAW DoDI 8520.02 and DoDI 8520.03.

8.2. PKI Guidance . The DoD and the CNSS PKIs have various tokens that are used with the DoD and AF. PKI hardware tokens provide two-factor authentication IAW DoDI 8520.02, to DoD and AF ISs and access to DoD and AF Directory Services domains on NIPRNet and SIPRNet. The DoD and the CNSS PKIs use asymmetric cryptography to identify and authenticate users to systems and networks for the NIPRNet and SIPRNet.

8.2.1. DoDI 8500.01 requires the use of certificates issued by DoD-approved identity credentials to authenticate to DoD ISs.

8.2.2. The CAC is the primary hardware token for identifying individuals for access to NIPRNet assets and physical access to DoD facilities according DoDI 8520.02, DoDM 1000.13, Volume 1, *DoD Identification (ID) Cards: ID Card Life-Cycle*, and AFI 31-101.

8.2.2.1. There are special instances where the CAC cannot be used. For these unique situations, the DoD CIO has approved the use of the Alternate Logon Token (ALT).

8.2.2.2. The NIPRNet Directory Services domain and SIPRNet legacy Directory Services domains are defined in the DISA STIGs as General Business Enclave LANs. All accounts and computers in Directory Services are required to use PKI.

8.2.2.2.1. Annotate smart card removal and screensaver exemptions that are allowed for very limited use cases in the enclave/system security authorization documentation IAW the applicable DISA Operating System STIG.

8.2.2.2.2. Submit Service Requests to AFSPC CYSS/CYZ PKI, (**afspc.cyss.cys.2@us.af.mil**) when a normal Directory Services-joined computer cannot fulfill the organizations requirements.

8.2.3. Identity Credential Determination. DoDI 8520.03 requires that the ISO determines the "Credential Strength" used to authenticate to the DoD IS by assessing the "Sensitivity Level" of the information contained in the DoD IS.

8.3. NIPRNet PKI. The most commonly used unclassified PKI hardware token or smart card is the CAC. The ALT can be issued in circumstances where the CAC cannot be issued to an individual. The Volunteer Logical Access Credential (VoLAC) can be issued to eligible volunteers. If there are validated circumstances where a NIPRNet token cannot be used, a NIPRNet Smart Card Logon (SCL) waiver allowing the use of username and password may be authorized. Contact AFSPC CYSS/CYZ PKI (**afspc.cyss.cys.2@us.af.mil**) for guidance.

8.3.1. AFI 36-3026 IP, Volume 1, *Identification (ID) Cards for Members of the Uniformed Services, Their Eligible Family Members, and Other Eligible Personnel*, identifies the individuals that are eligible for CACs. Individuals should be issued a separate CAC for each persona (e.g., Active Duty Service Member, Reserve or Guard Member, Government Civilian, Contractor) IAW DoDM 1000.13, Volume 1. This role or persona is commonly referred to as a Personnel Category Code (PCC).

8.3.1.1. For uniformed services personnel and DoD civilians, all submissions to DoD Enrollment Eligibility Reporting System (DEERS) can be made electronically via an authorized data source feed (e.g., Civilian Personnel Management Service).

8.3.1.2. The Defense Manpower Data Center (DMDC), as the administrator of DEERS and the Real-Time Automated Personnel Identification System (RAPIDS), requires the use of the Trusted Associate Sponsorship System (TASS) for requesting CACs for "DoD PKI Certificate Eligible Users," IAW DoDM 1000.13.

8.3.1.2.1. DoD PKI Certificate Eligible Users are authorized DoD volunteers, State, local, or tribal government employees, or interns as defined DoDI 8520.02. To begin the process for VoLAC issuance, to include completion of DD Form 2793, *Volunteer Agreement for Appropriated Fund Activities and Non-Appropriated Fund Instrumentalities,* contact supporting TASS Trusted Agent (TA). The TA establishes sponsorship of the applicant, verifies the access requirements, and initiates the application process in TASS.

8.3.1.2.1.1. The TASS application replaced the Contractor Verification System (CVS) and was designed to replace the paper application process using DD Form 1172-2, *Application for Department of Defense (DoD) CAC Defense Enrollment Eligibility Reporting System (DEERS) Enrollment.*

8.3.1.2.1.2. TASS allows "DoD PKI Certificate Eligible Users" requiring DoD Network access, DoD and Uniformed Service Contractors, Foreign Affiliates, Non-DoD Civil Service Employees, Non-Federal Agency Civilian Associates, Non-US Non-Appropriated Fund (NAF) Employees, outside the continental U.S. (OCONUS) Hires, Other Federal Agency Contractors to apply for a CAC or other government credential electronically through the Internet. Government sponsors of DoD contractor personnel should contact their supporting TASS TA to request an application for an eligible contractor to receive government credentials.

8.3.1.2.1.3. Follow the guidance provided in DoDM 1000.13 and the TASS TA user manual.

8.3.1.2.2. Unfunded contract options (annotated in the contract as the period of performance [PoP]) are considered in the determination of the length of contract. For example, a contractor hired under DoD contract with a base year plus two option years should be issued a CAC with a 3-year expiration. The expiration date of the PKI certificates on the CAC should match the expiration date on the card. If contract option years are not exercised, the COR notifies the TASS TA to revoke contractor access.

8.3.1.3. Dual-role personnel have more than one role/persona (e.g., Civilian and Reservist, Contractor and Air National Guard); the individual is required to have and use the appropriate CAC for each role. At issuance, the CAC should not have the individual's PCC appended to his or her Electronic Data Interchange Personal Identifier (EDI-PI). Append PCCs at the RAPIDS Self Service Portal (**https://www.dmdc.osd.mil/self_service/rapids/unauthenticated?execution=e2s1**). Set the CAC/Directory Services account that the individual uses the most with **EDI-PI@MIL**, and set the CAC/Directory Services account that is used the least with **EDI-PI.PCC@MIL**. Each time a new CAC is issued, append the PCC.

8.3.1.4. Authorized DoD volunteers, State, local, or tribal government employees, or interns are "DoD PKI Certificate Eligible Users" IAW DoDI 8520.02. Contact supporting TASS TA to begin the process for VoLAC issuance, to include completion of DD Form 2793. The TA enters user information into TASS.

8.3.1.5. Air Force Personnel Center (AFPC) manages the issuance of CACs through DEERS/RAPIDS. On AF installations, the AF Military Personnel Section (MPS) issues the CAC. On non-AF locations, any RAPIDS can issue a CAC to any authorized Service Member, Government Civilian, or DoD Contractor. DoD Contractors contact their unit's TASS TA prior to making an appointment with their supporting MPS to have their information entered or updated in DEERS.

8.3.1.6. Turn in expired, unneeded, or found CACs or VoLACs to the nearest RAPIDS facility by the individual, Contracting Officer's Representative (COR) for DoD contractors, or TASS TA.

8.3.2. The ALT is another form of a DoD authorized PKI hardware token or smart card that can be issued to individuals for logical access to NIPRNet. Currently, there is not an ALT-like capability on SIPRNet.

8.3.2.1. Individuals who are ineligible for receiving a CAC (e.g., Italian Nationals) or the support staff serving a General Officer (GO) or Senior Executive Service (SES) (e.g., PKI Tier-1) can be issued an ALT with DoD PKI certificates. See T.O. 31S5-4-7282-1, *Alternate Logon Token (ALT) Issuance Standard Operating Procedures,* for specific issuance criteria or eligibility.

8.3.2.2. The user/requestor should contact their base ALT TA, usually assigned to the supporting base communications unit or Communications Focal Point (CFP), to begin the ALT issuance process. For a list of each base's ALT TAs, see **https://afpki.lackland.af.mil/html/b-alttokencontacts.cfm**.

8.3.2.3. Turn in expired, unneeded, or found ALTs to the nearest AF base's ALT TA.

8.3.3. Most commercially available token readers (separate device or integrated into a keyboard) can be used on the NIPRNet; there is no approved or banned product list. Only use the latest approved version of middleware on NIPRNet. Remove all other middleware products from the IS.

8.3.4. Maintain positive control over hardware token at all times IAW AFI 36-3026.

8.3.4.1. Do not leave any unclassified PKI hardware token in an unattended computer.

8.3.4.2. The person who is issued a hardware token maintains positive control of the token at all times and the embedded certificates IAW the applicable CNSS guidance, DoD *Registration Practice Statement (RPS)*, or *United States Department of Defense X.509 Certificate Policy*.

8.3.4.3. Introduction of SIPRNet hardware tokens on NIPRNet ISs are not authorized. If a SIPRNet hardware token has been used on an unclassified IS, see paragraph 8.4.6 for guidance.

8.3.5. Implement SHA-256 algorithm on all DoD IT infrastructure (hardware and software) on both NIPRNet and SIPRNet IAW the *DoD Secure Hash Algorithm-256 Transition Plan*.

8.3.5.1. All DoD Components are required to support DoD-approved SHA-256 PKI credentials for digitally signing and encrypting emails, logging onto DoD networks, and authenticating to systems no later than September 30, 2017.

8.3.5.2. All NIPRNet Systems are required to be SHA-256 compliant according to SAF/CIO A6 or submit a POA&M to AFSPC CYSS/CYZ PKI (**afspc.cyss.cys.2@us.af.mil**). To be compliant, all systems, websites, web capabilities, network devices, and software should be capable of utilizing the SHA-256 certificate or SHA-256 certificates when issuance on the CAC begins.

8.3.5.3. Follow FIPS 180-4, FIPS 140-2, and the validation lists available through the NIST CMVP and the CAVP sites (**http://csrc.nist.gov/groups/STM/cmvp/index.html**).

8.4. SIPRNet PKI. The SIPRNet hardware token is the primary means for logical access to SIPRNet. If there are validated circumstances where a SIPRNet token cannot be used, a SIPRNet SCL exemption allowing the use of username and password may be allowed IAW MTO 2013-077-002C (or current update of the MTO). Contact AFSPC CYSS/CYZ PKI (**afspc.cyss.cys.2@us.af.mil**) for guidance.

8.4.1. Ensure all SIPRNet networks utilize the National Security Systems (NSS) Root Certificate Authority (CA) and are current with all PKI security patches and configuration settings IAW the applicable Certificate Practice Statement (CPS).

8.4.2. Individuals who have a SIPRNet Directory Services account are required to use SIPRNET hardware tokens IAW USCYBERCOM TASKORD J3-12-0863, Fragmentary Order (FRAGO) 2.

8.4.3. The LRA, normally residing at the supporting base normally within the base communications unit or CFP, issues the SIPRNet hardware token or smart card. The SIPRNet hardware token provides authorized users with an identity certificate, digital signature certificate, and an encryption certificate. With appropriate network configuration, the SIPRNet hardware token or smart card provides user authentication and non-repudiation for network logon.

8.4.4. The SIPRNet hardware token or smart card is a high-value unclassified item. Maintain the SIPRNet hardware token IAW CNSSI No. 1300, *National Security Systems Public Key Infrastructure X.509 Certificate Policy Under CNSS Policy No. 25,* and the *National Security Systems Public Key Infrastructure, Department of Defense Registration Practice Statement (RPS)*.

8.4.4.1. A SIPRNET token is classified SECRET when inserted into the SIPRNET hardware token reader and the personal identification number (PIN) is entered. It is considered unclassified when removed from the SIPRNET token reader or if it is inserted into the token reader but the PIN is not entered.

8.4.4.2. Do not leave the SIPRNet hardware token unattended in computer network resources.

8.4.4.3. Maintain the SIPRNet hardware token in the positive control of the authorized user, who is represented by the embedded certificates IAW the applicable CNSS policy or RPS. Turn-in expired, unneeded, or found SIPRNet hardware tokens to the nearest NSS LRA by the individual, COR for DoD Contractors, or TASS TA. *Note:* Do not return the found SIPRNet hardware token back to the individual. See paragraph 8.16 for key compromise guidance.

8.4.4.3.1. Positive control includes maintaining visual contact when in use, and retention on the person or secured when not in use. SIPRNET tokens are considered secured when locked or stored within a container (e.g., desk) inside a facility authorized for the protection of SECRET. Only the assigned user is authorized to use the SIPRNET token.

8.4.4.3.2. Contact the supporting LRA to revoke SIPRNet hardware token certificates when there is suspected loss of positive control or unauthorized use of the token or a certificate. Return any token determined to be temporarily out of the positive control of the assigned user to the LRA. When returned, zeroize the private keys and revoke the certificates. If zeroizing and revocation is not possible or if there is evidence of tampering with the SIPRNet hardware token, the LRA returns the token to NSA for investigation and/or destruction.

8.4.4.3.3. If the SIPRNet hardware token is lost or stolen and not recovered, immediately report this information to the LRA to initiate the revocation process IAW the applicable CPS. Issuance of a new SIPRNet hardware token is authorized after a dated and signed memorandum (wet or digital signature acceptable) on organizational letterhead by the requesters Commander authorizing the issuance, is provided to the LRA.

8.4.4.3.4. AF GO and/or SES members are authorized to retain their SIPRNet hardware token during a permanent change of station (PCS). All other AF SIPRNet users are required to turn–in their SIPRNet hardware token when undergoing a PCS or permanent change of assignment (PCA) (see paragraph 8.4.5.3.4.2).

8.4.4.3.4.1. The GO/SES or designated representative notifies the losing base LRA, either in person or through a digitally-signed e-mail stating that he/she is taking the SIPRNet hardware token to the new location and site code needs to be changed/updated. The losing base LRA changes the site code for the registration tied to the SIPRNet hardware token of the GO/SES in the Token Management System (TMS). The losing base LRA notifies the gaining base LRA of the transfer through a digitally signed e-mail.

8.4.4.3.4.2. Any user may retain their SIPRNet hardware token during PCA, if the issuing LRA remains the same.

8.4.4.3.5. Enclave or system ISSM/ISSO notifies the base LRA of expired accounts (see paragraph 4.6.1.2); the base LRA contacts users and recovers the SIPRNet hardware tokens from them.

8.4.4.3.6. Base communications unit will update their portion of the base out-processing checklist to ensure that all individuals have contacted their unit's CSS to terminate their SIPRNet account and have turned-in their SIPRNet hardware token to the base LRA prior to signing off the individual's Base Out-processing Checklist. **(T-1).** Contractors contact their unit's CSS to terminate their SIPRNet account and turn-in their SIPRNet hardware tokens to the base LRA at the end of the contract PoP.

8.4.5. Prohibit the introduction of (operational) SIPRNet hardware tokens on unclassified ISs and the introduction of unclassified tokens (e.g., CAC, ALT, Personal Identity Verification [PIV], VoLAC, and or Personal Identity Verification-Interoperable [PIV-I]) on classified ISs.

8.4.5.1. SIPRNet hardware tokens inserted into an unclassified IS may result in a security violation. Report suspected incidents to the WCO and local security manager to determine if the incident is a security violation. Follow the guidance in DoDM 5200.01, Volume 3. Note: This does not apply to SIPRNet hardware token testing cards on unclassified test beds.

8.4.5.2. The SIPRNet "90meter©" middleware configuration detects the NIPRNet token, blocks PIN entry, and blocks any service applets that do not require PIN entry.

8.4.5.3. An unclassified hardware token inserted into a SIPRNet IS may result in a security violation. Report suspected incidents to the WCO and local security manager to determine if the incident is a security violation. Follow the guidance in DoDM 5200.01, Volume 3.

8.4.6. Connect only authorized SIPRNet hardware token readers (i.e. Omnikey 3121, SCM 3310) to SIPRNet ISs. The connection of keyboards with built-in CAC readers and external USB CAC readers to classified ISs are not permitted.

8.4.6.1. Permit only the latest version of "90meter©" middleware and configure it to activate only SIPRNet hardware tokens initialized for use on the SIPRNet.

8.4.6.2. In the AF, "ActivClient©" middleware is not authorized on SIPRNet.

8.4.7. All SIPRNet Systems are required to be SHA-256 compliant according to SAF/CIO A6 or submit a POA&M to AFSPC CYSS/CYZ PKI (afspc.cyss.cys.2@us.af.mil). To be compliant, all systems, websites, web capabilities, network devices, and software should be capable of utilizing the SHA-256 certificate or SHA-256 certificates when issuance on the SIPRNet hardware token begins. Follow FIPS 180-4, FIPS 140-2, and the validation lists available through the NIST CMVP and the CAVP sites (http://csrc.nist.gov/groups/STM/cmvp/index.html).

8.5. User or Administrator Password/PIN Management. Passwords may be allowed only when the AF PKI SPO has evaluated the AF Information System and has validated that the use of PKI smart cards or other approved two factor authentication is not technologically feasible; contact AFSPC CYSS/CYZ PKI (**afspc.cyss.cys.2@us.af.mil**) for guidance. Specific procedural information for password/PIN management is located in MPTO 00-33B-5004. In addition to the AF-specific password guidance contained in the MPTO 00-33B-5004, configure IS password authentication IAW the applicable DISA Operating System STIGs. DISA STIG and/or USCYBERCOM TASKORD password requirements take precedence only if more restrictive than guidance in this publication.

8.5.1. Classify and protect passwords/PINs at the highest level of information processed on that system. As a minimum, safeguard passwords as FOUO. See DoDM 5200.01, Volume 1, for a detailed explanation of FOUO.

8.5.2. Classified passwords/PINs that are necessary for mission accomplishment (i.e., pre-established accounts for contingency or exercise) may be sealed in a properly marked envelope or annotated on a SF 700, *Security Container Information*, and stored in a GSA-approved container as specified in DoDM 5200.01, Volume 3.

8.5.3. Protect all passwords/PINs during transmission using FIPS-approved encryption IAW CJCSI 6510.01.

8.5.4. All passwords for AF ISs are required to comply with the following password management criteria.

8.5.4.1. To the extent capabilities permit, system mechanisms are implemented to enforce automatic expiration of passwords and to prevent password reuse, and processes are in place to validate that passwords are sufficiently strong to resist cracking and other attacks intended to discover a user's password. All factory set, default or standard-user IDs and passwords are removed or changed.

8.5.4.2. Authenticators are protected commensurate with the classification or sensitivity of the information accessed, they are not shared, and they are not embedded in access scripts or stored on function keys.

8.5.4.3. Passwords are encrypted both for storage and for transmission. Store passwords in an authentication system that minimizes their exposure to disclosure or unauthorized replacement. Encryption of electronically stored passwords and password files is required.

8.5.4.4. Service Account passwords have different requirements than user passwords; see paragraph 8.21.

8.5.4.5. Case sensitive, at least 15-character mix of two upper case letters, two lower case letters, two numbers, and two special characters. For password changes, change at least four characters when a new password is created.

8.5.4.6. The ISO ensures the establishment of procedures for manual or automatic password changes by users, administrators, and machine-to-machine interfaces; password changes occur at least every 60 days or more frequently as determined by the ISO, IAW CJCSI 6510.01.

8.5.5. For systems that are not joined to the Directory Services domain and require shared/group passwords, the system ISSM requests approval from the AO IAW CJCSI 6510.01. Implement system and physical auditing procedures to support non-repudiation and accountability. For more information on waiving DoD or AF PKI requirements, see paragraph 8.22.

8.5.5.1. Unauthorized sharing of passwords/PINs is a security incident IAW CJCSI 6510.01.

8.5.5.2. Incorporate electronic or paper tracking methods to account for user activity when using AO-approved shared passwords IAW CJCSI 6510.01.

8.5.6. In the event of a compromised password/PIN, the ISO and the ISSM ensures procedures are in place to implement immediate password/PIN change activities. A compromised PKI PIN warrants probable compromise of the associated certificates. See paragraph 8.16.

8.6. PIN Caching Setting . All NIPRNet and SIPRNet DoD ISs and Directory Services domains and domain-joined computers are required to be configured for PIN caching, set to 10 minutes.

8.7. Organizational Electronic Mailbox . Disable Directory Services objects that are associated with Organizational Mailboxes. Note: Organizational Mailboxes and Organizational Accounts are two different capabilities and are not related.

8.7.1. The Organizational Mailbox Manager should grant access from the actual Organizational Mailbox. The Organizational Mailbox Manager is the person whose name appears in Directory Services as the Manager of the Organizational Mailbox. Use IAO Express to add or change the Organizational Mailbox Manager in Directory Services/Exchange.

8.7.2. The sponsor appointed for the Organizational Mailbox manages the Encryption Certificate associated with the Organizational Mailbox. The Sponsor is the person who requests, issues, and manages the Encryption Certificate. The Organizational Mailbox Sponsor should follow the procedures for managing the Organizational Mailbox Encryption Certificate found on the AF PKI SPO website (**https://afpki.lackland.af.mil/**).

8.8. Organizational Accounts. Organizational Accounts are Active Accounts that individuals use to logon using DoD-approved PKI and accesses the electronic mailbox associated with the Organizational Account (e.g., AFSPC/CC, AFSPC/CCC, AFSPC/CCF). Each individual should have a unique identifier that the system can authenticate and provide an audit trail. The Organizational Accounts are unique since a DoD approved hardware token is used to logon to the associated Directory Services account to access files or email.

8.8.1. In order for multiple users to access the same Organizational Account, each person should possess a unique DoD approved hardware token (e.g., ALT). More than one person cannot share a single DoD approved hardware token.

8.9. Group Accounts Utilizing PKI. Group accounts (not to be confused with organizational accounts) are special case accounts where more than one person may access the same account using a DoD-approved PKI credential IAW DoDI 8520.02.

8.9.1. The approval authority for group accounts is one of the applicable AOs; see boundary specific appointment letters **https://cs1.eis.af.mil/sites/SAFCIOA6/A6S/afcks/AFAAP/Lists/DAA_Program/AO_Publ ic.aspx**.

8.9.1.1. For AFIN group accounts, the approval authority is the Enterprise AO. To begin the AFIN approval process, contact AFSPC CYSS/CYZ PKI (**afspc.cyss.cys.2@us.af.mil**) to determine if the appropriate solution is the use of a group account. AFSPC CYSS/CYZ PKI identifies the appropriate next step in the approval process.

8.9.1.2. For non-AFIN group accounts, the approval authority is the applicable AO for the specific boundary.

8.9.2. Authorized users request individual ALTs to access the group account; each token contains an individual identification certificate. See paragraph 8.3.2.

8.9.3. The ALT Sponsor maintains an inventory of token serial numbers and assigned users at all times.

8.9.4. Requests for group account ALTs should follow T.O. 31S5-4-7282-1.

8.10. External PKI. To begin the approval process for External PKI as authorized by DoDI 8520.02, contact AFSPC CYSS/CYZ PKI (**afspc.cyss.cys.2@us.af.mil**). AFSPC CYSS/CYZ PKI identifies the appropriate next step in the approval process.

8.11. Enterprise Certificate Trust Governance. Identity assurance must be applied to ensure strong identification and authentication, and to eliminate anonymity in DoD IS and PIT systems. DoD will public key-enable DoD ISs and implement a DoD-wide PKI solution that will be managed by the DoD PKI Program Management Office in accordance with DoDI 8520.02. The AF Certificate Trust baseline provides a white/black list of PKI Certificate Authorities (CAs) trust anchors (or roots) to secure AF systems from trusting unknown and/or untrusted issuing CAs. It includes a minimum number of roots required for the OS to operate and to support specific enterprise applications. The AF Certificate Trust Store Governance process exists to manage the baseline and provide a formal means to add and remove roots at the enterprise level.

8.11.1. If an AF IS user attempts to go to a website where the root CA has expired and is no longer being updated, a "Certificate Error" warning is displayed in the web browser.

8.11.1.1. For non-enterprise use (individual users), follow the procedures posted on the IACE.

8.11.1.2. For Enterprise use, the ISSM submits a request, on behalf of all users, to AFSPC CYSS/CYZ PKI (**afspc.cyss.cys.2@us.af.mil**) using the template found on the IACE.

8.12. Escrowed Certificates. The CA provides automatic escrow of the email encryption key IAW *United States Department of Defense X.509 Certificate Policy*. Perform recovery of escrowed encryption keys according to the CA associated practice statements. Recovery of Escrowed Certificates is required to read encrypted emails that were received by the user using the previous certificates.

8.12.1. Changing of employment roles (i.e. contractor-to-government civilian, military-to-contractor, etc.) may affect the users' need to know and requires the users to request manually the escrowed encryption certificate. For additional guidance, see the AF PKI SPO website (**https://afpki.lackland.af.mil/**).

8.13. Software Certificate Issuance and Control. The AF follows the methods for approving PKI certificates as prescribed in the DoD PKI RA/LRA CPS and DoD RPS, supported by the DoD X.509 Certificate Policy. AF RAs have overall management responsibility for certificate issuance with LRA/TA as base level points of contact. The AF Enterprise AO is the approving authority for each use of software certificates. To begin the approval process, the system/enclave ISSM should contact AFSPC CYSS/CYZ PKI (**afspc.cyss.cys.2@us.af.mil**).

8.13.1. AF PKI RAs, LRAs, CA Managers, CA Operators, System Administrators, and CA Security Managers comply with the detailed policy and procedures as applicable; see **https://afpki.lackland.af.mil/**.

8.13.2. Upon approval from the AO, the ISSM annotates the use in the authorization package (security control CM-6).

8.13.3. ISSMs ensure all devices are configured with an approved token reader or have AF Enterprise AO-approval to use software certificates IAW the DISA *Commercial Mobile Device (CMD) Policy* STIG. Identification, digital signature, and encryption software certificates are required for CMDs and have a designated sponsor appointed in writing; contact AFSPC CYSS/CYZ PKI (**afspc.cyss.cys.2@us.af.mil**). The AF Registration Authority (RA) or LRA, as appropriate, maintains a file of requirement validation documentation.. For organizational email mailboxes on CMDs, follow the appropriate DISA STIG. For additional guidance, see the AF PKI SPO website (**https://afpki.lackland.af.mil/**).

8.13.3.1. For organizations working to comply with the mandate to use CAC readers and requiring the use of software certificates on enterprise activated CMDs, submit a POA&M and the token reader exceptions to the AF PKI for review and recommendation to the AF Enterprise AO.

8.13.3.2. Once approved by AF Enterprise AO, use PKI software certificates for the minimum time necessary to comply with the token reader requirement. The ISSM adds the approval to the system/enclave authorization package; approval may be a memorandum, letter, or included in the SSP.

8.13.3.3. Organizations update user training materials and annotate certificate usage in block 12 of the AF Form 4433.

8.13.4. DoD PKI certificates and associated private keys are stored in a *Public-Key Cryptography Standards (PKCS)* #12 file on a removal storage medium. Do not leave PKCS#12 files in on-line file systems and are properly installed into the cryptographic module on an IS for use.

8.13.5. Do not share personal software certificate passwords; protect the media containing private keys from unauthorized access at all times IAW paragraph 8.5.

8.13.6. The Network Operations Squadrons (NOS) verify removal of software certificate installation files (.p12 or .pfx) from hard drives and other online storage devices weekly.

8.13.6.1. Removal of software certificate files does not prevent usage of software certificates for web servers, group, or role-based functions. The process only requires removal of the ".p12" or ".pfx" transportable file object that contains the private key corresponding to the DoD trusted certificate from online accessibility after installation. **NOTE:** Some applications create files with extensions of ".p12" or ".pfx" that are NOT certificate installation files. Removal of non-certificate installation files from systems is not required.

8.14. LRA Guidance. LRAs perform some aspects of certificate issuance and management at the local level. Designated LRAs have certificate issuance authority for the entire installation, including Tenant organizations and GSUs supported by the installation. Training, appointment, and eligibility information is available on the AF PKI SPO website at **https://afpki.lackland.af.mil**. AF MAJCOMS/Bases/Sites and AF supported COCOMS can establish and maintain AF LRAs who are designated IAW procedures outlined in the CPS and RPS, meeting needs of all base, site, and tenant organizations. Designated LRAs will attend a DISA approved AF LRA training course after the AF RA Office has vetted and approved the submission package. Detailed procedures for submitting LRA packages are available at **https://afpki.lackland.af.mil/html/**.

8.15. CMD Hardware Token Readers. ISSMs ensure all devices are configured with an approved token readers and/or an AO-approved process for installation of PKI software certificates IAW the DISA *Mobile Policy* SRG. See paragraph 8.5 for password requirements for devices not capable of supporting PKI and the DISA Mobility STIGs/SRGs for guidance setting up token readers.

8.16. Key Compromise. The ISSO immediately notifies the supporting TA, LRA, or the AF RA (**afpki.registration@us.af.mil**) directly by encrypted email if an AF PKI certificate holder (software certificate or token) suspects a compromise of the holder's private key.

8.16.1. Certificate revocation is necessary to terminate a certificate's use before its normal expiration date. Examples of reasons for revocations include private key compromise (e.g., lost or stolen token), loss of trust in a user, changes in a user's legal name, or departure from the DoD. The AF RA revokes certificates suspected of key compromise within 24 hours or the next duty day (whichever is first) after notification.

8.16.1.1. Revoke all other certificates (e.g., encryption and digital signature) on the token if there is a revocation of a user's ID certificate.

8.16.1.2. Enter the revoked certificates into a DoD Certificate Revocation List (CRL). All applications (i.e., websites, etc.) should check validity (e.g., the trust path, expiration, and revocation status) of the presented certificate prior to allowing access based on PKI authentication.

8.17. Server Certificates. The AF RA is the approving authority for the issuance of Medium-Assurance DoD PKI or NSS (SIPRNet) server certificates based on validation of the certificate used to digitally sign the email submitting the certificate request form (AF RA Form 2842-2). The certificate request form and specific instructions to obtain and load DoD server certificates are available on the AF PKI SPO website (**https://afpki.lackland.af.mil/**).

8.17.1. Reissue a server certificate when the fully qualified domain name (FQDN) for the server changes or after three years.

8.17.2. All AF Web servers are issued a DoD X.509 PKI Server certificate and have 128/256-bit encryption; enable the certificate at all times IAW DoDI 8520.02.

8.18. Code Signing and Mobile Code Certificates. Code signing and mobile code certificates are specially formatted certificates used for digitally signing executable program code in any number of languages or formats.

8.18.1. The sponsor is required to submit the request for code signing and mobile code certificates to the Code Signing Attribute Authority (CSAA), AFSPC CYSS/CYZ PKI (**afspc.cyss.cys.2@us.af.mil**), to begin the process for issuance on a hardware token by the AF RA/AF PKI SPO. The sponsor coordinates with the ISSM for inclusion into the security authorization package. For additional guidance, see the *Air Force Developer's Guide for Obtaining DoD Code Signing Certificates* at the AF PKI SPO website (**https://afpki.lackland.af.mil/**).

8.18.1.1. Designate individuals authorized to receive code-signing certificates; ensure that such designations are kept to a minimum consistent with operational requirements.

8.18.1.2. Upon approval from the AF Enterprise AO, the ISSM annotates compliance in the enclave/system authorization package that code signing and/or mobile code certificates are being used SC18 and CM-5/SA-10/SI-7).

8.19. Certificate Reissuance Prior to Expiration. Certificate Sponsors (owners) needing continued PKI services ensures reissuance of their certificates no earlier than 60 days prior to the certificate expiration date in order to prevent disruption in service.

8.20. Network Authentication. Enable all unclassified networks to use hardware tokens, DoD PKI certificate-based authentication, and set authorized user accounts to require SCL by selecting, "Smart card is required for Interactive Logon," in Windows Directory Services environments. Obtain exceptions to this policy from the AF Enterprise AO via AFSPC CYSS/CYZ PKI, (**afspc.cyss.cys.2@us.af.mil**).

8.21. Directory Services Service Accounts. Service accounts for Directory Services Service Accounts-joined servers (e.g., AREA52 or SIPRNet legacy domain) are required to comply with the mandate for all Directory Services Service Accounts to use SCL. Follow the password complexity requirements listed in paragraph 8.5.4.

8.21.1. Interactive logon is not allowed for any Directory Services Service Account; the use of smart cards for logon is not possible. Therefore, a SCL exemption can be granted for Use Cases that meet the SCL exemption guidance; the base enclave ISSM should contact AFSPC CYSS/CYZ PKI (**afspc.cyss.cys.2@us.af.mil**) for more information.

8.21.2. Approve service accounts through the Change Request process IAW MPTO 00-33A-1100, *AFNet Operational Change Management Process.* Comply with MPTO 00-33D-2001 and populate the required Directory Services attributes. The ISSM documents service account approval in the security authorization package.

8.21.3. The ISSM ensures the Service Account passwords are changed as required and documents compliance in the security authorization package.

8.22. PKI Waivers. Technical solutions should be evaluated before pursuing a waiver. Coordinate and submit all PKI waiver requests to AFSPC CYSS/CYZ PKI (**afspc.cyss.cys.2@us.af.mil**). See DoDI 8520.02 for PKI waiver guidance.

8.22.1. If AFSPC CYSS/CYZ PKI determines that a waiver is required, the ISO submits a waiver package (Authorization to Operate [ATO], DSAWG briefing package, topology diagram, and POA&M) through the system/enclave ISSM to AFSPC CYSS/CYZ PKI (**afspc.cyss.cys.2@us.af.mil**).

8.23. PKI LRA Assessments. LRAs perform annual self assessements using the *AF LRA PKI Self Assessment Checklist* (**https://afpki.lackland.af.mil/html/lra_trg.cfm**) and submit assessment results to the RAs.

8.24. Biometric Management. Biometrics should be fully integrated to conduct the AF mission in support of joint military operations IAW DoDD 8521.01E, *DoD Biometrics.* Configure biometric programs IAW the DISA *Biometric Security Checklist for the Access Control STIG.*

8.24.1. At the discretion of the installation commander, the collection and use of biometrics may occur at any time when a person requests or requires access to systems, facilities, and networks under the responsibility of the AF or according to host nation and Status of Forces Agreement (SOFA) agreements.

8.24.1.1. When used, biometrics are collected, matched, transmitted, stored, shared, archived, and received IAW AFI 33-332.

8.24.1.2. All biometrics data and associated information collected as a result of DoD operations or activities should be maintained or controlled by the DoD, unless otherwise specified by Defense Forensics and Biometrics Agency (DFBA) for DoD Biometrics at a later date.

8.24.2. All biometrics activities are coordinated via the sponsoring AF functional organization through the DFBA at **http://www.biometrics.dod.mil/** and approved by DoD Biometrics Executive Committee (EXCOM) before acquisition.

WILLIAM J. BENDER, Lt Gen, USAF
Chief of Information Dominance and
Chief Information Officer

Attachment 1

GLOSSARY OF REFERENCES AND SUPPORTING INFORMATION

References

Title 5 United States Code (U.S.C.), § 552a, *Privacy Act,* updated December 19, 2014

Title 8 Code of Federal Regulations (CFR), *Aliens and Nationality,* January 1, 2016

Title 10, U.S.C., § 2533a, *Requirement to Buy Certain Articles from American Sources; Exceptions*, January 2, 2013

Public Law 109-364, *Title V*, Section 561, *Military Personnel Policy*, October 17, 2006

Public Law 113-283, *Federal Information Security Modernization Act of 2014,* December 18, 2014

Federal Acquisition Regulation (FAR) Subpart 25.1, *Buy American – Supplies*, *25.103 Exceptions*, June 15, 2016

Defense Federal Acquisition Regulation Supplement (DFARS) Part 225 – *Foreign Acquisition*, *Subpart 225.1, Buy American – Supplies, 225.103 Exceptions*, June 30, 2016

CNSSI No. 1300, *National Security Systems Public Key Infrastructure X.509 Certificate Policy Under CNSS Policy No. 25,* December 2014

CNSSI 4009, *Committee on National Security Systems (CNSS) Glossary*, April 6, 2015

CNSSP No. 11, *Acquisition of Information Assurance (IA) and IA-Enabled Information Technology (IT) Products*, June 10, 2013

CNSSP No. 15, *National Information Assurance Policy on the Use of Public Standards for the Secure Sharing of Information Among National Security Systems,* October 1, 2012

National Security Telecommunications and Information Systems Security Policy (NSTISSP) No. 200, *National Policy on Controlled Access Protection*, July 15, 1987

National Institute of Standards and Technology (NIST) Special Publication (SP) 800-30, Revision 1, *Guide for Risk Assessments*, September 2012

NIST SP 800-46, Revision 1, *Guide to Enterprise Telework and Remote Access Security,* June 2009

NIST SP 800-53, Revision 4, *Security and Privacy Controls for Federal Information Systems and Organizations*, April 2013; Includes updates as of January 22, 2015

NIST SP 800-53A, Revision 4, *Assessing Security and Privacy Controls in Federal Information Systems and Organizations, Building Effective Security Assessment Plans*, December 2014; Includes updates as of December 18, 2014

NIST SP 800-88 Revision 1, *Guidelines for Media Sanitization,* December, 2014

NIST Federal Information Processing Standards (FIPS) 140-2, *Security Requirements for Cryptographic Modules*, May 2001; Includes updates as of December 3, 2002

NIST FIPS 180-4, *Secure Hash Standard (SHS),* August 2015

NIST FIPS 197, *Advanced Encryption Standard (AES)*, November 2001

NSA/CSS Policy Manual 9-12, *NSA/CSS Storage Device Sanitization Manual*, December 15, 2014

NSA MIT-005FS-2014, *Mitigations for Spillage of Classified Information onto Unclassified Mobile Devices (FOUO)*, August 2014

NIAP, *Mobile Device Fundamentals Protection Profile*, June 10, 2016

Intelligence Community Directive 503, *Intelligence Community Information Technology Systems Security Risk Management, Certification and Accreditation*, September 15, 2008; *Technical Amendment*, July 21, 2015

CJCSI 6211.02, *Defense Information System Network (DISN): Policy and Responsibilities*, January 24, 2012

CJCSI 6510.01, *Information Assurance (IA) and Support to Computer Network Defense (CND)*, February 9, 2011

Joint Publication 1-02, *Department of Defense Dictionary of Military and Associated Terms*, 8 November 2010; As Amended Through February 15, 2016

National Security Systems Public Key Infrastructure, Department of Defense Registration Practice Statement, Version 8, December 19, 2014

DoD Policy Memorandum, *Mobile Code Technologies Risk Category List Update*, March 14, 2011

DoD Secure Hash Algorithm-256 Transition Plan, June 11, 2013

DoD 5200.2-R, *Personnel Security Program*, January 1987, Administrative Reissuance Incorporating Through Change 3, February 23, 1996

DoD 5220.22-M, *National Industrial Security Program Operating Manual (NISPOM)*, February 28, 2006; Incorporating Change 2, May 18, 2016

DoD 5400.11-R, *Department of Defense Privacy Program*, May 14, 2007

DoD 8570.01-M, *IA Workforce Improvement Program*, December 19, 2005; Incorporating Change 4, November 10, 2015

DoDD 5230.11, *Disclosure of Classified Military Information to Foreign Governments and International Organizations*, June 16, 1992

DoDD 5230.20, *Visits and Assignments of Foreign Nationals*, June 22, 2005

DoDD 5230.25, *Withholding of Unclassified Technical Data from Public Disclosure*, November 6, 1984; Incorporating Change 1, August 18, 1995

DoDD 5400.7, *DoD Freedom of Information Act (FOIA) Program*, January 2, 2008

DoDD 5400.11, *DoD Privacy Program*, October 29, 2014

DoDD 8100.02, *Use of Commercial Wireless Devices, Services, and Technologies in the Department of Defense (DoD) Global Information Grid (GIG)*, April 14, 2004

DoDD 8140.01, *Cyberspace Workforce Management*, August 11, 2015

DoDD 8521.01E, *DoD Biometrics,* January 13, 2016

DoDI 1035.01, *Telework Policy,* April 4, 2012

DoDI 1100.21, *Voluntary Services in the Department of Defense,* March 11, 2002; Incorporating Change 1, December 26, 2002

DoDI 4161.02, *Accountability and Management of Government Contract Property,* April 27, 2012

DoDI 6025.22, *Assistive Technology (AT) for Wounded, Ill, and Injured Service Members,* January 30, 2015

DoDI 8100.04, *DoD Unified Capabilities (UC)*, December 9, 2010

DoDI 8500.01, *Cybersecurity*, March 14, 2014

DoDI 8510.01, *Risk Management Framework (RMF) for DoD Information Technology (IT)*, March 12, 2014; Incorporating Change 1, May 24, 2016

DoDI 8520.02, *Public Key Infrastructure (PKI) and Public Key (PK) Enabling,* May 24, 2011

DoDI 8520.03, *Identity Authentication for Information Systems,* May 13, 2011

DoDM 1000.13, Volume 1, *DoD Identification (ID) Cards: ID Card Life-Cycle,* January 23, 2014

DoDM 4160.21, Volume 2, *Defense Materiel Disposition Manual: Property Disposal and Reclamation*, October 22, 2015

DoDM 4160.21, Volume 4, *Defense Materiel Disposition Manual: Instructions for Hazardous Property and Other Special Processing Materiel*, October 22, 2015

DoDM 5200.01, Volume 1, *DoD Information Security Program: Overview, Classification, and Declassification, February 24, 2012*

DoDM 5200.01, Volume 2, *DoD Information Security Program: Marking of Classified Information*, February 24, 2012; Incorporating Change 2, March 19, 2013

DoDM 5200.01, Volume 3, *DoD Information Security Program: Protection of Classified Information*, February 24, 2012; Incorporating Change 2, March 19, 2013

DoDM 5200.01, Volume 4, *DoD Information Security Program: Controlled Unclassified Information (CUI)*, February 24, 2012

United States Department of Defense X.509 Certificate Policy Version 10.5, January 23, 2013

DoD Administration Instruction (AI) 117, *Telework Program*, March 31, 2015

USCYBERCOM CTO 07-015, *Public Key Infrastructure (PKI) Implementation, Phase 2,* December 11, 2007

USCYBERCOM CTO 08-001, *Encryption of Sensitive Unclassified Data at Rest (DAR) on Mobile Computing Devices and Removable Storage Media Used Within the Department of Defense (DoD),* January 8, 2008

USCYBERCOM TASKORD J3-12-0863, FRAGO 2, FOUO Title (U), July 1, 2013

USCYBERCOM TASKORD 2015-0102, *Implementation and Reporting of DoD Public Key Infrastructure (PKI) System Administrator and Privileged User Authentication*, July 6, 2015

AFPD 17-1, *Information Dominance Governance and Management*, April 12, 2016

AFI 10-712, *Cyberspace Defense Analysis (CDA) Operations and Notice and Consent Process*, December 17, 2015

AFI 16-107, *Military Personnel Exchange Program (MPEP)*, February 2, 2006

AFI 16-201, *Air Force Foreign Disclosure and Technology Transfer Program*, June 2, 2015

AFI 16-701, *Management, Administration and Oversite of Special Access Programs*, February 18, 2014

AFI 16-1404, *Air Force Information Security Program*, May 29, 2015

AFI 17-100, *Air Force Information Technology (IT) Service Management*, September 16, 2014

AFI 17-101, *Risk Management Framework (RMF) for Air Force Information Technology*, February 2, 2017

AFI 17-130, *Air Force Cybersecurity Program Management*, August 31, 2015

AFI 17-210, *Radio Management*, May 26, 2016

AFI 31-101, *Integrated Defense*, October 8, 2009; Incorporating Change 3, February 3, 2016

AFI 31-501, *Personnel Security Program Management*, January 27, 2005; Incorporating Change 2, November 29, 2012

AFI 33-332, *Air Force Privacy and Civil Liberties Program*, January 12, 2015

AFI 33-360, *Publications and Forms Management*, December 1, 2015

AFI 33-393, *Electronic and Information Technology Accessible to Individuals with Disabilities Section 508*, April 10, 2013; Incorporating Change 2, June 3, 2016

AFI 36-816, *Civilian Telework Program*, November 13, 2013

AFI 36-3026_IP, Volume 1, *Identification Cards for Members of the Uniformed Services, Their Eligible Family Members, and Other Eligible Personnel*, June 17, 2009

AFI 63-101/20-101, *Integrated Life Cycle Management*, March 7, 2013; Incorporating Change 3, February 23, 2015

AFI 90-201, *The Air Force Inspection System*, April 21, 2015; Incorporating Change 1, February 11, 2016

AFMAN 17-1201, *User Responsibilities and Guidance for Information Systems*, June 1, 2012

AFMAN 17-1202, *Collaboration Services and Voice Systems Management*, September 6, 2012

AFMAN 17-1203, *Information Technology (IT) Asset Management (ITAM)*, March 19, 2014; Incorporating Change 1, August 28, 2014

AFMAN 17-1302, *Communications Security (COMSEC) Operations, (U//FOUO)*, September 3, 2014; Incorporating Change 1, June 4, 2015

AFMAN 17-1303, *Cybersecurity Workforce Improvement Program*, March 20, 2015; Incorporating Change 1, May 26, 2016

DoD 5400.7-R_AFMAN 33-302, *Freedom of Information Act Program,* October 21, 2010; Incorporating Through Change 3, May 16, 2016

AFMAN 33-363, *Management of Records*, March 1, 2008; Incorporating Change 2, June 9, 2016

AFSPC/A6, *AF DAA Combined Implementation Guidance for USCYBERCOM CTO 10-084 and 10-133 Memorandum*, December 16, 2013

AFSPC/A6 Memorandum, *Guidance for Manual Data Transfers Across Security Domains*, January 10, 2012

Air Force Systems Security Instruction (AFSSI) 7700, *Emission Security*, October 24, 2007; Incorporating Change 1, April 14, 2009

MPTO 00-33A-1100, *AFNet Operational Change Management Process*, December 2, 2014

MPTO 00-33A-1202, *Air Force Network Account Management*, March 18, 2014

MPTO 00-33A-1301, *Foreign National NIPRNet Access Core Services,* April 4, 2016

MPTO 00-33B-5004, *Access Control for Information Systems*, July 23, 2015

MPTO 00-33B-5006, *End Point Security for Information Systems,* December, 19, 2012

MTPO 00-33B-5008, *Remanence Security for Information Systems,* December 19, 2012

MPTO 00-33D-2001, Active *Directory Naming Conventions*, April 17, 2015

MTO 2013-077-002C, FOUO Title (U), FOUO Date (U)

MTO 2014-295-001, FOUO Title (U), FOUO Date (U)

T.O. 31S5-4-7255-8-1, *Configuration and Operations Guide for Air Force Certificate-Based Smart Card Logon / Next Generation Using Personal Identity Verification (PIV) Certificate*, August 13, 2012

T.O. 31S5-4-7256-8-1, *Configuration and Operations Guide for Air Force Certificate-Based Smart Card Logon / Next Generation Using Alternate Security Identification (ALTSECID)*, December 13, 2011

T.O. 31S5-4-7282-1, *Alternate Logon Token (ALT) Issuance Standard Operating Procedures,* August 28, 2012, Incorporating Change 2, September 11, 2015

Air Force Developer's Guide for Obtaining DoD Code Signing Certificates, August 2014

Computer/Electronic Accommodations Program, *Handbook for Providing Assistive Technology to Wounded Service Members*, Version 1.1, November 9, 2010

AFQTP 3D0X3-211RA, *Information Assurance Manager's Handbook,* March 11, 2010

Prescribed Forms

AF RA Form 2842-2, *Air Force (AF) Registration Authority (RA) Public Key Infrastructure (PKI) Non Person Entity (NPE) Acceptance and Acknowledgement of Responsibilities*

AF Form 4433, *US Air Force Unclassified Wireless Mobile Device User Agreement*

Adopted Forms

SF 312, *Nondisclosure Agreement*

SF 700, *Security Container Information Form*

DD Form 1172-2, *Application for Department of Defense (DoD) CAC Defense Enrollment Eligibility Reporting System (DEERS) Enrollment*

DD Form 2793, *Volunteer Agreement for Appropriated Fund Activities and Non-Appropriated Fund Instrumentalities*

DD Form 2875, *System Authorization Access Request (SAAR)*

DD Form 2946, *Department of Defense Telework Agreement*

DD Form 2987, *CAP Accommodation Request*

AF Form 847, *Recommendation for Change of Publication*

AF Form 4394, *Air Force User Agreement Statement-Notice and Consent Provision*

Abbreviations and Acronyms

ADLS—Advanced Distributed Learning Service

ADMIN-I—Admin Identity

ADP—Automated Data Processing

AETC—Air Education and Training Command

AES—Advanced Encryption Standard

AF—Air Force

AFI—Air Force Instruction

AFIN—Air Force Information Network

AFIS—Air Force Inspection System

AFLCMC—Air Force Life Cycle Management Center

AFMAN—Air Force Manual

AFNET—Air Force Network

AFNET-S—Air Force Network-SIPRNet

AFNIC—Air Force Network Integration Center

AFPC—Air Force Personnel Center

AFPD—Air Force Policy Directive

AFQTP—Air Force Qualification Training Package

AFRIMS—Air Force Records Information Management System

AFSC—Air Force Specialty Code

AFSPC—Air Force Space Command

AFSSI—Air Force System Security Instruction

ALT—Alternate Logon Token

AO—Authorizing Official

APL—Approved Products List

ATO—Authorization to Operate

BPA—Blanket Purchase Agreement

CA—Certificate Authority

CA—Certifying Authority

CAA—Controlled Access Areas

CAC—Common Access Card

CAP—Computer/Electronic Accommodations Program

CAVP—Cryptographic Algorithm Validation Program

CCEVS—Common Criteria Evaluation and Validation Scheme

CD—Compact Disk

CDAR—Classified Data at Rest

CE—Computing Environment

CE—Continuing Education

CFP—Communications Focal Point

CFR—Code of Federal Regulation

CIO—Chief Information Officer

CISP—Commercial Internet Service Provider

CJCS—Chairman of the Joint Chiefs of Staff

CJCSI—Chairman of the Joint Chiefs of Staff Instruction

CMC—Classified Materiel Conversion

CMD—Commercial Mobile Device

CMI—Classified Message Incident

CMVP—Cryptographic Module Validation Program

CND—Computer Network Defense

CND-SP—Computer Network Defense Service Providers

CNSSI—Committee on National Security Systems Issuances

CNSSP—Committee on National Security Systems

COCOM—Combatant Command

COMPUSEC—Computer Security

COMSEC—Communications Security

COR—Contracting Officer's Representative

CPS—Certificate Practice Statement

CRL—Certificate Revocation List

CSAA—Code Signing Attribute Authority

CSS—Central Security Service

CSS—Commanders Support Staff

CST—Client Support Technician

CTTA—Certified TEMPEST Technical Authority

CTO—Communications Tasking Order

CUI—Controlled Unclassified Information

CYSS—Cyberspace Support Squadron

DAA—Designated Accrediting Authority

DAR—Data at Rest

DCS—Defense Collaboration Services

DEE—Defense Enterprise Email

DEERS—Defense Enrollment Eligibility Reporting System

DEMAN—Demanufacture

DFARS—Defense Federal Acquisition Regulation Supplement

DFBA—Defense Forensics and Biometrics Agency

DISA—Defense Information Systems Agency

DISN—Defense Information Systems Network

DLADS—Defense Logistics Agency Disposition Services

DMCC-S—DoD Mobility Classified Capability-Secret

DMDC—Defense Manpower Data Center

DMUC—DoD Mobility Unclassified Capability

DoD—Department of Defense

DoDD—Department of Defense Directive

DoDI—Department of Defense Instruction

DoDIN—Department of Defense Information Network

DoDM—Department of Defense Manual

DRAM—Dynamic Random-Access Memory

DRU—Direct Reporting Unit

DSAWG—Defense Information Assurance Security Accreditation Working Group

DSS—Defense Security Service

DTIC—Defense Technical Information Center

DVD—Digital Versatile Disc

DVS-G—DISA Video Service-Global

EDI-PI—Electronic Data Interchange Personal Identifier

EEPROM—Electrically Erasable Programmable Read Only Memory

eMASS—Enterprise Mission Assurance Support Service

EPL—Evaluated Products List

EPROM—Erasable Programmable Read Only Memory

ESD—Enterprise Service Desk

ETIMS—Enhanced Technical Information Management System

EXCOM—Executive Committee

FAR—Federal Acquisition Regulation

FDO—Foreign Disclosure Office

FIPS—Federal Information Processing Standards

FISMA—Federal Information Security Modernization Act

FiST—File Sanitization Tool

FN/LN—Foreign National/Local National

FOA—Field Operating Agency

FOIA—Freedom of Information Act

FOUO—For Official Use Only

FPGA—Field Programmable Gate Array

FQDN—Fully Qualified Domain Name

FRAGO—Fragmentary Order

FRAM—Ferroelectric RAM

GFE—Government Furnished Equipment

GIG—Global Information Grid

GO—General Officer

GSA—General Services Administration

GSU—Geographically Separated Unit

GVS—Global Video Services

HBSS—Host Based Security System

HDD—Hard Disk Drive

HIPAA—Health Insurance Portability and Accountability Act

HQ—Headquarters

IA—Information Assurance

IACE—Information Assurance Collaborative Environment

IACE-S—Information Assurance Collaborative Environment-SIPRNet

IAM—Information Assurance Management

IAM—Information Assurance Manager

IAO—Information Assurance Officer

IASAE—Information Assurance System Architects and Engineer

IASE—Information Assurance Support Environment

IAT—Information Assurance Technical

IAW—In Accordance With

IC—Intelligence Community

ICD—Intelligence Community Directive

ID—Identification

IG—Inspector General

IP—Information Protection

IR—Infrared

IS—Information System

ISDN—Integrated Services Digital Network

ISO—Information System Owner

ISP—Internet Service Provider

ISSM—Information Systems Security Manager

ISSO—Information Systems Security Officer

IT—Information Technology

ITCC—Information Technology Commodity Council

JPAS—Joint Personnel Adjudication System

JTIC—Joint Interoperability Test Command

JWICS—Joint Worldwide Intelligence Communications System

KVM—Keyboard, Video, Monitor

LAN—Local Area Network

LRA—Local Registration Authority

MAJCOM—Major Command

MICT—Management Internal Control Toolset

MFD—Multifunction Device

MPS—Military Personnel Section

MPTO—Methods and Procedures Technical Order

MRAM—Magnetic RAM

MTF—Medical Treatment Facilities

MTO—Maintenance Tasking Order

NAF—Non-Appropriated Fund

NEA—Non-Enterprise Activated

NIAP—National Information Assurance Partnership

NIPRNet—Non-classified Internet Protocol Router Network

NISPOM—National Industrial Security Program Operating Manual

NIST—National Institute of Standards and Technology

NLT—No Later Than

NOS—Network Operations Squadron

NSA—National Security Agency

NSS—National Security Systems

NSTISSP—National Security Telecommunications and Information Systems Security Policy

OCONUS——Outside the Continental U.S.

OPR—Office of Primary Responsibility

OS—Operating System

PCA—Permanent Change of Assignment

PCC—Personnel Category Code

PCS—Permanent Change of Station

PED—Portable Electronic Device

PII—Personally Identifiable Information

PIN—Personal Identification Number

PIT—Platform Information Technology

PIV—Personal Identity Verification

PIV-I—Personal Identity Verification-Interoperable

PKE—Public Key Enablement

PKI—Public Key Infrastructure

PMA—PKI Management Authority

POA&M—Plan of Actions and Milestones

PoP—Period of Performance

RA—Registration Authority

RAM—Random Access Memory

RAPIDS—Real-time Automated Personnel Identification System

RDS—Records Disposition Schedule

REMSEC—Remanence Security

RF—Radio Frequency

RMF—Risk Management Framework

ROM—Read Only Memory

RPS—Registration Practice Statement

SAAR—System Authorization Access Request

SAC—Self-Assessment Communicator

SAF—Secretary of the Air Force

SCI—Sensitive Compartmented Information

SCL—Smart Card Logon

SES—Senior Executive Service

SF—Standard Form

SHA—Secure Hash Algorithm

SHS—Secure Hash Standard

SII—Special Interest Item

SIPRNet—Secret Internet Protocol Router Network

SLA—Service Level Agreement

SME PED—Secure Mobile Environment PED

SOFA—Status of Forces Agreement

SPO—System Program Office

SP—Special Publication

SRAM—Static Random Access Memory

SRG—Security Requirements Guide

SSD—Solid State Drive

SSL—Secure Sockets Layer

SSP—System Security Plan

STIG—Security Technical Implementation Guide

TA—Trusted Agent

TASKORD—Tasking Order

TASS—Trusted Associate Sponsorship System

TDY—Temporary Duty

TLS—Transport Layer Security

TMS—Token Management System

TO—Technical Order

TODA—Technical Order Distribution Account

UC—Unified Capabilities

USB—Universal Serial Bus

U.S.C—United States Code

USCYBERCOM—United States Cyber Command

UCCO—Unified Capabilities Certification Office

US—United States

UVEPROM—Ultra-Violet EPROM

VAR—Visit Authorization Request

VoIP—Voice over Internet Protocol

VoLAC—Volunteer Logical Access Credential

VVoIP—Voice and Video over Internet Protocol

VPN—Virtual Private Network

VTC—Video Teleconferencing

WCO—Wing Cybersecurity Office

WTO GPA—World Trade Organization Government Procurement Agreement

Terms

Air Force Information Network (AFIN)—AF provisioned portion of the DoDIN.

Alternate Logon Token (ALT)—A portable, user-controlled, physical device used to generate, store, and protect cryptographic information, and to perform cryptographic functions. (DoDI 8520.02)

Assistive Technology (AT)—AT refers to a service or device that is used to increase, maintain, or improve functional capabilities of individuals with disabilities. AT solutions may include compact keyboards, breath-controlled keyboard/mouse devices, alternative pointing devices, assistive listening devices (wired, FM, and Bluetooth), video phones, screen reader software, screen magnification software, voice recognition software, etc.

Authorized User—Any appropriately cleared individual with a requirement to access a DoD information system in order to perform or assist in a lawful and authorized governmental function. Authorized users include DoD employees, contractors, and guest researchers. (DoD 8570.01-M).

Biometrics—Measurable physical characteristics or personal behavioral traits used to identify, or verify the claimed identity, of an individual. Facial images, fingerprints, and handwriting samples are all examples of biometrics. (CNSSI 4009 and DoDD 8521.01)

Certification Authority (CA)—An entity authorized to create, sign, and issue public key certificates. (CNSSI No. 1300)

Certification Authority System (CAS)—The collection of hardware, software, and operating personnel that create, sign, and issue public key certificates to subscribers. (CNSSI No. 1300)

Classified Message Incident (CMI)—A higher classification level of data is transferred to a lower classification level system/device via messaging systems, e.g., email, instant messaging, etc. (AFI 16-1404)

Classified Information Spillage—Security incident that occurs whenever classified data is spilled either onto an unclassified IS or to an IS with a lower level of classification. (CNSSI 4009)

Collaborative Computing—Applications and technology (e.g., white boarding, group conferencing) that allow two or more individuals to share information real time in an inter- or intra-enterprise environment. (CNSSI 4009)

Common Criteria—Governing document that provides a comprehensive, rigorous method for specifying security function and assurance requirements for products and systems. (CNSSI 4009)

Commercial Mobile Device (CMD)—A subset of PED as defined in DoDD 8100.02 that provide one or more commercial wireless interfaces along with a compact user input interface (Touch Screen, Miniature Keyboard, etc.) and exclude PEDs running a multi-user operating system (Windows OS, Mac OS, etc.). This definition includes, but is not limited to smart phones, tablets, and e-readers.

Computer Security—Measures and controls that ensure confidentiality, integrity, and availability of information system assets including hardware, software, firmware, and information being processed, stored, and communicated. (CNSSI 4009)

Countermeasures—Actions, devices, procedures, or techniques that meet or oppose(i.e., counters) a threat, a vulnerability, or an attack by eliminating or preventing it, by minimizing the harm it can cause, or by discovering and reporting it so that corrective action can be taken. (CNSSI 4009)

Cybersecurity—Prevention of damage to, protection of, and restoration of computers, electronic communications systems, electronic communications services, wire communication, and electronic communication, including information contained therein, to ensure its availability, integrity, authentication, confidentiality, and nonrepudiation. (DoDI 8500.01)

Cybersecurity Workforce—Personnel who secure, defend, and preserve data, networks, net-centric capabilities, and other designated systems by ensuring appropriate security controls and measures are in place, and taking internal defense actions. This includes access to system controls, monitoring, administration, and integration of cybersecurity into all aspects of engineering and acquisition of cyberspace capabilities. (DoDD 8140.01).

Data Spillage—Security incident that results in the transfer of classified or CUI information onto an information system not accredited (i.e., authorized) for the appropriate security level. (CNSSI 4009)

Declassification—An administrative decision/action, based on a consideration of risk by the owner, whereby the classification of a properly sanitized storage device is downgraded to UNCLASSIFIED. (NSA Policy Manual 9-12)

Degaussing (or Demagnetizing)—Process for reducing the magnetization of a storage

device to zero by applying a reverse (coercive) magnetizing force, rendering any previously stored data unreadable and unintelligible, and ensuring that it cannot be recovered by any technology known to exist. (NSA Policy Manual 9-12)

Destroy—A method of Sanitization that renders Target Data recovery infeasible using state of the art laboratory techniques and results in the subsequent inability to use the media for storage of data. (NIST SP 800-88)

Department of Defense Information Network (DoDIN)—The set of information capabilities, and associated processes for collecting, processing, storing, disseminating, and managing information on-demand to warfighters, policy makers, and support personnel, whether interconnected or standalone, including owned and leased communications and computing systems and services, software (including applications), data, security services, other associated services, and national security systems. Formerly known as the Global Information Grid (GIG). (JP1-02)

Flash Media—Devices or products that maintain stored data without any external power source. Data can be electro-magnetically written, erased, and/or reprogrammed. General storage and example devices used for data transfers between ISs and other digital products are items such as memory cards, USB flash drives, and solid-state drives. (CNSS 4009)

Foreign Disclosure Office (FDO)—A U.S. Government official designated in writing whose primary responsibilities are to authorize disclosure of classified military information or CUI and manage and implement a disclosure program for their command or organization. (AFI 16-201)

Foreign National (FN)—Any person other than a U.S. citizen, U.S. permanent or temporary legal resident alien, or person in U.S. custody. (JP 1-02)**High Impact Personally Identifiable**

Information (PII)—Any Defense-wide, organizational (e.g., unit or office), program or project level compilation of electronic records containing PII on 500 or more individuals stored on a single device or accessible through a single application or service, whether or not the compilation is subject to the Privacy Act. Any compilation of electronic records containing PII on less than 500 individuals identified by the Information or Data Owner as requiring additional protection measures. Examples: A single mobile computing or storage device containing PII on 500 or more individuals, even if the PII is distributed across multiple files or directories, is considered High Impact PII. A DoD enclave of 500 or more users, with the PII for each user embedded in his/her individual workstation, is not considered High Impact PII. (DoD Memorandum, *Department of Defense (DoD) Guidance on Protecting Personally Identifiable Information (PII)*)

IA-Enabled Product—Product whose primary role is not security, but provides security services as an associated feature of its intended operating capabilities. **Note:** Examples include such products as security-enabled web browsers, screening routers, trusted operating systems, and security enabling messaging systems. (CNSSI 4009)

IT Position Category—Applicable to unclassified DoD ISs, a designator that indicates the level of IT access required to execute the responsibilities of the position. It is based on the potential for an individual assigned to the position to adversely impact DoD missions or functions. IT Position categories include: IT-I (Privileged), IT-II (Limited Privileged) and IT-III (Non-Privileged), as outlined in DoD 5200.2-R, Appendix 10. Investigative requirements for each category vary, depending on role and whether the incumbent is a U.S. military member, U.S. civilian government employee, U.S. civilian contractor, or a foreign national, as outlined in DoD 5200.2-R in **Chapter 3.**

Note:—The term IT Position is synonymous with the older term Automated Data Processing (ADP) Position outlined in DoD 5200.2-R. (DoD 5200.2-R)

Least Privilege—The principle that a security architecture should be designed so that each entity is granted the minimum system resources and authorizations that the entity needs to perform its function. (CNSSI 4009)

Management Internal Control Toolset (MICT)—the AF program of record to communicate a unit's current status of SAC, HAF Self-Assessment Communicator Fragmentary Order (SAC FRAGO) and Special Interest Item (SII) compliance. (AFI 90-201)

Moderate Impact PII—Any electronic records containing PII not identified as High Impact (DoD Memorandum, *Department of Defense [DoD] Guidance on Protecting Personally Identifiable Information (PII)*).

Mobile Code—Software programs or parts of programs obtained from remote ISs, transmitted across a network, and executed on a local information system without explicit installation or execution by the recipient. **Note:** Some examples of software technologies that provide the mechanisms for the production and use of mobile code include Java, JavaScript, ActiveX, VBScript, etc. (CNSSI 4009)

Non-Enterprise Activated (NEA) CMD—A non-enterprise activated (NEA) device is any DoD mobile handheld device that is not connected at any time to a DoD network or enterprise, and does not process sensitive or classified DoD data or voice communications. Sensitive data or information is defined as any DoD data or information that has not been deemed as publicly releasable by a DoD Public Affairs Officer. (Mobile Policy SRG Overview)

Nonrepudiation—Assurance that the sender of information is provided with proof of delivery and the recipient is provided with proof of the sender's identity, so neither can later deny having processed the information. (CNSSI 4009)

Protection against an individual falsely denying having performed a particular action. Provides the capability to determine whether a given individual took a particular action such as creating information, sending a message, approving information, and receiving a message. (NIST 800-53)

Overwriting—The process of writing data on top of the physical location of data stored on the media. (NIST SP 800-88)

Periods Processing—The processing of various levels of classified and unclassified information at distinctly different times. Under the concept of periods processing, the system must be purged of all information from one processing period before transitioning to the next. (CNSSI 4009)

Privileged User—A user that is authorized (and, therefore, trusted) to perform security-relevant functions that ordinary users are not authorized to perform. (CNSSI 4009)

Have the same requirements as an authorized user, but have additional permissions to configure IA-enabled software products and systems. These uses must hold baseline commercial certifications IAW DoD 8570.01-M and be placed in unit manning documented positions that require privileged access. (DoDI 8500.01)

Public Key Enable—The incorporation of the use of certificates for people, networks, systems and applications to provide security services such as strong identification, authentication, confidentiality, data integrity, and non-repudiation. (DoDI 8500.01, DoDI 8520.02, and DoDI 8520.03).

Public Key Infrastructure (PKI)—The framework and services that provide for the generation, production, distribution, control, accounting, and destruction of public key certificates. Components include the personnel, policies, processes, server platforms, software, and workstations used for the purpose of administering certificates and public-private key pairs, including the ability to issue, maintain, recover, and revoke public key certificates. (CNSSI 4009)

Registration Authority (RA)—An entity (hardware, software, and individual) authorized by the (Certification Authority System) CAS to collect, verify, and submit information provided by potential subscribers that is to be entered into public key certificates. (CNSSI No. 1300)

Registration Practice Statement (RPS)—A document representing a statement of practices a RA employs when performing RA duties for a CAS. (CNSSI No. 1300)

Remanence—Residual information remaining on data media after clearing. (CNSSI 4009)

Removable Media—Portable electronic storage media such as magnetic, optical, and solid state devices, which can be inserted into and removed from a computing device for the purpose of storing text, video, audio, and image information. Such devices lack independent processing capabilities. Examples include hard disks, floppy disks, zip drives, compact disks (CD), thumb drives, pen drives, and similar USB storage devices. (CNSSI 4009)

Sanitization—The removal of information from the storage device such that data recovery using any known technique or analysis is prevented. Sanitization includes the removal of data from the storage device, as well as the removal of all labels, markings, and activity logs. The method of sanitization varies depending upon the storage device in question, and may include degaussing, incineration, shredding, grinding, embossing, etc. (NSA Policy Manual 9-12)

Sanitize—A process to render access to Target Data on the media infeasible for a given level of effort. Clear, Purge, and Destroy are actions that can be taken to sanitize media. (NIST SP 800-88)

Self-Assessment Communicator (SAC)—A SAC is a two-way communication tool designed to improve compliance with published guidance and communicate risk and program health up and down the chain of command in near real-time. Compliance with a SAC does not relieve individual Airmen from complying with all statutory and regulatory requirements in AFIs and directives at the local, state, or federal level. (AFI 90-201)

Sensitive Information—Information that the loss, misuse, or unauthorized access to or modification of could adversely affect the national interest or the conduct of federal programs, or the privacy to which individuals are entitled under *Title 5 U.S.C.* Section 552a (Privacy Act), but that has not been specifically authorized under criteria established by an Executive Order or an act of Congress to be kept secret in the interest of national defense or foreign policy. **Note:** Systems that are not national security systems, but contain sensitive information are subject to be protected IAW the requirements of the Computer Security Act of 1987 (Public Law 100-235). (CNSSI 4009)

Sensitivity Level—Sensitivity levels relate the relative importance of information residing in a system or on a network to the potential impact that could be caused by unauthorized access or modification of that information. There are four sensitivity levels for unclassified information and three sensitivity levels for classified as Secret or Confidential. (DoDI 8520.03)

Telehealth Monitoring Devices—Electronic monitoring devices (pacemakers, implanted medical devices, personal life support systems, etc.)

Two-Factor Authentication—A method of authenticating a user's identity using a combination of something the user has (private key) and something the user knows (PIN). (NIST Interagency Report 7849)

Vulnerability—Weakness in an information system, system security procedures, internal controls, or implementation that could be exploited by a threat source. (CNSSI 4009).

BY ORDER OF THE SECRETARY
OF THE AIR FORCE

AIR FORCE INSTRUCTION 17-203

16 MARCH 2017

Operations

CYBER INCIDENT HANDLING

COMPLIANCE WITH THIS PUBLICATION IS MANDATORY

ACCESSIBILITY: Publications and forms are available for downloading or ordering on the e-Publishing website at **www.e-Publishing.af.mil**

RELEASABILITY: There are no releasability restrictions on this publication

---

OPR: SAF/CIO A3CW

Certified by: SAF/CIO A3C/A6C
(Brig Gen Kevin B. Kennedy)
Pages: 28

This instruction implements Air Force Policy Directive (AFPD) 17-2, *Cyberspace Operations*. It describes and provides broad guidance for implementing the Air Force (AF) and Department of Defense (DoD) Cyber Incident Handling Program, the major processes that take place within that program, and the interactions with related U.S. government Defensive Cyberspace Operations (DCO) and DoD Information Networks (DoDIN) Operations activities. It applies to all military and civilian AF personnel, members of the AF Reserve, Air National Guard, DoD contractors, and individuals or activities under legal agreements or obligations with the Department of the AF. Refer recommended changes and questions about this publication to the Office of Primary Responsibility (OPR) using the AF Form 847, *Recommendation for Change of Publication*; route AF Form 847s from the field through Major Command (MAJCOM) publications/forms managers to HQ USAF/A6S. The authorities to waive wing/unit level requirements in this publication are identified with a Tier ("T-0, T-1, T-2, T-3") number following the compliance statement. See AFI 33-360, *Publications and Forms Management*, Table 1.1 for a description of the authorities associated with the Tier numbers. Submit requests for waivers as directed in the appropriate paragraphs of this Instruction. Ensure that all records created as a result of processes prescribed in this publication are maintained in accordance with AF Manual (AFMAN) 33-363, *Management of Records*, and disposed of in accordance with the Air Force Records Disposition Schedule (RDS) located in the AF Records Information Management System (AFRIMS).

Chapter 1

INTRODUCTION

1.1. Introduction. The AF relies on networked electronic systems to plan and execute its full range of missions around the world. While these systems help us to maintain our military dominance, they also provide our adversaries a means by which to gain an asymmetric advantage via network attack and/or the exploitation of networked systems. AF networks are probed and scanned by domestic and foreign sources thousands of times each day. To counter, negate and mitigate unauthorized activity on its networks, the AF and DoD conduct a wide range of actions collectively known as DCO.

1.1.1. DCO are passive and active cyberspace operations intended to preserve the ability to utilize friendly cyberspace capabilities and protect data, networks, and net-centric capabilities.

1.1.2. This Instruction provides guidance on AF DCO and the conduct of network incident handling. For the purposes of this instruction, DCO and DoDIN Operations refer to day-to-day network monitoring, analysis, detection, and response. They do not refer to missions/actions associated with deliberate mission planning for named defensive operations.

1.1.3. This Instruction also applies to incidents involving systems which are not directly connected to or part of an AF network, e.g., supervisory control and data acquisition (SCADA) systems or information systems that are an integral part of a weapon system and may connect to the DoDIN indirectly through the use of removable media or a wireless connection.

1.1.4. This Instruction does not apply to AF Intelligence Community (IC) and Intelligence, Surveillance, and Reconnaissance systems, networks and assets. These assets fall under the purview of Office of the Director for National Intelligence (ODNI) and HQ USAF/A2.

1.2. Applicability. CJCSM 6510.01B, *Cyber Incident Handling Program*, breaks down adverse actions that occur on DoD networks into ten categories (see Table 1.1). The terms "event" and "incident" are also used to further categorize the actions and to help prioritize the counteractions necessary to detect and prevent future adversary activity of that type.

1.2.1. Event. Committee on National Security Systems (CNSS) Instruction 4009 defines an "event" as any observable occurrence in a system and/or network. Events sometimes provide indication that an incident is occurring. Occurrences determined to be Category (CAT) 0, 3, 5, 6, 8, and 9 activity are referred to as events.

1.2.2. Incident. CNSS Instruction 4009 defines an "incident" as an assessed occurrence that actually or potentially jeopardizes the confidentiality, integrity, or availability of an information system (IS); or the information the system processes, stores, or transmits; or that constitutes a violation or imminent threat of violation of security policies, security procedures, or acceptable use policies. For purposes of this AFI, "information system" includes weapon systems and platform information technology (IT). Occurrences assessed to be CAT 1, 2, 4, and 7 are called incidents. Do not confuse the term "incident" as used in this Instruction with the alternative use of the term to describe network maintenance types of occurrences (i.e., an "incident" consisting of a customer not being able to access email because his/her account was incorrectly configured by a system administrator).

1.2.3. Incidents Involving Breaches of Personally Identifiable Information (PII). In addition to the procedures specified in this Instruction, incidents which may involve the compromise of PII will also be reported according to the guidelines in paragraph 1.1.2.4 of AFI 33-332, *The Air Force Privacy and Civil Liberties Program*, and Appendix A, Table 1, of Office of the Secretary of Defense (OSD) Memorandum OSD 06227-09, *Safeguarding Against and Responding to the Breach of Personally Identifiable Information.* **(T-0)**

Table 1.1. Categories of Events (0, 3, 5, 6, 8, and 9) and Incidents (1, 2, 4, and 7).

Category	Description
0	Training and Exercises (Event): Operations performed for training purposes and support to Combatant Command/Service/Agency/Field Activity (CC/S/A/FA) exercises.
1	Root-Level Intrusion (Incident): Privileged access, often referred to as administrative or root access, provides unrestricted access to an IS. This category includes unauthorized access to information or unauthorized access to account credentials that could be used to perform administrative functions (e.g., domain administrator). If the IS is compromised with malicious code that provides remote interactive control, it will be reported in this category.
2	User-Level Intrusion (Incident): Unauthorized non-privileged access to an IS. Non-privileged access, often referred to as user-level access, provides restricted access to the IS based on the privileges granted to the user. This includes unauthorized access to information or unauthorized access to account credentials that could be used to perform user functions such as accessing Web applications, Web portals, or other similar information resources. If the IS is compromised with malicious code that provides remote interactive control, it will be reported in this category.
3	Unsuccessful Activity Attempt (Event): Deliberate attempts to gain unauthorized access to an IS that are defeated by normal defensive mechanisms. Attacker fails to gain access to the IS (i.e., attacker attempts valid or potentially valid username and password combinations) and the activity cannot be characterized as exploratory scanning. Note the above CAT 3 explanation does not cover the "run-of-the-mill" virus that is defeated/deleted by AV software. "Run-of-the-mill" viruses that are defeated/deleted by AV software are not reportable events or incidents and should not be annotated in the Joint Information Management System (JIMS).
4	Denial of Service (Incident): Activity that denies, degrades, or disrupts normal functionality of an IS or DoD information network.

5	Non-Compliance Activity (Event): Activity that potentially exposes ISs or networks to increased risk as a result of the action or inaction of authorized users. This includes administrative and user actions such as failure to apply security patches, connections across security domains, installation of vulnerable applications, and other breaches of existing AF or DoD policy.
6	Reconnaissance (Event): Activity that seeks to gather information used to characterize ISs, applications, DoD information networks, and users that may be useful in formulating an attack. This includes activity such as mapping DoD information networks, IS devices and applications, interconnectivity, and their users or reporting structure. This activity does not directly result in a compromise.
7	Malicious Logic (Incident): Installation of software designed and/or deployed by adversaries with malicious intentions for the purpose of gaining access to resources or information without the consent or knowledge of the user. This only includes malicious code that does not provide remote interactive control of the compromised IS. Malicious code that has allowed interactive access should be categorized as Category 1 or Category 2 incidents, not Category 7. Interactive active access may include automated tools that establish an open channel of communications to and/or from an IS. Unless otherwise directed, only those computers that were infected will be reported as a Category 7 incident.
8	Investigating (Event): Events that are potentially malicious or anomalous activity deemed suspicious and warrant, or are undergoing, further review. No event will be closed out as a Category 8. Category 8 will be re-categorized to appropriate Category 1-7 or 9 prior to closure.
9	Explained Anomaly (Event): Suspicious events that, after further investigation, are determined to be non-malicious activity and do not fit the criteria for any other categories. This includes events such as system malfunctions and false alarms. When reporting these events, clearly specify the reason for which it cannot be otherwise categorized.

1.3. DoD DCO and DoDIN Operations Operational Hierarchy. DoD has a three-tiered structure to conduct DCO and DoDIN Operations. NOTE: Do not confuse this with the tier hierarchy used for IT incident management (i.e., network trouble tickets), in which tiers I through III are used with lower numbers corresponding to lower echelons.

1.3.1. Tier One provides DoD-wide DCO and DoDIN Operations operational direction and support to all Combatant Commanders, Services and Agencies (C/S/As). Tier One entities include US Strategic Command (USSTRATCOM) and the US Cyber Command (USCYBERCOM).

1.3.2. Tier Two provides C/S/As DCO and DoDIN Operations direction and support and responds to direction from Tier One. Tier Two includes 24th AF (AFCYBER) with the 624

Operations Center (624 OC) acting as its operational command and control (C2) arm, operating the Cyberspace Command and Control Mission System (C3MS) and providing AF-level command and control (C2) of DCO and DoDIN Operations. It also includes units which operate the Air Force Cyberspace Defense (ACD) weapon system to provide the 624 OC and AF units with incident handling, computer/network forensics analysis, and countermeasures development support. It also includes the 26th Network Operations Squadron (NOS), which operates the AF Intranet Control weapon system and provides support to DCO and DoDIN Operations. Finally, Tier Two also includes assets of 25th Air Force (25AF) (ACC) that provide the ACD weapon system and 624 OC with computer/network foreign threat analysis.

1.3.3. Tier Three provides operational direction and support to local DCO and DoDIN Operations and responds to direction from a designated Tier Two entity. Tier Three includes regionally-focused organizations such as the Network Operations Squadrons (NOS), the MAJCOM Communications Coordination Centers (MCCC)/AFFOR Communications Control Center (ACCC), and local elements such as the base-level Communications Focal Points (CFPs). For purposes of this Instruction, the term MCCC also includes organizational structures established at the discretion of a MAJCOM which perform the same functions as an MCCC.

1.4. Air Force Office of Special Investigations (AFOSI) and other Law Enforcement & Counterintelligence (LE/CI) Agencies. These organizations are not organized within the "tiered" structure. However, they support and operate throughout all tiers. As an LE/CI agency, AFOSI is a critical contributor to effective DCO and DoDIN Operations by providing cyber threat indicators and warnings to commanders; AFOSI establishes and enables attribution and is charged with investigating intrusions and other illegal activity impacting AF information systems and networks. AFOSI's authorities offer access to the civilian/commercial sector not otherwise available to the USAF.

1.5. Other Partners. Other important partners include the Intelligence Community, defense industrial base, and the commercial sector (e.g., anti-virus vendors). These groups have access to resources that can augment and enhance DCO, DoDIN Operations, and incident handling, analysis, and response capabilities.

Chapter 2

ROLES AND RESPONSIBILITIES

2.1. Directorate of Cyberspace Strategy and Policy (S AF/CIO A6S). Serves as the OPR for Headquarters Air Force development and coordination of policies and guidelines for cyber incident handling.

2.2. Directorate of Security, Special Access Program Oversight and Information Protection (SAF/AAZ).

2.2.1. In coordination with AF/A3, SAF/A6 and SAF/AQ, recommends security protection of new projects/capabilities in accordance with established classification guidance and Department of Defense Instruction (DoDI) O-3600.02, Information Operation (IO) Security Classification Guidance.

2.2.2. Is designated Computer Network Defense Service Provider (CNDSP) Certification Authority (CA) for Special Access Program (SAP) networks and is responsible for coordinating and directing SAP enclave-wide CNDSP activities.

2.3. The AF Inspector General (SAF/IG). SAF/IG provides administrative guidance and oversight to the AFOSI, and provides Executive Agent oversight for the Defense Cyber Crime Center (DC3) as delegated by the SecAF in accordance with DoDD 5505.13e, *DOD Executive Agent (EA) for the Defense Cyber Crime Center (DC3).*

2.3.1. AFOSI is a Federal Law Enforcement (LE) agency and a member of the Intelligence Community (IC) as executor of the AF's counterintelligence (CI) mission. The AFOSI:

2.3.1.1. Is the sole AF entity with responsibility for conducting felony criminal investigations and counterintelligence activities in and through cyberspace. It is also the sole AF agency responsible for conducting liaison with federal, state, local and foreign nation law enforcement, counterintelligence, and security agencies for matters falling within the AFOSI mission.

2.3.1.2. Provides releasable LE/CI information, threat analysis and indications and warnings (I&W) support to the 624 OC and larger AF DCO and DoDIN Operations community when appropriate.

2.3.1.3. Counters cyber threats by enabling criminal prosecution or conducting counterintelligence activities.

2.3.2. The Defense Cyber Crime Center (DC3). DC3 provides support in intrusion forensics, cyber training for incident response, cyber investigations, digital forensics, and cyber analysis via its Defense Computer Forensics Laboratory and Defense Cyber Investigations Training Academy as well as capabilities in cyber analytics via the DC3 Analytical Group and DoD Defense Industrial Base Collaborative Information Sharing Environment.

2.4. Other Air Staff Offices. Coordinate with SAF/A6S on development of all cyberspace operations-related policy and guidance.

2.5. MAJCOMs, Numbered Air Forces (NAFs), Field Operating Agencies (FOAs) and Direct Reporting Units (DRUs).

2.5.1. **Air Force Space Command (AFSPC).** AFSPC is the lead command for Cyberspace Operations with responsibilities as outlined in AFPD 10-9, Lead Command Designation and Responsibilities For Weapon Systems. In accordance with AFI 17-201, Command and Control for Cyberspace Operations, the Commander, AF Space Command (AFSPC/CC) is responsible for the overall command and control, security and defense of the AF Information Network (AFIN), and for the command, control, implementation, security, operation, maintenance, sustainment, configuration, and defense of the AF Network (AFNET)/AF Network-Secure (AFNET-S). These day-to-day authorities may be delegated.

2.5.1.1. 24 AF / AFCYBER. AFCYBER is the Air Force component to USCYBERCOM. 24 AF/CC, when acting as AFCYBER/CC or when executing missions delegated by AFSPC/CC:

2.5.1.1.1. Issues cyber orders to subordinate 24 AF wings, MAJCOMs, wings, NOSs, and CFPs via the 624 OC and/or the AFSPC Command Center as needed for response to cyber incidents.

2.5.1.1.2. Exercises specific compliance enforcement and directive authority to task the NOSs in response to network events that involve multiple MAJCOMs, affect the preponderance of the AF network, or are time-critical to assure network availability and security. This authority extends to all systems and applications that expose AF networks to a vulnerability or impact operations.

2.5.1.1.3. Provides the Intelligence Community with requirements for priority intelligence and I&W of potential attacks against AF information systems and computer networks.

2.5.1.1.4. Establishes requirements and direction for AF Attack, Sensing and Warning under responsibilities for the National Security Incident Program.

2.5.1.1.5. Engages with the owners of functional systems that are employed and in-use on the AF network, and with appropriate Authorizing Officials (AOs) and their staffs, to ensure that information needed for management of incidents involving those systems is disseminated to levels were it is required to enable appropriate action.

2.5.1.1.6. In his/her role as AF component commander (AFCYBER/CC) to USCYBERCOM, 24 AF/CC ensures AF forces perform the mission and tasks assigned by USCYBERCOM to include the reporting and coordination of network events and incidents.

2.5.1.1.7. 24 AF is designated as the AF CNDSP for AF General Services (GENSER) on NIPRNet and SIPRNet. In this role, 24 AF:

2.5.1.1.7.1. Coordinates and directs AF-wide CNDSP activities in accordance with DoDD O-8530.1, Computer Network Defense (CND).

2.5.1.1.7.2. Supports USCYBERCOM in Mission Analysis development.

2.5.1.1.7.3. Provides functional expertise in Mission Analysis, leveraging established doctrine, tactics, techniques and procedures.

2.5.1.1.7.4. Develops and implements procedures to coordinate with NOSs, MCCCs/ACCCs (if applicable), CFPs and other AF organizations to collect timely and accurate information and to ensure effective C2 of executed COAs.

2.5.1.1.7.5. Notifies MCCCs and NOSs of cyber incidents occurring in their respective AORs to facilitate mission impact analysis. NOSs will coordinate through the 624 OC with 24 AF, if necessary, to determine if additional protections are required to prevent future similar incidents.

2.5.1.1.8. 24 AF operates the appropriate key weapon systems and associated infrastructure to support cyber incident handling. Air Force Cyber Defense (ACD) performs continuous operations to prevent, detect and respond to intrusions and attacks against Air Force networks.

2.5.2. **Air Combat Command (ACC).** AF intelligence, surveillance, and reconnaissance (ISR) assets belonging to 25th AF (ACC) provide foreign cyber threat Indications and Warnings (I&W), Attack Sensing & Warning (AS&W), in-depth entity profiling, in-depth incident analysis, and detailed sensor data analysis of foreign threats to AF computers for the ACD weapon system and 624 OC. This information is reported in a Network Intelligence Report (NIR), threat tipper, or AS&W advisory.

2.5.3. **I-NOSCs.** The I-NOSC is one of three functions provided by the Cyberspace Security and Control System (CSCS). There are three I-NOSCs: they are operated by the 83d Network Operations Squadron (83 NOS), the 561st Network Operations Squadron (561 NOS), and the Air National Guard's 299th Network Operations Security Squadron (299 NOSS). In support of DCO operations, I-NOSCs provide commanders real-time situational awareness of the network within their area of responsibility. The I-NOSCs:

2.5.3.1. Coordinate with and inform MCCCs/ACCCs (if applicable) and CFPs under their purview in response to DCO events that cross their area of responsibility. Accomplish tasking using the most expeditious means available (voice, electrical message, ACT, etc.), and direct organizations to report completion of required actions.

2.5.3.2. Report suspected/confirmed events to the ACD units in accordance with standing rules of engagement.

2.5.3.3. Coordinate with and inform the 624 OC, MCCC, CFP, and appropriate weapon system units on all corrective actions associated with the investigation and mitigation of events and incidents.

2.5.4. **MCCCs.** MCCCs, or similar structures established at the discretion of the MAJCOM, provide network situational awareness to MAJCOM/CCs and manage MAJCOM-unique systems and applications. MCCCs:

2.5.4.1. Coordinate with the functional communities within their area of responsibility to maintain a situational awareness picture of all MAJCOM-unique systems and applications on AF networks.

2.5.4.2. Coordinate DCO and DoDIN Operations COA planning and execution with the appropriate I-NOSC, the 624 OC and applicable 24 AF-designated units as appropriate. Provide operational impact data to assist efforts to investigate and mitigate events and incidents involving systems within their area of responsibility.

2.5.5. **CFPs/Communications Squadrons.** CFPs, and those Communication Squadrons at locations without a servicing CFP, provide an on-site technical capability to implement physical and logical network changes, modifications, and restoration of faulty network transmission equipment and circuits. CFPs implement Cyber Tasking Orders (CTOs) and messages received from the 624 OC and/or the AFSPC Command Center. CFPs:

2.5.5.1. Execute the operational direction of the 624 OC and CSCS units for DCO and DoDIN Operations COA development and execution. Coordinate with and inform the lead C3MS unit, MCCC/ACCC (if applicable), and other tasked/participating units on all corrective actions associated with the investigating and mitigation of events and incidents.

2.5.5.2. Provide the servicing ACCC/MCCC (if applicable), CSCS units, ACD units, and 624 OC all necessary information and data (i.e., system and anti-virus logs) requested to assist with incident/event investigations within the timelines specified. If unable to provide the necessary information/data or meet the specified timelines due to technical limitations or other factors, provide a detailed explanation (along with a get well date, if applicable) to the 624 OC, CSCS units, ACD units, other tasked/participating units, and ACCC/MCCC (if applicable), for tracking, COA modification, and trending purposes.

Chapter 3

INCIDENT HANDLING

3.1. General. Units operating the ACD and AFINC weapon systems monitor and record suspicious and unauthorized network and information systems access and activity on AF networks. Suspicious activity may include network scanning, multiple connection attempts to a network device from an unknown entity, or other reportable activity detected at any level. Intrusion activity may include the presence of unusual or excessive activity on the network, or unauthorized individuals gaining full (root) or limited (user) access to a network device or information system. Report data spillages and classified message incidents as a security incident in accordance with AFI 16-1404, *Air Force Information Security Program.*

3.2. Incident Handling Process and Life Cycle. The basic process for cyber incident handling consists of six phases:

3.2.1. Detection and reporting of events.

3.2.2. Preliminary analysis and identification.

3.2.3. Preliminary response actions.

3.2.4. Incident analysis.

3.2.5. Response and recovery.

3.2.6. Post-incident analysis.

3.3. Detection and Reporting of Events. The AF detects activity through a variety of means and capabilities. These range from detection via weapon systems utilizing network intrusion detection/prevention sensors to local personnel identifying questionable activity via Enterprise Information Technology Service Management (EITSM) records, trend analysis, or problem management investigations. Depending upon the identifying source and method used to detect the activity, all affected parties and tasked units gather/report preliminary information and coordinate reporting and response actions among themselves and with other organizations as appropriate.

3.3.1. **Objectives.**

3.3.2.1. Ensure all suspicious activity is detected and reported so that further analysis can take place to determine if it is a reportable event or incident.

3.3.2.2. Ensure suspicious activity is reported in a timely manner consistent with required reporting timelines. Reporting accurate incident information as close to near-real-time as possible is crucial to an effective response. If the incident meets OPREP-3 criteria, report the operational impact in accordance with AFI 10-206, Operational Reporting, Chapter 3.

3.3.2.3. Coordinate with command channels, DoD organizations, and assigned Authorizing Officials (AO) or their staffs as required.

3.4. Preliminary Analysis and Identification. Upon detection of a possible event by internal or external sources, the 624 OC and ACD units will initiate notification procedures in accordance with AFI 10-206, CJCSM 6510.01B, and established Standard Operating Procedures

(SOPs) of the affected units **(T-2)**. Notification messages must be properly classified (see paragraph 3.4.4.3 below) **(T-2)**.

3.4.1. Refer to paragraph 4 for guidance on identifying exercise incidents/events reported, and the processes for de-conflicting real world and exercise activities.

3.4.2. In cases when the cause/intent of a possible event is not readily apparent, initially categorize detected activity as a CAT 8 investigation. During this time, the ACD unit coordinates with the 624 OC, and other participating units, as applicable, to gather additional information to assist in the investigation. Information typically requested during the course of an investigation includes: data showing the true source of system affected by the activity, anti-virus and system log data, and initial forensics data obtained either remotely or locally by using appropriate forensics tools as directed. The ACD unit may also request the victim system's hard drive for an in-depth forensic analysis.

3.4.2.1. As the investigation of an event progresses and additional information is obtained, the assigned category may be changed to reflect the new data. For example, an initial CAT 8 event may be re-designated as a root-level intrusion (CAT 1 incident) or a result of non-compliance activity (CAT 5 event).

3.4.2.2. In order to support incident investigation, CSCS units and other applicable units will retain proxy server, firewall and Domain Name Server audit logs for a minimum of one year in accordance with the AF Records Disposition Schedule, Series 33, Table 25, Rule 8.00 (T 33-25 R 8), unless a longer retention period is specified in other guidance **(T-2)**.

3.4.2.3. Upon detecting a suspected or verified incident, notify the Primary Recipient according to the guidance in Table 3.1.

Table 3.1. Incident Reporting Action Matrix.

If the originator / recipient of the incident report (IR) is	then take the indicated Actions	and the Primary Recipient will be	and Informational Recipients will be
End user	1	Client Support Technician (CST)/ Cybersecurity Liaison (CSL)	N/A
CST/CSL	2, 7	CFP	Supporting NOS
Functional System Administrator (FSA)	2, 7	CFP	ACCC/MCCC/NOS
NCC/CFP	2, 7	Appropriate CSCS unit, ACCC/MCCC	624 OC, ACD unit
I-NOSC	3-7	624 OC	ACD unit, ACCC/MCCC

Actions	
1	Upon detection of an incident, end users will immediately notify their assigned CST/CSL and provide information as requested. **(T-2)**
2	Upon detection or notification of an incident, the CST/CSL will notify their servicing CFP. After notifying the CFP, the CST/CSL will prepare and transmit an IR to the servicing CFP. If there is no servicing CFP, send the IR directly to the supporting I-NOSC. Support the ACD unit as directed during investigation of incident. **(T-2)**
3	Upon detection or notification of an incident, contact the 624 OC for assessment of the incident and assignment of an Incident Report Identifier (IRID) (upon validation). **(T-2)**
4	After making initial contact with the 624 OC, follow-up by submitting an initial IR. **(T-2)**
5	Submit an updated IR every 7 days until all actions required to resolve the incident are complete. **(T-2)**
6	Submit a final IR within 24 hours of the all action related to the incident being completed. **(T-2)**
7	Send an informational copy of all IRs to the Informational Recipients indicated. **(T-2)**

3.4.3. **Objectives.**

3.4.3.1. Determine whether a detected event is a reportable event or incident.

3.4.3.2. Ensure all appropriate DoD organizations, to include assigned Authorizing Officials (AO) and their staffs, are notified through technical and operational reporting channels.

3.4.3.3. Ensure the timely submission, by the organization that first discovers and reports the incident, of an initial incident report that contains as much complete and useful information as is available (or possible). This includes timely submissions into the DoD's Joint Incident Management System (JIMS).

3.4.4. **Methodology.**

3.4.4.1. Assess and Categorize. Assess the event against the incident criteria to determine if it is a reportable event or incident (See Table 1.1, Incident Categories). In cases where more than one category applies, use the category of highest precedence as outlined in the Table 1.1.

3.4.4.2. Classification of Incident Reports. Incident reports may be either classified or unclassified. The individual responsible for developing the incident report will review either DoDI O-3600.02 or the AF Cyberspace Operation Security Classification Guide (SCG) to determine if the report should be classified. **(T-1)** If it is determined the report is unclassified the author should mark the report in accordance with AFI 16-1404 using the standards for controlled unclassified information. The author may contact the Wing Information Protection Office for additional guidance on marking reports.

3.4.4.3. Based on the incident category, nature, and impact of the incident, determine if the computer forensics process should be initiated per CJCSM 6510.01B **(T-2)**.

3.5. Preliminary Response Actions. Preliminary response actions are the immediate steps taken once an incident has been detected and declared. They provide information to help protect the systems and network from more damage while more detailed analysis is completed. More detailed response steps may be taken after a more thorough analysis is performed. These will be based on the nature, scope, and potential impact of the incident. Preliminary response actions should not result in a self-imposed denial of service; that is, wherever possible, affected systems/networks should be kept in operation to support the unit mission.

3.5.1. **Objectives.**

3.5.1.1. Isolate and contain the reportable event from causing further damage to AF networks.

3.5.1.2. Maintain control of the affected system(s) and surrounding environment.

3.5.1.3. As directed by AFOSI and the 624 OC, begin chain of custody documentation and ensure forensically sound acquisition of required data as determined by preliminary analysis and identification; reference paragraphs 3.4.2 and 3.5.2.5.

3.5.1.4. Maintain and update the incident report and communicate updates through the appropriate technical and operational command channels.

3.5.1.5. AFOSI will notify ACD unit preliminary responders if AFOSI will conduct an investigation. If AFOSI elects to conduct a criminal investigation or counterintelligence operation, ensure data acquisition, storage and release is conducted according to case agent (in consultation with 624 OC) direction. Resulting data may be controlled as Law Enforcement Sensitive (LES) and details will be provided to those with a need to know via trusted agents. **(T-2)**

3.5.2. **Methodology.**

3.5.2.1. Network technicians and incident handling personnel contain the incident and/or potential threat to protect the affected system or network and prevent any further contamination, intrusion, or malicious activity.

3.5.2.1.1. Containment can be done by an automated detection system or by incident handling staff working in conjunction with technical and management staff.

3.5.2.1.2. Network technicians and incident handling personnel coordinate containment with the supporting CNDSP. The commander and supporting CNDSP will coordinate with LE/CI when initial investigation indicates the possibility of criminal or hostile intelligence activity **(T-2)**.

3.5.2.1.3. Carefully decide on containment actions that may affect the ability to acquire and preserve data about the incident. When making these decisions, it is important to assess the relative value of ensuring mission success by preventing further damage against the potential for containment actions to hinder further analysis.

3.5.2.2. Acquire and Preserve Data. Safely acquire and preserve the integrity of all data (as directed by incident handling, law enforcement, or counterintelligence personnel) to allow for further incident analysis. This may include making primary and working images(s) of affected system(s) in a forensically sound manner as directed by AFOSI, the supporting CNDSP, or the 624 OC.

3.6. Incident Analysis . Incident analysis is a series of analytical steps taken to find out what happened in an incident. Include the mission owner in the process. The purpose of this analysis is to understand the technical details, root cause(s), and potential impact of the incident. This understanding helps determine what additional information to gather, coordinate information sharing with others, and facilitate working with the MAJCOM and other organizations as needed to develop a COA for response and prevention.

3.6.1. **Objectives.**

3.6.1.1. Ensure the accuracy and completeness of incident reports.

3.6.1.2. Characterize and communicate the potential impact of the incident. This includes identifying and sanitizing any compromised AF data.

3.6.1.3. Systematically capture the methods used in the attack and identify security controls that could prevent future occurrences.

3.6.1.4. Research actions that can be taken to respond to and eradicate the risk and/or threat.

3.6.1.5. Understand patterns of activity to characterize the threat and direct protective and defensive strategies.

3.6.1.6. Identify the likely root cause(s) of the incident through technical analysis.

3.6.2. **Methodology.**

3.6.2.1. Gather information. All involved personnel should identify and collect all relevant information about the incident for use in incident analysis. Information gathered may include data previously acquired and preserved, external logs, personal accounts, all-source intelligence, technical information, or the current operational situation.

3.6.2.2. Validate the incident. Personnel should continuously review, corroborate, and update (if applicable) the reported incident to ensure the accuracy of all information.

3.6.2.3. Determine the operational impact. Operational impact refers to detrimental impacts on an organization's ability to perform its mission. This may include direct and/or indirect effects that diminish or incapacitate system or network capabilities, the compromise and/or loss of mission critical data, or the temporary or permanent loss of mission critical applications or systems. Coordinate as necessary with the HQ USAF Damage Assessment Management Office (AF-DAMO), the lead CDA unit for Cyber Operations Risk Assessments (CORA), or other organizations for assistance in preparing an impact assessment.

3.6.2.4. Coordinate with the victim system's owning CFP, NOS, and MCCC (as appropriate) to determine the Mission Assurance Category level of the system.

3.6.2.5. Determine within one hour if the event or incident meets AF Operational Reporting (OPREP-3) and/or USSTRATCOM or USCYBERCOM Commander's Critical Information Requirements (CCIR) reporting requirements.

3.7. Response and Recovery. Response and recovery includes the detailed response steps performed to prevent further damage, restore the integrity of affected systems, and implement follow-up strategies to prevent the incident from happening again. The local CFP, with the assistance of the mission owner, the servicing MCCC/ACCC and applicable CSCS units, will develop a Plan of Action and Milestones (POA&M) detailing the required actions and responsible offices/individuals to guide system restoration and prevention of similar incidents in the future **(T-2)**.

3.7.1. **Objectives.**

3.7.1.1. Resolve the incident according to this instruction, CJCSM 6510.01B, and local guidance.

3.7.1.2. Eliminate the risk or threat.

3.7.1.3. Either restore the integrity of the system and return it to an operational state, or properly destroy the information/media according to AFMAN 17-1301, *Computer Security (COMPUSEC)*.

3.7.1.4. Implement proactive and reactive defensive and protective measures to prevent similar incidents from occurring in the future. Coordinate with the appropriate AFSPC Weapon System Team Leads to ensure that lessons learned can be used to improve existing capabilities or justify the development of new ones.

3.7.1.5. Collaborate with LE or IC partners to identify investigative or intelligence equities which may need to be considered before certain containment measures are taken.

3.7.2. Methodology.

3.7.2.1. If applicable, implement additional containment actions to regain control of or isolate the system and prevent further malicious activity.

3.7.2.2. Containment strategies vary based on the type of incident. Common strategies include restoring the compromised system to a pristine condition and/or formally decommissioning the system if it cannot be restored.

3.7.2.3. Examples of strategies include modifying network access controls (e.g., firewall), installing new antivirus or intrusion detection/prevention sensor signatures, or making physical changes to the infrastructure. As more network intrusion prevention sensors are added to the AF toolbox, assigned ACD, AFINC, and CSCS weapon system units will, as directed by the 624 OC, determine the appropriate thresholds for automated/real-time blocking of suspect activity **(T-2)**. The 624 OC should coordinate with MAJCOMs, Air National Guard (ANG), and numbered air force/warfighting headquarters to review and adjust blocking thresholds as needed.

3.7.2.4. The decision to restore a system without identifying the root cause(s) of an incident must be weighed carefully as it may leave the system vulnerable. Local commanders, with the assistance of the supporting communications element, will determine the adequacy of final restoration or decommissioning actions, and are responsible for ensuring the actions are completed **(T-2)**.

3.7.2.5. Applicable ACD, CSCS, and AFINC weapon system units, MCCCs/ACCCs, and CFPs conduct scans, as capabilities permit, to ensure fix actions are complete, Technical Orders (TOs) are implemented, and all known vulnerabilities are patched/mitigated.

3.7.3. Post-Incident Analysis.

3.7.3.1. Post-incident analysis involves the postmortem analysis of an incident to review the effectiveness and efficiency of incident handling. Data captured in the postmortem includes lessons learned, initial root cause, problems with executing COAs, missing policies and procedures, and inadequate infrastructure defenses. Post-incident analysis reporting will be provided to the affected MAJCOM/unit so that corrective actions can be taken **(T-2)**.

3.7.3.2. The ACD unit drafts a Cyber Incident Report (CIR), which provides a detailed analysis to include the affected system, probable attacker, attack vector used, and technical and operational impacts (if known). A general CIR format with detailed instructions can be found in CJCSI 6510.01B, Appendix B to Enclosure C.

3.7.3.3. 25AF provides intelligence support to the ACD unit CIR incident reporting process through the production of a Network Intelligence Report (NIR), an all-source report which focuses on an incident, group of incidents, or network activity or on a foreign individual, group, or organization identified as a threat or potential threat to DOD networks. A general NIR format with detailed instructions can be found in CJCSI 6510.01B, Appendix B to Enclosure F.

3.8. LE & CI Incidents . An incident/event investigation involving LE/CI (e.g., investigation of insider activity) may deviate from "typical" cyber incident handling processes depending upon the nature and sensitivity of the investigation. In such cases, information may be "law enforcement sensitive" or subject to other handling restrictions, with limited distribution to the general AF community.

3.8.1. An incident/event investigation involving the IC may deviate from "typical" cyber incident handling processes depending upon the nature and sensitivity of the operation. In such cases, adversary activity may be allowed to continue in order for friendly forces to gain actionable intelligence or allow for the continuation of friendly classified operations.

Table 3.2. Incident Handling and Support Activities.

This table presents the relationship between the ongoing support activities and the basic phases of incident handling.			
	Reporting & Notification	Documentation	Coordination
Detection of Events	Submission of report of events of interest	Initial documentation of event activity	Global information sharing and gathering between tiers, with other DCO and DoDIN Operations components, LE/CI or IC
Preliminary Analysis & Identification	Submission of initial incident report	If no documentation has been started initial documentation should occur here	Coordination to identify additional sources of information and artifacts
Preliminary Response Action	Update of actions taken	Documentation of any actions taken	Coordination of technical and organizational steps taken to implement preliminary actions across all affected C/S/As
Incident Analysis	More detailed updates of analysis performed	Documentation of analysis results	Coordination of incident analysis activities between DCO, DoDIN Operations, mission owners, technical and management components and internal/external subject matter experts
Response & Recovery	Updates on actions taken and submission of final report for closure	Documentation of response plan, analysis performed, and COAs	Coordination of response actions between C/S/As and field activities, CNDSPs, mission owners, Installations and DCO Service subscribers, DoDIN Operations, and with LE/CI and IC, and others as required
Post-Incident Analysis	Submission of Post-Incident Analysis report	Documentation of lessons learned and resulting improvement plan	Coordination between DoD components to implement any process improvement activities resulting from post-incident analysis

Chapter 4

EXERCISES

4.1. Exercises on Operational Networks. Organizations that conduct exercises on operational networks run the risk of confusing exercise incidents with real world incidents. Any organization that participates in exercises conducted on operational networks will ensure procedures are in place to manage real world and exercise incidents.

4.2. Joint Exercises. The sponsoring command should provide the rules of engagement (ROEs) and standard operating procedures (SOPs) for the exercise. The senior Air Force representative from each participating organization will ensure the ROEs and SOPs address the issue of managing real world and exercise events and incidents. Participating organizations will attend planning conferences to ensure their equities are represented.

4.3. Air Force Exercises. The sponsoring command will establish the ROEs and SOPs for the exercise participants and will ensure the ROEs and SOPs address the issue of managing real world and exercise events and incidents. Participating organizations will attend planning conferences to ensure their equities are represented.

4.4. MAJCOM Exercises. The sponsoring MAJCOM Staff element will establish the ROEs and SOPs for the exercise participants and will ensure the ROEs and SOPs address the issue of managing real world and exercise events and incidents. Participating organizations will attend planning conferences to ensure their equities are represented.

4.5. Internal Exercises. Organizations conducting internal exercises on operational networks will establish the ROEs and SOPs for the exercise participants.

MARK. C. NOWLAND, Lt Gen, USAF
Deputy Chief of Staff, Operations

Attachment 1

GLOSSARY OF REFERENCES AND SUPPORTING INFORMATION

References

DoDD 3600.01, *Information Operations*, 2 May 2013

DoDD 5400.7-R_AFMAN 33-302, *Freedom of Information Act Program*, 21 October 2010

DoDD 5400.11, *DoD Privacy Program*, 29 October 2014

DoDD 5505.13E, *DoD Executive Agent (EA) for the DoD Cyber Crime Center (DC3),* 1 March 2010

DoDD O-8530.1, *Computer Network Defense (CND)*, 8 January 2001

DoDD O-8530.1-M, *DoD Computer Network Defense (CND) Service Provider Certification and Accreditation Process,* 8 January 2001

DoDI O-3600.02, *Information Operations (IO) Security Classification Guidance*, 28 November 2005

DoDI 8500.01, *Cybersecurity*, 14 March 2014

DoDI O-8530.2, *Support to Computer Network Defense (CND)*, 9 March 2001

Office of the Secretary of Defense (OSD) Memorandum OSD 06227-09, *Safeguarding Against and Responding to the Breach of Personally Identifiable Information*, 5 June 2009

CJCSI 3121.01B, *Standing Rules Of Engagement/Standing Rules For The Use Of Force For US Forces*, 13 Jun 2005

CJCSI 3213.01D, *Joint Operations Security*, 7 May 2012

CJCSI 6510.01F, *Information Assurance (IA) and Support to Computer Network Defense (CND)*, 09 February 2011

CJCSM 6510.01B, *Cyber Incident Handling Program*, 10 July 2012 (current as of 18 December 2014)

National Security Telecommunications and Information Systems Security Directive 503, *Incident Response and Vulnerability Reporting for National Security Systems Security*

Committee on National Security Systems (CNSS) Instruction 4009, Jun 06 (revised 26 April 2010)

JP 3-12, *Cyberspace Operations*, 5 February 2013

AF Doctrine Annex 3-12, *Cyberspace Operations*, 30 November 2011

AFPD 10-9, *Lead Command Designation and Responsibilities for Weapon Systems*, 8 March 2007

AFPD 17-2, *Cyberspace Operations*, 31 July 2012

AFI 10-206, *Operational Reporting*, 11 June 2014

AFI 17-201, *Command and Control for Cyberspace Operations*, 5 March 2014

AFI 16-1404, *Air Force Information Security Program*, 29 May 2015

AFI 17-100, *Air Force Information Technology (IT) Service Management*, 16 September 2014

AFI 17-130, *Air Force Cybersecurity Program Management*, 31 August 2015

AFI 33-360, *Publications and Forms Management*, 1 December 2015

AFMAN 17-1301, *Computer Security (COMPUSEC)*, 27 March 2012

AFI 33-332, *The Air Force Privacy and Civil Liberties Program*, 12 January 2015

AFMAN 33-363, *Management of Records*, 1 March 2008

USAF Interim Computer Network Attack (CNA) Security Classification Guidance, 3 June 2002, with Change 2, 1 June 2006

Adopted Form

AF Form 847, Recommendation for Change of Publication

Abbreviations and Acronyms

25AF—25th Air Force

624 OC—624 Operations Center

ACC— Air Combat Command

ACCC— AFFOR Communications Coordination Center

ACT—AFNETOPS Compliance Tracker

AETC— Air Education and Training Command

AF— Air Force

AFCERT— Air Force Computer Emergency Response Team

AFCYBER—Air Forces Cyber (24AF)

AFDD— Air Force Doctrine Document

AFI— Air Force Instruction

AFIN— Air Force Information Network

AFMAN—Air Force Manual

AFMC— Air Force Materiel Command

AFNIC— Air Force Network Integration Center

AFOSI— Air Force Office of Special Investigations

AFPD— Air Force Policy Directive

AFRC— Air Force Reserve Command

AFSPC— Air Force Space Command

ANG— Air National Guard

C2— Command and Control

CAT— Category (i.e., CAT 1 root level intrusion)

CCDR— Combatant Commander

CCIR— Commander's Critical Information Requirements

CERT— Computer Emergency Response Team

CFP—Communications Focal Point

CI— Counterintelligence

CIO— Chief Information Officer

CIR— Cyber Incident Report

CJCS— Chairman, Joint Chiefs of Staff

CJCSI— Chairman, Joint Chiefs of Staff Instruction

CJCSM— Chairman, Joint Chiefs of Staff Manual

CNDSP— Computer Network Defense Service Provider

CNA—Computer Network Attack

CNSS—Committee on National Security Systems

COA— Course of Action

CoR— Certificate of Reconstitution

CORA— Cyber Operations Risk Assessment

C/S/As— Combatant Commands/Services/Agencies

CSL—Cybersecurity Liaison

CST—Client Service Technician

CTO— Communications Tasking Order

DC3—Defense Cyber Crime Center

DCO— Defensive Cyberspace Operations

DoD— Department of Defense

DoDD— Department of Defense Directive

DoDI— Department of Defense Instruction

DoDIN—Department of Defense Information Networks

EITSM— Enterprise Information Technology Service Management

HQ— Headquarters

I&W— Indications & Warnings

IA— Information Assurance

IC— Intelligence Community

I—NOSC – Integrated Network Operations Security Center

IO— Information Operations

IP—Information Protection

IS—Information System

ISR— Intelligence, Surveillance, and Reconnaissance

IT—Information Technology

JIMS—Joint Incident Management System

JP— Joint Publication

LE— Law Enforcement

MAJCOM— Major Command

MCCC— MAJCOM Communications Coordination Center

NOS—Network Operations Squadron

OPR— Office of Primary Responsibility

PII—Personally Identifiable Information

SOPs— Standard Operating Procedures

TCTO— Time Compliant Technical Order

TO— Technical Order

USAF— United States Air Force

USCYBERCOM—United States Cyber Command

USSTRATCOM—United States Strategic Command

Terms

Attack Sensing and Warning (AS&W)—The detection, correlation, identification and characterization of intentional unauthorized activity, including computer intrusion or attack, across a large spectrum coupled with the notification to command and decision makers so that an appropriate response can be developed. Attack sensing and warning also includes attack/intrusion related intelligence collection tasking and dissemination; limited immediate response recommendations; and limited potential impact assessments.

Classified Message Incident.—A form of data spillage which results when classified information is transmitted over unclassified channels, or via channels not approved for its level of classification.

Client Support Technician (CST).—An individual who supports customers with resolving issues relating to information technology devices, such as personal computers, personal digital assistants, and printers. (AFMAN 17-1201)

Counterintelligence (CI).—Information gathered and activities conducted to protect against espionage, other intelligence activities, sabotage, or assassinations conducted for or on behalf of foreign powers, organizations, or persons, or international terrorist activities, but not including personnel, physical, document, or communications security programs. (DoDI 5200.1-R)

Cyber (adj.).—Of or pertaining to the cyberspace environment, capabilities, plans, or operations. (AFPD 17-2)

Cybersecurity Liaison.—An individual responsible for ensuring that the appropriate operational cybersecurity posture is maintained for an AF information system or organization. (AFI 17-130)

Cyberspace.—A global domain within the information environment consisting of the interdependent networks of information technology infrastructures and resident data, including the Internet, telecommunications networks, computer systems, and embedded processors and controllers. (JP 1-02)

Cyberspace Operations—The employment of cyber capabilities where the primary purpose is to achieve objectives in or through cyberspace. (JP 3-12)

Data Spillage—Spillage occurs when classified data is entered into a system/device not accredited for its level of classification. For example, if a user copies a classified data file to removable media (e.g. thumb drive, DVD or CD) from SIPRNET and then uploads the data onto a NIPRNET computer, spillage results.

Defensive Cyberspace Operations (DCO).—Passive and active cyberspace operations intended to preserve the ability to utilize friendly cyberspace capabilities and protect data, networks, and net-centric capabilities. (JP 3-12)

Department of Defense Information Networks (DoDIN).—The globally interconnected, end-to-end set of information capabilities, and associated processes for collecting, processing, storing, disseminating, and managing information on-demand to warfighters, policy makers, and support personnel, including owned and leased communications and computing systems and services, software (including applications), data, security services, other associated services, and national security systems. (JP 3-12)

Department of Defense Information Network (DoDIN) Operations.—Operations to design, build, configure, secure, operate, maintain, and sustain Department of Defense networks to create and preserve information assurance on the Department of Defense information Networks. (JP 3-12)

Event.—Any observable occurrence in a system and/or network. Events sometimes provide indication that an incident is occurring. (CNSSI 4009)

Incident.—An assessed occurrence that actually or potentially jeopardizes the confidentiality, integrity, or availability of an information system; or the information the system processes, stores, or transmits; or that constitutes a violation or imminent threat of violation of security policies, security procedures, or acceptable use policies. (CNSSI 4009)

Indications & Warning (I&W)—Intelligence activities to detect and report time-sensitive intelligence information on foreign developments that could involve a threat to the United States or allied/coalition military, political, or economic interests or to U.S. citizens abroad. It includes forewarning of enemy actions or intentions; the imminence of hostilities; insurgency;

nuclear/non-nuclear attack on the United States, its overseas forces, or allied/coalition nations; hostile reactions to U.S. reconnaissance activities; terrorists' attacks; and other similar events.

Information Assurance (IA).—Measures that protect and defend information and information systems by ensuring their availability, integrity, authentication, confidentiality, and nonrepudiation. This includes providing for restoration of information systems by incorporating protection, detection, and reaction capabilities. (JP 1-02)

Information Operations (IO).—The integrated employment, during military operations, of information-related capabilities (IRC's) in concert with other lines of operation to influence, disrupt, corrupt, or usurp the decision-making of adversaries and potential adversaries while protecting our own. (JP 13-3)

Attachment 2

AF CYBERSPACE WEAPON SYSTEMS

A2.1. There are six CSAF -approved cyberspace weapon systems with their associated infrastructure and other major systems which are impacted by this AFI. This list does not include every weapon system nor is it intended to be an all-inclusive list as new weapon systems may be introduced in the future to operate, defend and C2 the DoDIN and its operations.

A2.1.1. Air Force Cyberspace Defense (ACD). ACD prevents, detects, responds to, and provides forensics of intrusions into unclassified and classified AF networks.

A2.1.2. Air Force Intranet Control (AFINC). AFINC is the top level boundary and entry point into the Air Force Information Network (AFIN), and controls the flow of all external and inter-base traffic through standard, centrally managed gateways.

A2.1.3. Cyber Command and Control Mission System (C3MS). C3MS is the single AF weapon system providing overarching 24/7/365 awareness, management and control of the AF portion of the cyberspace domain. It ensures unfettered access, mission assurance, and joint warfighter use of networks and information processing systems to accomplish worldwide operations.

A2.1.4. Cyberspace Defense Analysis (CDA). CDA monitors, collects, analyzes, and reports on sensitive information released from friendly unclassified systems, such as computer networks, telephones, email, and USAF websites. Also, CDA conducts Cyberspace Operational Risk Assessment (CORA) activities which assesses data compromised through intrusions into AF networks with the objective of determining the associated impact to operations resulting from that data loss.

A2.1.5. Air Force Cyber Security and Control System (CSCS). CSCS provides 24/7 network operations and management functions and enables key enterprise services within Air Force unclassified and classified networks.

A2.1.6. Cyberspace Vulnerability Assessment/Hunter (CVA/Hunter). CVA/Hunter executes vulnerability, compliance, defense and non-technical assessments, best practice reviews, penetration testing and Hunter missions on AF and DoD networks & systems. Hunter operations characterize and then eliminate threats for the purpose of mission assurance. The weapon system can perform defensive sorties world-wide via remote or on-site access.

Cybersecurity Titles Published by 4th Watch Publishing Co.

NIST SP 500-288	Specification for WS-Biometric Devices (WS-BD)
NIST SP 500-291 V2	NIST Cloud Computing Standards Roadmap
NIST SP 500-292	NIST Cloud Computing Reference Architecture
NIST SP 500-293 V1 & V2	US Government Cloud Computing Technology Roadmap
NIST SP 500-293 V3	US Government Cloud Computing Technology Roadmap
NIST SP 500-299	NIST Cloud Computing Security Reference Architecture
NIST SP 500-304	Data Format for the Interchange of Fingerprint, Facial & Other Biometric Information
NIST SP 800-12 R1	An Introduction to Information Security
NIST SP 800-16 R1	A Role-Based Model for Federal Information Technology/Cybersecurity Training
NIST SP 800-18 R1	Developing Security Plans for Federal Information Systems
NIST SP 800-22 R1a	A Statistical Test Suite for Random and Pseudorandom Number Generators for Cryptographic Applications
NIST SP 800-30	Guide for Conducting Risk Assessments
NIST SP 800-31	Intrusion Detection Systems
NIST SP 800-32	Public Key Technology and the Federal PKI Infrastructure
NIST SP 800-34 R1	Contingency Planning Guide for Federal Information Systems
NIST SP 800-35	Guide to Information Technology Security Services
NIST SP 800-36	Guide to Selecting Information Technology Security Products
NIST SP 800-37 R2	Applying Risk Management Framework to Federal Information
NIST SP 800-38	Recommendation for Block Cipher Modes of Operation
NIST SP 800-38A Addendum	Block Cipher Modes of Operation: Three Variants of Ciphertext Stealing for CBC Mode
NIST SP 800-38B	Block Cipher Modes of Operation: The CMAC Mode for Authentication
NIST SP 800-38C	Block Cipher Modes of Operation: The CCM Mode for Authentication and Confidentiality
NIST SP 800-38D	Block Cipher Modes of Operation: Galois/Counter Mode (GCM) and GMAC
NIST SP 800-38E	Block Cipher Modes of Operation: The XTS-AES Mode for Confidentiality on Storage Devices
NIST SP 800-38F	Block Cipher Modes of Operation: Methods for Key Wrapping
NIST SP 800-38G	Block Cipher Modes of Operation: Methods for Format-Preserving Encryption
NIST SP 800-39	Managing Information Security Risk
NIST SP 800-40 R3	Guide to Enterprise Patch Management Technologies
NIST SP 800-41	Guidelines on Firewalls and Firewall Policy
NIST SP 800-44 V2	Guidelines on Securing Public Web Servers
NIST SP 800-45 V2	Guidelines on Electronic Mail Security
NIST SP 800-46 R2	Guide to Enterprise Telework, Remote Access, and Bring Your Own Device (BYOD) Security
NIST SP 800-47	Security Guide for Interconnecting Information Technology Systems
NIST SP 800-48	Guide to Securing Legacy IEEE 802.11 Wireless Networks
NIST SP 800-49	Federal S/MIME V3 Client Profile
NIST SP 800-50	Building an Information Technology Security Awareness and Training Program
NIST SP 800-52 R1	Guidelines for the Selection, Configuration, and Use of Transport Layer Security (TLS) Implementations
NIST SP 800-53 R5	Security and Privacy Controls for Information Systems and Organizations
NIST SP 800-53A R4	Assessing Security and Privacy Controls
NIST SP 800-54	Border Gateway Protocol Security
NIST SP 800-56A R3	Pair-Wise Key-Establishment Schemes Using Discrete Logarithm Cryptography
NIST SP 56B R 1	Recommendation for Pair-Wise Key-Establishment Schemes Using Integer Factorization Cryptography
NIST SP 800-56C R1	Recommendation for Key-Derivation Methods in Key-Establishment Schemes - Draft
NIST SP 800-57 R4	Recommendation for Key Management
NIST SP 800-58	Security Considerations for Voice Over IP Systems
NIST SP 800-60	Guide for Mapping Types of Information and Information Systems to Security Categories
NIST SP 800-61 R2	Computer Security Incident Handling Guide
NIST SP 800-63-3	Digital Identity Guidelines
NIST SP 800-63a	Digital Identity Guidelines - Enrollment and Identity Proofing
NIST SP 800-63b	Digital Identity Guidelines - Authentication and Lifecycle Management
NIST SP 800-63c	Digital Identity Guidelines- Federation and Assertions
NIST SP 800-64 R2	Security Considerations in the System Development Life Cycle
NIST SP 800-66	Implementing the Health Insurance Portability and Accountability Act (HIPAA) Security Rule
NIST SP 800-67 R2	Recommendation for Triple Data Encryption Algorithm (TDEA) Block Cipher - Draft
NIST SP 800-70 R4	National Checklist Program for IT Products
NIST SP 800-72	Guidelines on PDA Forensics
NIST SP 800-73-4	Interfaces for Personal Identity Verification
NIST SP 800-76-2	Biometric Specifications for Personal Identity Verification
NIST SP 800-77	Guide to IPsec VPNs
NIST SP 800-79-2	Authorization of Personal Identity Verification Card Issuers (PCI) and Derived PIV Credential Issuers (DPCI)
NIST SP 800-81-2	Secure Domain Name System (DNS) Deployment Guide
NIST SP 800-82 R2	Guide to Industrial Control Systems (ICS) Security
NIST SP 800-83	Guide to Malware Incident Prevention and Handling for Desktops and Laptops
NIST SP 800-84	Guide to Test, Training, and Exercise Programs for IT Plans and Capabilities
NIST SP 800-85A-4 PIV	Card Application and Middleware Interface Test Guidelines
NIST SP 800-85B-4 PIV	Data Model Test Guidelines - Draft
NIST SP 800-86	Guide to Integrating Forensic Techniques into Incident Response

NIST SP 1800-4a & 4b Mobile Device Security: Cloud and Hybrid Builds
NIST SP 1800-4c Mobile Device Security: Cloud and Hybrid Builds
NIST SP 1800-5 IT Asset Management: Financial Services
NIST SP 1800-6 Domain Name Systems-Based Electronic Mail Security
NIST SP 1800-7 Situational Awareness for Electric Utilities
NIST SP 1800-8 Securing Wireless Infusion Pumps
NIST SP 1800-9a & 9b Access Rights Management for the Financial Services Sector
NIST SP 1800-9c Access Rights Management for the Financial Services Sector - How To Guide
NIST SP 1800-11a & 11b Data Integrity Recovering from Ransomware and Other Destructive Events
NIST SP 1800-11c Data Integrity Recovering from Ransomware and Other Destructive Events - How To Guide
NIST SP 1800-12 Derived Personal Identity Verification (PIV) Credentials
NISTIR 7298 R2 Glossary of Key Information Security Terms
NISTIR 7316 Assessment of Access Control Systems
NISTIR 7497 Security Architecture Design Process for Health Information Exchanges (HIEs)
NISTIR 7511 R4 V1.2 Security Content Automation Protocol (SCAP) Version 1.2 Validation Program Test Requirements
NISTIR 7628 R1 Vol 1 Guidelines for Smart Grid Cybersecurity - Architecture, and High-Level Requirements
NISTIR 7628 R1 Vol 2 Guidelines for Smart Grid Cybersecurity - Privacy and the Smart Grid
NISTIR 7628 R1 Vol 3 Guidelines for Smart Grid Cybersecurity - Supportive Analyses and References
NISTIR 7756 CAESARS Framework Extension: An Enterprise Continuous Monitoring Technical Refer
NISTIR 7788 Security Risk Analysis of Enterprise Networks Using Probabilistic Attack Graphs
NISTIR 7823 Advanced Metering Infrastructure Smart Meter Upgradeability Test Framework
NISTIR 7874 Guidelines for Access Control System Evaluation Metrics
NISTIR 7904 Trusted Geolocation in the Cloud: Proof of Concept Implementation
NISTIR 7924 Reference Certificate Policy
NISTIR 7987 Policy Machine: Features, Architecture, and Specification
NISTIR 8006 NIST Cloud Computing Forensic Science Challenges
NISTIR 8011 Vol 1 Automation Support for Security Control Assessments
NISTIR 8011 Vol 2 Automation Support for Security Control Assessments
NISTIR 8040 Measuring the Usability and Security of Permuted Passwords on Mobile Platforms
NISTIR 8053 De-Identification of Personal Information
NISTIR 8054 NSTIC Pilots: Catalyzing the Identity Ecosystem
NISTIR 8055 Derived Personal Identity Verification (PIV) Credentials (DPC) Proof of Concept Research
NISTIR 8060 Guidelines for the Creation of Interoperable Software Identification (SWID) Tags
NISTIR 8062 Introduction to Privacy Engineering and Risk Management in Federal Systems
NISTIR 8074 Vol 1 & Vol 2 Strategic U.S. Government Engagement in International Standardization to Achieve U.S. Objectives for Cybersecurity
NISTIR 8080 Usability and Security Considerations for Public Safety Mobile Authentication
NISTIR 8089 An Industrial Control System Cybersecurity Performance Testbed
NISTIR 8112 Attribute Metadata - Draft
NISTIR 8135 Identifying and Categorizing Data Types for Public Safety Mobile Applications
NISTIR 8138 Vulnerability Description Ontology (VDO)
NISTIR 8144 Assessing Threats to Mobile Devices & Infrastructure
NISTIR 8151 Dramatically Reducing Software Vulnerabilities
NISTIR 8170 The Cybersecurity Framework
NISTIR 8176 Security Assurance Requirements for Linux Application Container Deployments
NISTIR 8179 Criticality Analysis Process Model
NISTIR 8183 Cybersecurity Framework Manufacturing Profile
NISTIR 8192 Enhancing Resilience of the Internet and Communications Ecosystem
Whitepaper Cybersecurity Framework Manufacturing Profile
Whitepaper NIST Framework for Improving Critical Infrastructure Cybersecurity
Whitepaper Challenging Security Requirements for US Government Cloud Computing Adoption
FIPS PUBS 140-2 Security Requirements for Cryptographic Modules
FIPS PUBS 140-2 Annex A Approved Security Functions
FIPS PUBS 140-2 Annex B Approved Protection Profiles
FIPS PUBS 140-2 Annex C Approved Random Number Generators
FIPS PUBS 140-2 Annex D Approved Key Establishment Techniques
FIPS PUBS 180-4 Secure Hash Standard (SHS)
FIPS PUBS 186-4 Digital Signature Standard (DSS)
FIPS PUBS 197 Advanced Encryption Standard (AES)
FIPS PUBS 198-1 The Keyed-Hash Message Authentication Code (HMAC)
FIPS PUBS 199 Standards for Security Categorization of Federal Information and Information Systems
FIPS PUBS 200 Minimum Security Requirements for Federal Information and Information Systems
FIPS PUBS 201-2 Personal Identity Verification (PIV) of Federal Employees and Contractors
FIPS PUBS 202 SHA-3 Standard: Permutation-Based Hash and Extendable-Output Functions

DHS Study DHS Study on Mobile Device Security

OMB A-130 / FISMA OMB A-130/Federal Information Security Modernization Act
GAO Federal Information System Controls Audit Manual

DoD	
UFC 3-430-11	Boiler Control Systems
UFC 4-010-06	Cybersecurity of Facility-Related Control Systems
FC 4-141-05N	Navy and Marine Corps Industrial Control Systems Monitoring Stations
MIL-HDBK-232A	RED/BLACK Engineering-Installation Guidelines
MIL-HDBK 1195	Radio Frequency Shielded Enclosures
TM 5-601	Supervisory Control and Data Acquisition (SCADA) Systems for C4ISR Facilities
ESTCP	Facility-Related Control Systems Cybersecurity Guideline
ESTCP	Facility-Related Control Systems Ver 4.0
DoD	Self-Assessing Security Vulnerabilities & Risks of Industrial Controls
DoD	Program Manager's Guidebook for Integrating the Cybersecurity Risk Management Framework (RMF) into the System Acquisition Lifecycle
DoD	Advanced Cyber Industrial Control System Tactics, Techniques, and Procedures (ACI TTP)
DoD 4140.1	Supply Chain Materiel Management Procedures
AFI 17-2NAS	Air Force Network Attack System (NAS) Volume 1, 2 & 3
AFI 10-1703	Air Force Cybercrew Volume 1, 2 & 3
AFI 17-2ACD	Air Force Cyberspace Defense (ACD) Volume 1, 2 & 3
AFI 17-2CDA	Air Force Cyberspace Defense Analysis (CDA) Volume 1, 2 & 3
AFPD 17-2	Cyberspace Operations

www.ingramcontent.com/pod-product-compliance
Lightning Source LLC
LaVergne TN
LVHW060140070326
832902LV00018B/2875